INDIANA GENEALOGICAL RESEARCH

by

George K. Schweitzer, Ph.D., Sc.D.
407 Ascot Court
Knoxville, TN 37923-5807

WITHDRAWN

Wordprocessing by
Anne M. Smalley

TABLE OF CONTENTS

Chapter 1. INDIANA BACKGROUND 5
  1. Geography 5
  2. The French period 8
  3. The British period 12
  4. The Northwest Territory period 13
  5. The IN Territorial period 15
  6. Early IN statehood 17
  7. The Civil War era 21
  8. The Post-Civil War era 24
  9. Indiana's counties 25
  10. Recommended readings 34

Chapter 2. TYPES OF RECORDS 37
  1. Introduction 37
  2. Bible records 39
  3. Biographies 40
  4. Birth records 44
  5. Cemetery records 45
  6. Census records 47
  7. Church records 52
  8. City directories 62
  9. City and county histories 62
  10. Court records 63
  11. DAR records 66
  12. Death records 66
  13. Divorce records 67
  14. Emigration and immmigration records 68
  15. Ethnic records 70
  16. Gazetteers, atlases, and maps 72
  17. Genealogical compilations and indexes 74
  18. Genealogical periodicals 75
  19. Genealogical and historical societies 76
  20. Land records 77
  21. Manuscripts 80
  22. Marriage records 81
  23. Military records: Revolutionary War 83
  24. Military records: 1812-48 86
  25. Military records: Civil War 88
  26. Mortuary records 91
  27. Naturalization records 91
  28. Newspaper records 93
  29. Published genealogies 93

30. Regional publications 94
31. Tax lists 96
32. Wills and probate records 97
33. WPA works 98

Chapter 3. RECORD LOCATIONS 101
1. Introduction 101
2. The IN State Library 106
3. The IN State Archives 111
4. The IN Historical Society 114
5. The Allen County Public Library 115
6. The Public Library of Cincinnati 118
7. The Family History Library and its Branch
       Family History Centers 119
8. The National Archives 124
9. Regional libraries 126
10. Local repositories 127
11. Large genealogical libraries 127

Chapter 4. RESEARCH PROCEDURE AND
       COUNTY LISTINGS 129
1. Introduction 129
2. Finding the county 130
3. Research approaches 133
4. Format of county listings 135
5. Adams County 137
6. Allen County 137
7. Bartholomew County 138
8. Benton County 138
9. Blackford County 139
10. Boone County 139
11. Brown County 140
12. Carroll County 140
13. Cass County 141
14. Clark County 141
15. Clay County 142
16. Clinton County 142
17. Crawford County 143
18. Daviess County 143
19. Dearborn County 144
20. Decatur County 144
21. Dekalb County 145
22. Delaware County 145
23. Dubois County 146

24. Elkhart County 146
25. Fayette County 147
26. Floyd County 147
27. Fountain County 148
28. Franklin County 148
29. Fulton County 149
30. Gibson County 150
31. Grant County 150
32. Greene County 151
33. Hamilton County 151
34. Hancock County 152
35. Harrison County 152
36. Hendricks County 153
37. Henry County 153
38. Howard County 154
39. Huntington County 154
40. Jackson County 155
41. Jasper County 155
42. Jay County 156
43. Jefferson County 156
44. Jennings County 157
45. Johnson County 157
46. Knox County 158
47. Kosciusko County 159
48. Lagrange County 159
49. Lake County 160
50. La Porte County 160
51. Lawrence County 161
52. Madison County 161
53. Marion County 162
54. Marshall County 162
55. Martin County 163
56. Miami County 163
57. Monroe County 164
58. Montgomery County 165
59. Morgan County 165
60. Newton County 166
61. Noble County 166
62. Ohio County 167
63. Orange County 167
64. Owen County 167
65. Parke County 168
66. Perry County 168
67. Pike County 169

68. Porter County 169
69. Posey County 170
70. Pulaski County 170
71. Putnam County 171
72. Randolph County 171
73. Ripley County 172
74. Rush County 172
75. St. Joseph County 173
76. Scott County 174
77. Shelby County 174
78. Spencer County 175
79. Starke County 175
80. Steuben County 176
81. Sullivan County 176
82. Switzerland County 176
83. Tippecanoe County 177
84. Tipton County 177
85. Union County 178
86. Vanderburgh County 178
87. Vermillion County 179
88. Vigo County 179
89. Wabash County 180
90. Warren County 180
91. Warrick County 181
92. Washington County 181
93. Wayne County 182
94. Wells County 183
95. White County 183
96. Whitley County 184

Chapter 1

INDIANA BACKGROUND

1. Geography The state of Indiana (hereafter IN), which was admitted to the US in 1816 as the 19th state, is located in the northeastern section of the Midwest. The state is in the shape of a rough upright rectangle with the lower right-hand corner cut off slightly. It is about 270 miles high and about 160 miles wide at its extremes. See Figure 1. IN is bordered in the north by MI and Lake MI, on the east by OH, on the west by IL, and on the south by the OH River, across which rests KY. Its capital city Indianapolis is centrally located, and is also IN's largest city (731 K population). The other large cities in the state are Fort Wayne (173 K) in the northeast, Evansville (126 K) in the southwest, Gary (117 K) in the northwest, South Bend (106K) in the north center, and Hammond (84 K) in the northwest.

The state of IN has three major land regions, the Lake Plains in the north, the Central Plains in the center, and the Hills and Lowlands in the south. These are depicted in Figure 2. The LAKE PLAINS region is an area of gently-rolling fertile lowlands with many small lakes and low hills. Sand dunes border Lake MI, but south of them is rich, black soil. The northwest corner was originally swamps and marshes, but when they were drained, they left very good ground, exceptionally suitable for farming. The CENTRAL PLAINS are generally fairly flat, have rich soil, and many sections are good grazing lands. There are some low hills and shallow valleys, particularly in the west. The HILLS AND LOWLANDS region is the most varied area in the state. In the west are the lowlands surrounding the mouth of the Wabash River, a flat fertile area. The remainder is made up of deep valleys, ridges, rugged bluffs, and scenic knobs. Most of the region is underlain with limestone, whose erosion has given rise to sinkholes, underground rivers, caverns, mineral springs, bluffs, natural bridges, and waterfalls.

Most of the land contained within the IN borders slopes from up near the northeastern corner downward to the southwestern corner. Three minor exceptions are the westward slope of the northwest corner, the northward slope of the north central portion, and the northeastward slope of the northeast corner. The result is that over 95% of IN drains toward the southwest corner, at which point the Wabash River enters the

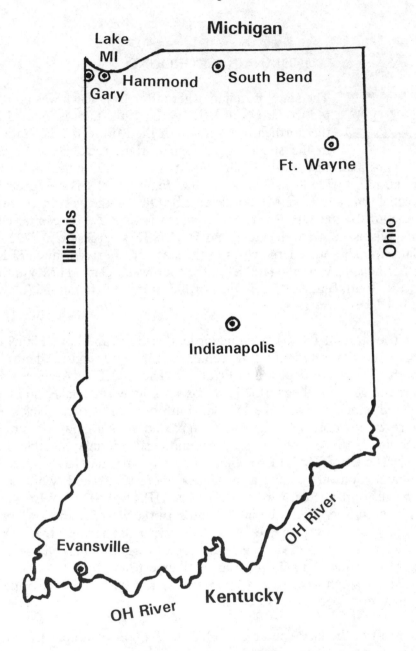

Figure 1. Indiana

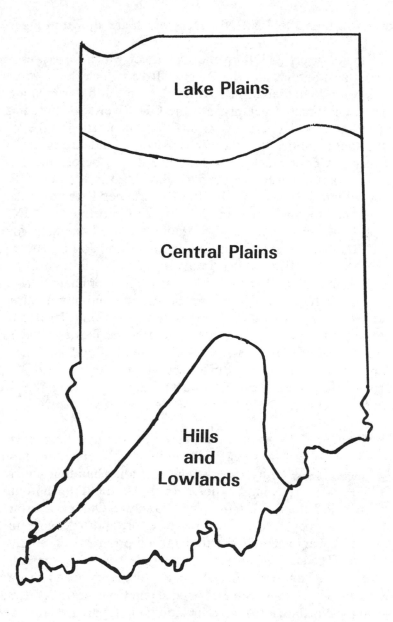

Figure 2. Indiana Land Regions

OH River. Now take a look at IN's rivers which are shown in Figure 3.

The major rivers of IN are the OH River which flows westward along the southern border, and the Wabash River which flows westward across north central IN, then turns southwest, then south to run along the IN-IL border, and finally to empty into the OH River. Its most important tributaries are the Tippecanoe River (T) in the north and the White River in the south. Notice that the White River is made up of the West Fork and the East Fork which come together shortly before the confluence with the Wabash River. In northwestern IN, the Kankakee River flows westward into IL where it joins the Des Plaines River to make up the IL River when then runs into the MS River. In north central IN, the Saint Joseph River runs north into MI, then west into Lake MI. And in northeast IN the Saint Marys River and another Saint Joseph River join to form the Maumee River which drains toward and through OH into Lake Erie. It is important that you understand this river geography of IN since the rivers of IN were its early transportation and communication routes and thereby influenced its pioneer settlement and development. Two important portages in northern IN are the one between the Saint Joseph and Kankakee Rivers at the site of South Bend and the one between the Maumee and Wabash Rivers at the site of Fort Wayne. These portages allowed early travelers into IN to transfer from the Great Lakes waterway network to the OH-MS Rivers waterway network.

2. The French period

As of about 1600, the area now defined by IN was essentially uninhabited, except for temporary expeditions of Indian hunting and trapping parties. In 1604, the French founded Port Royal (now in Nova Scotia), then in 1608 settled Quebec to establish New France. They began to explore the interior, and to engage in fur trading and missionary activities, as they moved progressively southwest and west from Quebec. About the same time, in 1607, the English planted a colony at Jamestown in VA, and settlements began to spread north, south, and west of that center. The second Charter of VA, framed in 1609, gave the Northwest Country, including the IN area, to the colony of VA. By 1670, the French had penetrated into the western Great Lakes area and had gotten into the upper MS Valley. In the process, some explorers, traders, and missionaries had probably passed through what is now northern IN. About this time, or a little earlier, small numbers of Indians had begun to move into IN and to soon diffuse southward down the Wabash River Valley. The Miami located across northern IN, the Wea settled on the Wabash River around present-day

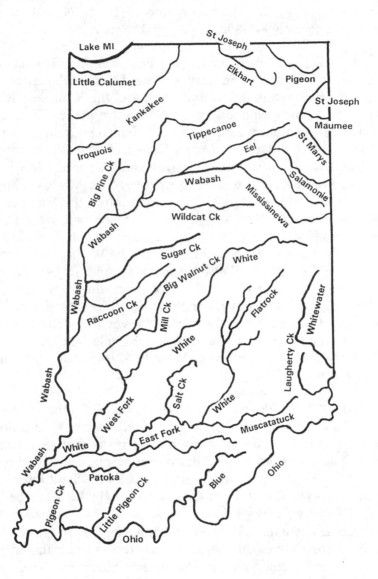

Figure 3. Indiana Rivers

Lafayette, and the Piankashaw further down the Wabash River. The Potawatomi would follow the Miami into northern IN, and the Shawnee would use central IN as a hunting ground.

By 1672, a French fur-trading post was in place on the Saint Joseph River of Lake MI in northwestern IN, probably at or near the portage which connects the Saint Joseph and the Kankakee Rivers. In 1679-81, the French explorer LaSalle crossed northern IN at least two times during exploratory expeditions between the Great Lakes and the MS River. He used the Saint Joseph-Kankakee portage (near the site of South Bend) to proceed to the IL River and then to the MS River. He made firm France's claim to all the territory of the MS River and named the lower MS River area Louisiana. Shortly after, the Maumee-Wabash portage near today's Fort Wayne proved to be better for fur traders because it was located to the east of the Saint Joseph-Kankakee connection. This more easterly portage lead down the Wabash River to the OH River to the MS River. During the 1680s and 1690s, the fur trade increased and a number of temporary fur-trading posts were set up, including ones at Kekionga (Fort Wayne), Vincennes (lower Wabash), and perhaps Quiatenon (on the Wabash River near Lafayette). Meanwhile, Louisiana began to be settled, Mobile and Biloxi in 1699, Natchitoches in 1714, and New Orleans in 1718. Four years later, New Orleans was made the capital.

By 1700, the French had made friends with most of the Indians who were now coming into IN, and they were carrying out a flourishing fur trade with them. As temporary trading posts came and went in the IN area, four sites slowly settled down into permanence: Kekionga (Fort Wayne), Quiatenon (Lafayette), Vincennes, and the Saint Joseph River of Lake MI site. The first three of these stood along the Maumee-Wabash-OH-MS Rivers trade route. However, some English fur traders had now begun coming down the OH River and entering the areas of OH and IN. As their numbers increased, they began to present an escalating challenge to the French fur enterprise, so the French began fortifying several of their more strategic trading posts. In 1720, a French fort was built at Quiatenon (Lafayette), in 1722 at Kekionga (Fort Wayne), and in 1732 at Vincennes. Small French settlements grew up around these forts, the most notable one being at Vincennes. Vincennes at this time was under the governance of French Louisiana, while the other two were under the rule of New France.

The English fur traders, chiefly from VA and PA, continued to increase in the IN area. They were paying more for the furs, and were giving the Indians better trading goods at lower prices, so the Indians were slowly abandoning the French market for the English. As of 1744, Vincennes had a French-Indian community with 40 French and about 150 Indians, and an active Roman Catholic church. Fort Quiatenon (Lafayette) had about 20 French and a number of Indians, and the situation was about the same at Kekionga or Fort Miami (Fort Wayne). In 1747, the English built a large trading center and warehouse in OH at Pickawillany (near present-day Piqua). This facility attracted more Indian traders, and even more of the fur trade was taken from the French. In order to redress this trend, the French destroyed Pickawillany in 1752, and began building a series of forts in the areas that are now OH and western PA. The most strategically-located of these forts was Fort Duquesne which was set up in 1754 at the present-day site of Pittsburgh. At this time, there were slightly under 2000 French people in the IN-IL region.

In this same year of 1754, the French and Indian War broke out in North America. This conflict was an extension of French-British warfare in Europe. The major actions of the War took place to the east of the IN country, with many Indians siding with the French and the Iroquois fighting on the British side. At first the French prevailed, but soon the British took the upper hand, and in 1758, the major French bulwark in PA, Fort Duquesne, fell to the British forces. It was renamed Fort Pitt. In the succeeding year, 1789, Quebec fell to the British, and then in 1760, Montreal was conquered. These major British victories forced France to relinquish the Northwest area including the northern half of IN. Vincennes, which was under the French province of Louisiana, was not given over. The British held a conference at the newly established Fort Pitt, and over 1000 Indians attended, including many from the IN area. The British promised them good prices for furs and a plentiful supply of inexpensive commodities in exchange for their loyalty. Very quickly, British forces were dispatched to take over the fortifications at Fort Pontchartrain (Detroit), Fort Miami Kekionga (Fort Wayne), and Fort Quiatenon (Lafayette). In 1763, the Treaty of Paris ended the French and Indian War, and resulted in the transfer of almost everything east of the MS River to Britain, including Vincennes and all the rest of IN. The British also received Florida from Spain, and Spain received New Orleans and the French lands west of the MS River.

3. The British period

No sooner had the French and Indian War ended than the Indians were stirred up by a charismatic leader. He encouraged them to rise up and retake the lands that the English had now received from the French. The challenge was taken up by the Ottawa Indian chief Pontiac, who united several tribes, then put Detroit under seige. Many Indians of the IN country joined the effort and soon captured Forts Miami (Fort Wayne) and Quiatenon (Lafayette). Other forts fell, so that by the middle of 1763 nine British outposts had fallen to the Indians, and Fort Pitt was also under seige. As winter came on, and supplies became scarce, Pontiac's forces dwindled, the captured forts were abandoned, and the seiges were lifted. To placate the Indians, the British issued the Proclamation of 1763, which forbid colonists to settle west of the Appalachian Mountains, the area being reserved for Indians and fur traders. A British agent Croghan was dispatched to the northwest area to make peace with the Indians for the British occupation. He found about 85 French families at Vincennes, about 15 at Ouiatenon (Lafayette), and about 10 at Fort Miami (Fort Wayne). The French were permitted to stay, to practice their Catholic religion, and peace was made with the Indians. The Proclamation of 1763 was not effective in keeping land speculators and settlers back in the east. In the 1760s they flooded into western PA, and in the 1770s, they surged into KY. In order to attempt to forestall the occupation of the northwest country by these illegals, the British attached the area to Quebec in 1774.

In 1775, the American Revolution broke out between the thirteen colonies along the eastern coast and the mother country. The fundamental issue was the denial to the colonials of their rights and freedoms as British citizens. In the west, the British set up military headquarters at Detroit, and from there, they supported Indian raids into western PA and KY. Vincennes was strengthened and the Indians in that area were armed. George Rogers Clark of KY (a VA county) was commissioned to suppress the Indian raids and to take the British forts in the area northwest of the OH River. In 1778, Clark took the British outpost at Kaskaskia in southwestern IL, then he marched eastward to Vincennes and took over that fortress also. Upon receiving word of the loss of Vincennes, a British force was dispatched from Detroit. They attacked Vincennes and regained it, but a second expedition from Kaskasia under Clark retook the fort in early 1779. On the basis of this victory, VA organized the area into Illinois County, VA, with the county seat at Kaskaskia. A county official was sent there, and civil and criminal court jurisdiction was initiated. The court at Vincennes granted land to numerous settlers. In 1780, the VA legislature awarded Clark and his men 150,000 acres of land in southern IN just across the OH River from the Falls of the OH (now Louisville). In 1783, peace was signed between Britain and the new United States in Paris, and the entire northwestern country was given over to the US. However, the British delayed abandoning several of their forts up near the Canadian border, including Fort Miami(Fort Wayne) and Ouiatenon (Lafayette) in the IN country. Late in the year, the state of VA conveyed all of these northwestern lands over to the US, except for the Clark tract and a large area in OH called the VA Military Tract.

4. The Northwest Territory period

Clark and a number of his men settled in their alloted tracts across the OH River from Louisville. There was, however, constant danger from Indian attacks, and ceaseless Indian warfare would beset the IN country for the next dozen years. KY was a major destination of settlers after the Revolutionary War, and the population there was to rise to over 70,000 in the next seven years. As KY filled, some frontiersmen began to settle on the north side of the OH River, particularly in or near Clark's area and at Vincennes. The US, recognizing that settlers were about to stream into the area northwest of the OH River, in 1785 enacted a Land Ordinance which provided for the survey of the region into square townships six miles on a side. Each township was then subdivided into 36 numbered square-mile sections. This would allow every bit of land to be identified for purposes of sale. The new ordinance provided for land to be sold at auctions held in the East, and the minimum purchase was set at 640 acres. This arrangement was not satisfactory for many would-be settlers and they protested vigorously. The US Army was stationed along the OH River to protect surveyors, and two companies of troops occupied a fort just opposite Louisville. In 1787, about 100 soldiers were stationed at Vincennes, which had grown to have 900 French and 400 American inhabitants.

In that same year (1787) the US Congress passed the Northwest Ordinance which set up the Northwest Territory and provided for its government. The territory included all of what is now OH, IN, IL, MI, WI, and part of MN. The act provided for a governor, a court of three judges, and a secretary. It provided for an elected legislature when the population reached 5000 voters, and for statehood when the population reached 60,000. The capital was established at Marietta (now in OH). In the year following, about 20,000 pioneers entered the Northwest Territory, coming across from KY or down the OH River. Most of these people were of Scots-Irish extraction. Indian raids increased, and the territorial government organized a militia composed of all males of ages 16 to 50. In the middle of 1790 Knox County was created from the Northwest Territory. The county contained all of IN, and parts of OH, MI, IL, and WI. Vincennes was made the county seat. The intensification of Indian aggression caused Harmar and his troops to march north from Cincinnati. They burned Indian towns and crops in the Kekionga (Fort Wayne) area, but the force was subsequently badly defeated by the Indians. Small forces led by Hamtramck and Wilkinson in the next few months destroyed Indian towns in central IN. Then late in 1791, Governor St. Clair led a sizable number of troops to the northwest-OH-northeast-IN region. The Indians dealt them a stunning defeat, with more than two-thirds of them wounded or killed. In the year following, President Washington appointed Wayne to take charge of the army in the Northwest Territory, and 5000 troops were authorized. As Wayne began to train his soldiers, a peace treaty was signed with the Indians in the area of Vincennes. In 1793, Wayne moved his forces north, building forts as he went, and in 1794, he soundly defeated the Indians in the Battle of Fallen Timbers near the site of present-day Toledo, OH. He then moved westward, destroying Indian towns, and built Fort Wayne on the foundations of older forts. Six companies of soldiers were stationed there to keep the area under control.

The year 1795 saw two momentous events. The first was a treaty with the British which brought about their pullout from IN over the next two years. The second event was the Treaty of Greenville with the Indians. This agreement opened for settlement two-thirds of OH and a thin triangular slice in southeast IN. It also included the US completely taking over Fort Wayne, Ouiatenon, Vincennes, and Clark's Grant. By 1798, the Northwest Territory qualified to enter the second stage of its government. A lower legislative house was elected, and an upper house was appointed. The first Protestant church meeting in IN took place in Clark's Grant, this being the beginnings of Baptist activity in IN. In May of 1800, most of the land west of the present IN-OH line was split off from the Northwest Territory. It was constituted as a new territory, the IN Territory, with Vincennes as its capital. A small narrow triangular section (the Gore) in the southeast corner of today's IN was not included in the IN Territory. There were about 5600 people in the entire IN Territorial area, about 3000 being in what is present-day IN. The old arrangement for land sales was amended in 1800 to make it easier for settlers to obtain land in the territories. This new Land Act of 1800 reduced the minimum purchase to 320 acres, set up land offices near the land, and permitted sales on credit. The liberalized regulations led to a flood of migration into the new territories. A land office was set up at Cincinnati, and large amounts of land were rapidly sold, including land in the Gore.

---

5. The IN Territorial period

The new IN Territory received a governor, a secretary, and a court with three judges. Harrison, the new governor, immediately began negotiations with the Indians, and a number of treaties followed in the next decade and a half. In 1801, Clark County was split off Knox County. Its county seat was first at Springville (1801-1802), but was soon transfered to Jeffersonville (1802-1810), and then to Charleston. In 1803, two other counties were established: Wayne County and Dearborn County. This latter county was created from the Gore Tract which OH gave over to the IN Territory when OH became a state. In 1804, a land office was established at Vincennes, and sales began in 1805. In the same year, IN elected a Territorial assembly, set up an upper house, and the MI Territory was split off. Most of present-day MI was included plus the northernmost strip of today's IN. The most important of the governor's treaties with the Indians included (1) one at Fort Wayne in 1803 which defined the Vincennes tract, (2) two at Vincennes in 1804 transferring to IN a strip north of the OH River and south of Vincennes, (3) one at Grouseland in 1805 adding to the tract obtained in 1804, and (4) two at Fort Wayne in 1809 transferring a tract north of Vincennes and a tract in central IN near the OH border. These cessions constituted the southern third of IN, which was now essentially cleared for settlement.

Methodist circuit riders had begun serving the people in 1804, a Quaker meeting was organized at the site of Richmond in 1807, and a Shaker colony was set up on the Wabash River in 1808. A land office was opened at Jeffersonville in 1807. In 1809, the IL Territory (IL, WI, part of MN) was split from the IN Territory, leaving the IN Territory with its present state boundaries, minus that strip along the MI Territory border, and plus the western half of Upper MI. The census of 1810 recorded an IN Territory population of about 25,000 including approximately 250 slaves. This small number of slaves was a reflection that IN settlers were largely anti-slave. For several years, an Indian called the Prophet and Tecumseh had been uniting tribes in northern and central IN to oppose the white takeover. In 1811, while Tecumseh was off trying to enlist some central IN tribes, Harrison marched the 4th US Regiment north and camped close to the headquarters of the Prophet. The Indians attacked the encampment, were repulsed, then beaten in the Battle of Tippecanoe. Southern IN was made more accesssible in this year by virtue of the coming of the steamboat to the OH River. The next year saw the breaking out of the War of 1812, with the northern IN Indians siding with the British against the US. The IN militia built a string of forts across the center of the Territory, but Indian raids increased driving many settlers back toward the OH River. Then the US lost Fort Dearborn (Chicago) and Detroit to the British, and more Indians joined the British. Harrison led troops to lift the Indian-British seige of Fort Wayne, Fort Harrison (Terre Haute) repulsed an Indian attack, and then OH troops entered northeastern IN to destroy Indian towns and fight a group of Indians to a tie. The destructions of the towns so disheartened the Indians that this was the last battle fought in IN, although some Indian raids continued.

The capital of IN Territory was moved in 1813 from Vincennes to Corydon, where it was to remain for 12 years. In that year, Harrison and his soldiers took Detroit, then defeated the British and Tecumseh and his Indians at the Battle of the Thames River in Canada, just east of Detroit. Tecumseh was killed in the battle, and the disheartened Indians fought very little thereafter. IN Territory was no longer a battlefield. The War ended in late 1814, and many Indians retreated west. This stemming of Indian hostilities opened IN up even further for settlement, and the new arrivals swelled the population toward that required for statehood. In 1814, some German Rappites came from PA and purchased a site on the Wabash River south of Vincennes. The Rappites or Harmonists, a celibate religious community, had originally come from Württemberg in Germany to escape persecution. The entire colony came in 1815 and built an amazingly progressive village called Harmonie. The community established a highly profitable agricultural and manufacturing enterprise. The Territorial census of 1815 indicated a population of almost 64,000, and a petition to Congress was made for statehood. The petition was granted in 1816, a constitutional convention was held, a constitution was approved, and IN was admitted to the Union late that year. The new state faced numerous challenges: the people were largely poor farmers, there were no sizable towns, the government had no sizable source of income, settlers were exempt from land tax for five years, and the upper two-thirds of the state was largely wilderness owned by Indians.

6. Early IN statehood

The attainment of statehood by IN served as a further attraction for settlers, because they could be assured of better local governmental control. So, increasing numbers entered and purchased land at the land offices in Cincinnati (east of southeastern IN), Vincennes (southwest IN) and Jeffersonville (southeast IN). In 1818, almost all of central IN south of the Wabash River was purchased from the Indians. This was designated the New Purchase. In 1819 a land office was set up at Brookville (east central IN), and the area was opened for settlement in 1820. This latter year showed a population of about 147K in IN, and another land office was opened at Terre Haute (west central IN). The Federal Land Act of 1820 did away with credit sales of land, but lower prices were set and the minimum that could be purchased was dropped to 80 acres. The year 1821 was beset with financial panic, depression, and widespread epidemics (much of it ague or malaria) in the southern counties. Responding to the release of Indian land, a land office at Fort Wayne was opened in 1823, and in the following year, a mail stage started operating across southern IN between Louisville (just across from Jeffersonville) and Vincennes.

As settlement progressed from south to north, the legislature deemed it advisable to move the capital to a more centrally-located site. Such was realized in 1825, when Indianapolis replaced Corydon as the capital city. With the establishment of the new capital, the land office at Brookville was moved to Indianapolis. The German Rappites who had settled in southwestern IN gave their communal experiment up in 1825, and they sold Harmonie to a Scotsman Robert Owen, who set up another utopian community. The community attracted many brilliant people who made the place a center of education and knowledge. However, even though it failed economically in 1827, it left many progressive individuals who would influence the future of IN very favorably. A treaty with the Potawatomi Indians in 1826 released land for the construction of the MI Road, a road from south to north, which was planned to connect the OH River at Madison with Shelbyville, then Indianapolis, then Logansport, then South Bend, and on to Lake MI and into MI. The cession of most of the land north and west of the Wabash River was also brought about. The Federal government, which owned all the IN land not yet granted, in 1827 gave the state land to build a canal from Lake Erie to the Wabash River. This canal would function as an extension of the Erie Canal and would provide an excellent transportation route into and beyond IN. A survey was also initiated for an extension of the National Road, and the survey was completed from Richmond to Indianapolis. The town of

Indianapolis had grown to about 1000, this being quite large for an IN town, because the great majority of people were on farms. The next year, 1828, saw the opening of a stage route from Madison (in southeast IN on the OH River) to Indianapolis. During this year, the Terre Haute land office was moved a short distance northeast to Crawfordsville, and construction was begun on the MI Road.

Following on the heels of the beginning of construction on the MI Road, construction on the National Road was started at Richmond in 1829. All this construction was accompanied by many other lesser canal and road projects meant to enhance the transportation system in IN, especially so that IN farm products could be shipped economically to out-of-state markets. The IN State Historical Society was organized in 1830, a year in which the state population exceeded 343K people. As part of the continuing transportation route increases, the Wabash and Erie Canal construction was started at Fort Wayne in 1832. IN soldiers went to participate in the Black Hawk War in this year, but the war was over before they arrived. This was a conflict in northern IL between the US and Sac and Fox Indians under the leadership of Black Hawk. Many IN citizens used the incident to demand that all Indians were dangerous and should be removed from IN. The state chartered eight railroad projects for rail lines between the OH River and Indianapolis, again responding to the need for better transportation. In 1833 a land office was opened at LaPorte in northwestern IN, most of the area having been ceded by the Indians in 1826 and 1832. In 1834, the first segment of railroad was built near Shelbyville, and in the year following the middle section of the Erie and Wabash Canal was opened. These two events signaled the canal-railroad competition which was to grow, with the railroads rapidly winning out.

The MI Road was finished in 1836. But transportation became even more pressing, so the IN Legislature passed a 13 million dollar improvement bill to finance canals, railroads, and roads. This large amount of money (for then) represented a sizable overextension of the state's capabilities, and it was followed by wild speculation. The result was that the state went bankrupt in 1837, and the ensuing panic economically devastated all IN. In 1838, coal was discovered and mines were started in Cannelton along the OH River in southcentral IN. The coal became important as steamboat fuel and was a large source of income. The year 1838 saw the completion of the National Road all across the state to Terre Haute on its western border. And the fears which grew out of the Black Hawk War came to be realized in the requirement that all Indians leave IN to be located in AR, OK, and KS. The LaPorte land office was moved a short distance south to Winamac in 1839. And, once again, epidemics beset the countryside, this time there being ague, cholera, and milk sickness. As of 1840, the end of IN's pioneer period, the population stood at 686K people, the last Indian treaty had almost cleared the state, about 80% of the public land had been taken up, and there were only three towns with over 2500 population: New Albany, Indianapolis, and Madison.

Now, several genealogically-pertinent trends which occurred during the pioneer period need to be recognized. The first of these is that the state was settled from the south to the north, the major reason being the positions of the Indians. This is readily seen by the opening dates of the land offices: (1) in the south, Cincinnati in 1800, Vincennes in 1804, Jeffersonville in 1807, (2) in the center, Brookville in 1819 and Terre Haute in 1820, and (3) in the north, Fort Wayne in 1823 and LaPorte in 1833. The second item that is of import is the people who settled IN. The first immigrants who came into the southern portion were people of Ulster-Scot derivation (with some Germans and English Quakers) who came from KY, TN, western VA, western NC, northwestern SC, and western PA. The main routes their ancestors and they used were (1) from PA to western VA to western NC (or SC) to TN to KY to IN, (2) from PA to western VA to KY to IN, (3) from PA to western VA to TN to KY to IN, (4) from VA to western VA down the Kanawha River down the OH River to IN, (5) from PA to western PA down the OH River to IN. The next immigrants who settled the central portion of the state were also from the southeastern state uplands (as above), from southern IN, and a very large number of people from the mid-Atlantic states east of IN (PA, MD, DE, NJ, OH). Most of this last group came down the OH River or through the state of OH. The last section to be settled was north IN, and those settlers came from the mid-Altantic states, from central IN, and from the northeastern states (NY, NJ, New England). Many of the last group came into IN across the northern lakeshore routes, west on the Erie Canal, and on the Great Lakes. Not too many foreign-born immigrants came into IN early, but in the 1830s, Germans and Irish were coming in goodly numbers. As of 1840, it is estimated that about 5% of IN's population was from New England, 20% from the Mid-Atlantic including NY, 30% from OH, and 45% from the southeastern states. IN had more southerners in it than any state that came out of the Northwest Territory.

The _third_ facet of IN's pioneer history that is genealogically relevant is its economy and transportation. The first residents were subsistence farmers, who quickly developed a surplus of produce, especially corn and hogs. That surplus could be turned into prosperity only by developing good transportation to and from the farms. The earliest farmers had only horrible roads and the rivers, plus the blockage to the east of the Appalachian Mountains and the westward flow of the rivers. In order to reach eastern markets, IN produce had to go down the OH River to the MS River to New Orleans, then by sailboat to the Atlantic ports. The demand for improvements grew more pressing year by year. After the War of 1812, steamboat traffic reversed the direction on the OH River, and improved canals and roads fed products from non-River farms to the OH River. Then, in the 1820s, steaamboat operation on the Great Lakes was well under way. By 1836, all the MI Road was open, and by 1838, the National Road had crossed the state. It had reached the state at Richmond in 1829, and was to be the main land route to the east for many years thereafter. The Wabash and Erie Canal had penetrated much of the interior of IN (90 miles) by 1840, and was facilitating a northern route to the east.

The _fourth_ aspect of the early statehood of IN is its religious situation. As you will recall, the pre-territorial period of the IN country was Catholic by virtue of the French control of the area. However, much of this was lost when the British took over, the main Catholic remnant being at Vincennes. When settlement by Americans began in the late 1700s, the predominant type of early religion was an evangelical Protestantism. This was due to the predominance of people from the upcountry of VA, NC, SC, TN, and KY during the territorial and early state years. Baptists came first in the 1790s, followed by Methodists in the late 1790s. Baptist ministers were usually unpaid and uneducated farmer-preachers, who farmed six days a week and preached most of the day Sunday and on Wednesday evening. They conducted marriages and funerals, held emotionally-laden meetings, and kept church members under strict moral regulation. Methodist ministers were usually circuit riders (horseback travellers), who moved from one group to another for preaching services, established new congregations, and ministered to the spiritual needs of the people. They were not as emotionally oriented as the Baptists, but they also could get a good rousing revival going. Gradually, the congregations of these groups grew and began to build churches, the Methodists hiring permanent pastors. It is not to be inferred that all early settlers were church goers. To the contrary, many, if not most, were not actively concerned with organized religion.

Adherents of other denominations also came early as is indicated by the first IN Dunkard (German Baptist) Church in 1803, the first Presbyterian Church in 1805, and the first Quaker Monthly Meeting in 1809. The Presbyterians differed considerably from the Baptists and Methodists in that they had a paid educated clergy, and therefore attracted people who were socially different. Their growth was thereby somewhat slower. As IN was being settled in the early 1800s, the people were participating in what came to be known as the Second Great Awakening. Sweeping the country were emotional revivals and camp meetings which were adding large numbers to the churches, including many of the unchurched of IN. The churches were providing important elements to IN's social structure: spiritual needs, moral stability, recreation, community, and emotional release. In 1832, a new religious group was organized in an attempt to do away with denominations. They believed that there were no denominations, there were only individuals who could be simply called Disciples or Christians. The movement, which began in KY and PA, quickly spread into IN, and many people rapidly embraced it. The result, as one might suspect, was the development of a new denomination, one called the Disciples of Christ. Catholic regrowth was sufficient by 1834 that a Catholic bishop was seated at Vincennes. By the end of the pioneer period (1840), the leading IN churches in order of their numbers were Methodist, Baptist, Presbyterian, Disciples of Christ, Quaker, Roman Catholic, and Lutheran. Smaller-numbered groups were the Primitive Baptists, Freewill Baptists, United Brethren, Mennonites, Amish Mennonites, Dunkards, Congregationalists, Moravians, and Episcopalians.

---

7. The Civil War era

The next period of IN's history is termed the Civil War era, which dates from 1840 to 1865. This name is chosen because the issues involved in the War were those that increasingly set the national agenda during these years. The northern states and the southern states had been in controversy over slave-holding, slave law enforcement, tariffs, and admissions of new states for a sizable number of years. However, the differences had been settled by compromise and trade-offs. In the 1850s, the differences became more extreme, and there was a growing sense that peaceful resolution might not continue to work. The two opposite forces were strongly at work in IN, with many people supporting and implementing the Underground Railroad and many people expressing strong sympathies toward the southern positions. This latter was largely due to the fact that many IN citizens had their origins in slave states. In 1843, the Wabash and Erie Canal was opened at Fort

Wayne, and construction was started toward the Wabash River. The year 1846 saw the last of the Indians of IN moved to KS. In the following year, married women were given the right to make a will indicating increasing activity toward equal treatment. Other reforms that came to fruition at this time were the building of a state hospital for the mentally ill and the establishing of a state school for the blind. The first steam train connecting Indianapolis with Madison on the OH River was put into operation, launching an extensive railroad construction era. The Mexican War was fought 1846-48, with IN contributing over 5000 participants, over 500 of them dying of wounds or disease. In 1848, the first IN Jewish congregation was organized in Fort Wayne. By 1849, the Wabash and Erie Canal had reached Terre Haute, and construction was continued southward from there.

In 1850, the population of IN had grown to about 990K, approximately 400K of which were born out of IN, 29K were German, 13K were Irish, and 7K had come from England or Canada. The major event of the 1850s for the US was the growing animosity between the states. For IN, however, the major event of the 1850s was the acceptance of a new state constitution in 1851. The structure of government was not radically changed, but greater emphasis was placed on free elementary public education. The constitution gave more power to the executive branch, prohibited the state from participating in business, prohibited a state debt, and forbid free blacks from entering. The year 1854 saw a coalition of anti-democrat, pro-temperance, anti-slavery advocates who favored citizenship as a requirement for suffrage meet together in Indianapolis. Out of this came the Republican Party, which would undergo an astonishing growth, allowing it to win the national elections in 1860. IN's economy grew in the 1850s, as farming prospered, manufacturing industries made several small starts, transportation (canals, roads, railroads) improved, mines and quarries opened, and more markets called for the state's produce. The increased trade with the north and the east led to a weakening of the ties of IN with the south. The towns began to increase in size, and professionals and skilled laborers began to practice in them. The Wabash and Erie Canal reached Evansville in 1853, just as railroads were taking the traffic away from canals, and almost 700 township libraries were set up by the state government. German and Irish immigration increased, many of the Germans and most of the Irish being Catholic.

The population stood at about 1350K in 1860, 2100 miles of railroad track were in place and being heavily used, strong connections by rail had been established to the east, and Indianapolis had now become the largest town, even though it had only 19K people. In early 1861, southern states challenged the Union by bombarding and capturing the Federal Fort Sumter in Charleston, SC. This marked the outbreak of the Civil War, with IN facing the conflict divided by sympathy for the south and loyalty to the north. When Lincoln called for troops, IN met its quota with twice the number called for. As the War wore on, more and more wounded and dead shocked IN into the realization that it would be a long, hard struggle. Popularity for the Union declined, there rose organizations advocating letting the southern states go, the draft was viewed unfavorably, desertions increased, and the political split between the Democrats and Republicans grew. In 1862, the state elected a Democratic legislature, but retained its Republican governor. The resulting hostility caused constitutional government in IN to collapse, as the governor continued to favor the Union, but the legislature voted not to grant him any funds. The governor had to run the state, its schools, its institutions, and its military operations on borrowed money. And anti-conscription violence broke out in over 30 counties, mainly in the south. In the summer of 1862, a band of Confederates crossed the OH River and raided and pillaged Newburgh (near Evansville).

About a year later, Confederate General Morgan crossed the OH with about 2500 troops. They defeated about 400 Corydon Home Guards, then raided Palmyra, Salem, Vienna, and Lexington. The forces were checked by militia at Vernon, some of them were captured, and the remainder went into southern OH where they continued raiding, and were finally captured. Southern IN developed active groups of southern collaborators (known as Copperheads) who belonged to treasonable organizations such as the Sons of Liberty and the Knights of the Golden Circle. In 1864, many of their leaders were indicted by the Federal government on charges of conspiracy and planning to kidnap the governor, and the movements were dissolved. IN troops had helped open the war at Philippi, VA (now WV), in 1861, and they assisted in its close at Palmetto Ranch, TX, in May of 1865. Of about 300K eligible men, IN had fielded over 197K for the Union, with over 25K losing their lives. Many IN voters were reluctant to accept the 13th, 14th, and 15th amendments to the US Constitution (slavery abolished, rights of citizenship not to be limited, vote not to be denied on basis of race), but IN ratified them all. During Reconstruction, IN harbored both a demand for punishment of the south and a demand for leniency and forgiveness, but the former attitude prevailed both in the state and nationally. This attitude gradually faded, and by the early 1870s, its strength was largely dissipated. In spite of the turbulence of the War, German and Irish immigrants kept coming in larger numbers to IN during 1840-70.

---

8. The Post-Civil War era

During the War Between the States, IN's farming, mining, forestry, and industry had developed to support the military effort. These trends continued at an ever acceler-ating pace after the conflict. Large-scale mechanized agriculture increased as agricultural implements, machinery, techniques, and fertilizers were improved. The increased profits from the increased produce were mainly put back into land development which greatly increased the land under cultivation. To protect their interests, IN farmers organized as the Grange and the Greenbacks in the 1870s and the Farmers' Alliance in the 1880s. Substantial industrial growth was also brought about, as mills and factories were set up in towns. This increased the growth of towns, but IN still remained predominantly rural well up into the 20th century. In 1893, IN participated in the national economic panic of the country. This resulted in factory closures, bank failures, labor unrest, and hard times for much of the population. Recovery was fairly rapid, and was well underway when the US fought the Spanish-American War of 1898. Only a few IN men participated. By 1910, Indianapolis had become an automobile city, manufacturing the vehicles in large numbers. Standard Oil then constructed large oil refineries in the village of Whiting, Inland Steel built at Hammond and East Chicago, and US Steel established the city of Gary around its mills. German and Irish immigrations continued from 1870 onwards, then these newcomers were joined about 1880 by Polish people, then with the development of the large industries in northwestern IN, people from southeastern Europe came.

The industrial growth of IN was further stimulated by the needs of the US in World War I. IN provided over 130K troops for this War, losing about 3K, and its citizens bought large quantities of war bonds. By 1920, IN's production was more industrial than agricultural, and its population was for the first time more urban than rural. In spite of the coming of immigrant workers, in 1920 IN showed the lowest percentage of foreign born than any state, namely about 5%. After a post-War depression in 1921, IN's industry recovered rapidly, but much of its agriculture remained unprofitable, thus increasing the rural-to-urban migration. In the industrial recovery, many blacks workers from the south were attracted to the heavy industrial cities. A general depression began in the US in 1929, and in the early 1930s, IN suffered failed banks, farm mortgage foreclosures, industrial bankruptcies, and widespread unemployment. Government programs were put in place to assist the people and provide jobs, but a general degree of economic depression persisted until the outbreak of World War II in 1941. IN sent over 362K into the armed forces, and about 10K lost their lives. The economy of the state showed good strength after the War, with most people well off and many prospering. There have been several periods of slack economy since that time, the Korean War, the Vietnam War, and the collapse of Communism. IN, the Hoosier State, remains a land of promise for many people, with its notable agricultural, industrial, technological, and educational enterprises being among the best.

---

9. Indiana's counties

Figure 4 presents the 92 counties of the State of IN as they have been since 1860 (except for some very small alterations in the western and northern boundaries of Morgan County). These counties arose in the following order. The counties which represent land in the present State of IN and which were set up by the OH Territory are: (1790) Knox, Hamilton. Those established by the IN Territory are: (1801) Clark, (1803) Dearborn created out of the IN portion of Hamilton County, OH, leaving no Hamilton County in Indiana, (1808) Harrison, (1810) Jefferson, Franklin, Wayne, (1813) Gibson, Warrick, Washington, (1814) Perry, Posey, Switzerland, (1815) Jackson, Orange. The counties created by the State of IN are: (1816) Pike, Daviess, Jennings, Ripley, Sullivan, (1817) DuBois, (1818) Lawrence, Vanderburgh, Randolph, Spencer, Monroe, Vigo, Crawford, Owen, Fayette, (1819) Floyd, (1820) Scott, Martin, (1821) Union, Greene, Bartholomew, Parke, Decatur, Henry, Marion, Morgan, Putnam, Rush, Shelby, (1822) Montgomery, Johnson, (1823) Madison, (1823) Hamilton, Allen, Hendricks, (1824) Vermillion, (1825) Clay, Fountain, (1826) Tippecanoe, (1827) Warren, Delaware, Hancock, (1828) Carroll, Cass, (1830) Boone, Clinton, Elkhart, St. Joseph, (1832) LaPorte, Huntington, LaGrange, Miami, Wabash, (1834) White, Adams, DeKalb, Fulton, Jasper, Jay, Kosciusko, Newton which was not organized, and therefore re-created in 1859, Starke, Steuben, Wells, Whitley, (1836) Lake, Brown, (1838) Blackford, (1840) Benton, (1844) Ohio, Howard, Tipton, (1859) Newton.

The following abbreviations are those used for the 92 counties in Figure 4 and will be used for Figures 5 through 10:

Ad=Adams	Hn=Hancock	Pi=Pike
Al=Allen	Ho=Howard	Pk=Pulaski
Ba=Bartholomew	Hs=Hendricks	Po=Posey
Be=Benton	Hu=Huntington	Pr=Porter
Bl=Blackford	Ja=Jackson	Pu=Putnam
Bo=Boone	Je=Jennings	Ra=Randolph
Br=Brown	Jf=Jefferson	Ri=Ripley
Ca=Carroll	Jo=Johnson	Ru=Rush
Cl=Clark	Js=Jasper	Sb=Steuben
Cn=Clinton	Jy=Jay	Sc=Scott
Cr=Crawford	Kn=Knox	Sh=Shelby
Cs=Cass	Ko=Kosciusko	Sk=Starke
Cy=Clay	La=Lawrence	Sp=Spencer
Da=Daviess	Lg=LaGrange	St=St. Joseph
De=Decatur	Lk=Lake	Su=Sullivan
Dk=Dekalb	Lp=LaPorte	Sw=Switzerland
Dl=Delaware	Ma=Marion	Ti=Tippecanoe
Dr=Dearborn	Md=Madison	Tn=Tipton
Du=Dubois	Mg=Montgomery	Un=Union
El=Elkhart	Mi=Miami	Va=Vanderburgh
Fa=Fayette	Mn=Martin	Ve=Vermillion
Fl=Floyd	Mo=Monroe	Vi=Vigo
Fo=Fountain	Mr=Morgan	Wa=Washington
Fr=Franklin	Ms=Marshall	Wb=Wabash
Fu=Fulton	Ne =Newton	We=Wells
Gi=Gibson	No=Noble	Wh=White
Gn=Grant	Oh=Ohio	Wi=Whitley
Gr=Greene	Or=Orange	Wn=Warren
Ha=Harrison	Ow=Owen	Wr=Warrick
He=Henry	Pa=Parke	Wy=Wayne
Hm=Hamilton	Pe=Perry	

Figures 5, 6, 7, 8, 9, and 10 show the counties in the land area that is now the State of IN as they were in 1800, 1810, 1820, 1830, 1840, and 1850. Notice that the county formation proceeds from south to north, reflecting the settlement pattern of IN. For considerable detail on the formation of IN counties and the consequent boundary changes, see:

Figure 4. Indiana Counties, 1860-

Figure 5. Indiana Counties in 1800

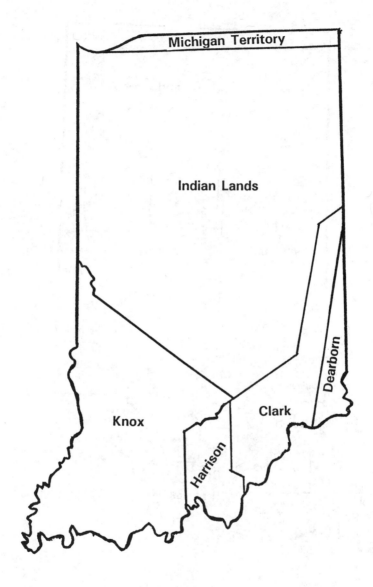

Figure 6. Indiana Counties in 1810

Figure 7. Indiana Counties in 1820

Figure 8. Indiana Counties in 1830

Figure 9. Indiana Counties in 1840

Figure 10. Indiana Counties in 1850

___C. Pence and N. C. Armstrong, IN BOUNDARIES, IN Historical Bureau, Indianapolis, IN, 1933.

![bar]
10. Recommended readings
![bar]

A knowledge of the history, geography, government, and laws of IN and its local regions is of extreme importance for tracing the genealogies of its former inhabitants. This chapter has been a brief treatment of some of these. Your next step should be the reading of two of the following relatively short one-volumed works:

___J. H. Madison, THE IN WAY, A STATE HISTORY, IN University Press, Bloomington, IN, 1986.

___R. M. Taylor, Jr., IN, A NEW HISTORICAL GUIDE, IHS, Indianapolis, IN, 1989.

___H. Peckham, IN, A BICENTENNIAL HISTORY, Norton, New York, NY, 1978.

___W. E. Wilson, IN, A HISTORY, IN University Press, Bloomington, IN, 1966.

___J. B. Martin, IN, AN INTERPRETATION, Knopf, New York, NY, 1947.

___I. Leibowitz, MY IN, Prentice-Hall, Engleewood Cliffs, NJ, 1964.

___J. Carter and D. Jones, IN, Graphics Arts Center, Portland, OR, 1984.

Three good multi-volumed works for detailed information on special topics and particular periods of IN's history are:

___J. D. Barnhart, D. L. Riker, and numerous others, THE HISTORY OF IN, IN Historical Society, Indianapolis, IN, 1965-, 6 volumes. First volume covers through 1816, the second 1816-50, the third 1850-80, the fourth 1880-1920, the fifth 1920-45, and the sixth 1945-.

___J. D. Barnhart and D. J. Carmody, IN FROM FRONTIER TO INDUSTRIAL COMMONWEALTH, Lewis Historical Publishing Co., New York, NY, 1954, 4 volumes.

___J. P. Dunn, IN AND INDIANANS, A HISTORY OF ABORIGINAL AND TERRITORIAL IN AND THE CENTURY OF STATEHOOD, American Historical Society, Chicago, IL, 1919, 6 volumes.

Some specialized volumes of particular interest include:

___R. E. Banta, THE WABASH, Farrar and Rinehart, New York, NY, 1950.

___R. C. Buley, THE OLD NORTHWEST, PIONEER PERIOD, 1815-40, IN Historical Society, Indianapolis, IN, 1950.

___D. J. Carmody, IN, A SELF-APPRAISAL, IN University Press, Bloomington, IN, 1966.

___J. B. Dillon, THE HISTORY OF IN FROM ITS EARLIEST EXPLORATION TO THE CLOSE OF THE TERRITORIAL GOVERNMENT in 1816, Sheets and Co., Indianapolis, IN, 1843.

___L. Esarey, THE IN HOME, IN University Press, Bloomington, IN, 1953. IN frontier life.

___L. Esarey, A HISTORY OF IN FROM ITS EXPLORATION TO 1850, Stewart Co., Indianapolis, IN, 1915.

___P. J. Furlong, IN, AN ILLUSTRATED HISTORY, Windsor Publns., Northridge, CA, 1985.

___R. D. Gray, THE HOOSIER STATE, READINGS in IN HISTORY, Eerdmans, Grand Rapids, MI, 1980, 2 volumes.

___D. W. Hoover, A PICTORAL HISTORY OF IN, IN University Press, Bloomington, IN, 1980.

___H, Lindley, IN AS SEEN BY EARLY TRAVELERS, IN Historical Commission, Indianapolis, IN, 1916.

___S. S. McCord, TRAVEL ACCOUNTS OF IN, 1679-1961, IN Historical Bureau, Indianapolis, IN, 1970.

___M. J. Rohrbough, THE TRANS-APPALACHIAN FRONTIER, PEOPLE, SOCIETIES, AND INSTITUTIONS, 1775-1850, Oxford Univ. Press, New York, NY, 1978.

___R. S. Simons, THE RIVERS OF IN, IN University Press, Bloomington, IN, 1985.

Definitely not to be overlooked is the major historical periodical dealing with IN. This journal is a gold mine of historical information, much of which is pertinent to IN genealogical research.

___IN MAGAZINE OF HISTORY, quarterly, Department of History, IN University, Bloomington, IN, 1905-present. With three 25-year collective indexes and also annual indexes.

LIST OF ABBREVIATIONS

ACPL	=	Allen County Public Library, Ft. Wayne, IN
AGLL	=	American Genealogical Lending Library, Bountiful, UT
CH	=	Courthouse(s)
D	=	Mortality (death) census(es)
DAR	=	Daughters of the American Revolution
F	=	Farm and ranch census(es)
FHC	=	Family History Center(s)
FHL	=	Family History Library, Salt Lake City, UT
IN	=	Indiana
IHS	=	IN Historical Society, Indianapolis, IN
ISA	=	IN State Archives, Indianapolis, IN
ISL	=	IN State Library, Indianapolis, IN
LGL	=	Large genealogical library(ies)
LL	=	Local library(ies)
M	=	Manufactures census(es)
NA	=	National Archives, Washington, DC
P	=	Revolutionary War pension census
R	=	Regular federal census(es)
RBNA	=	Regional Branches of the National Archives
RL	=	Regional library(ies)
T	=	Territorial census(es)

Chapter 2

TYPES OF RECORDS

██████████████ The state of IN is relatively rich in genealogical
1. Introduction   source materials, although there are some gaps in
                  the early years and there are some problems with
██████████████ the loss of records in court house (CH) fires, which
                  were fairly common in the 19th century. A great
deal of work has been done in accumulating, preserving, photocopying,
transcribing, and indexing records, and therefore many are readily
available. The best collections of IN materials are to be found in the
following repositories:

___(ISL) IN State Library, 140 North Senate Avenue, Indianapolis, IN,
    46204.

___(ISA) IN State Archives, Commission on Public Records, 140 North
    Senate Avenue, Indianapolis, IN, 46204.

___(IHS) IN Historical Society, Genealogy Division, 315 West Ohio
    Street, Indianapolis, IN 46202.

___(FHL) Family History Library, Genealogical Library of the Church of
    Jesus Christ of Latter-day Saints, 35 North West Temple, Salt
    Lake City, UT 84150.

___(FHC) Family History Center(s), over 1700 of them, located all over
    the world. They are local branch affiliates of the Family History
    Library (FHL). They can be found in most major US cities, in-
    cluding 9 in IN.

___(ACPL) Allen County Public Library, Historical Genealogy
    Department, 900 Webster Street, Fort Wayne, IN 46802.

Three major repositories for IN genealogical materials are
clustered together in Indianapolis: the IN State Library (ISL), the IN State
Archives (ISA), and the IN Historical Society (IHS). Together they
constitute the best place in the world to do IN genealogical research. All
three are located in the IN State Library and Historical Building.

The IN State Library (ISL) has three divisions which are of direct
interest to family researchers: the Genealogy Division, the IN Division,
and the Newspaper Division. The Genealogy Division holds about 40
thousand books, microfiche, and microfilms dealing with these sorts of
records: birth, cemetery, census, church, court, death, deed, family
histories, genealogical compilations, Indian, land, marriage, military,
mortality, naturalization, pension, probate, tax, and will, plus indexes to

many of them. The IN Division has in its holdings the following items of genealogical interest: biographical collections, city directories, city histories, church histories, county histories, manuscripts, maps, military histories, periodicals, state histories, territorial histories, and town histories. The Newspaper Division, as the name indicates, has a very large newspaper collection (over 1600) with several finding aids.

The IN State Archives (ISA) of the IN Commission on Public Records is the official repository for state records. Its chief genealogically-related materials include a large surname index and records relating to federal land, state military, state land, and veterans' graves.

The IN Historical Society is a private organization with its library on the third floor of the IN State Library and Historical Building. Its collection is made up of rare books, manuscripts, maps, business records, journals, pamphlets, and historical materials relating to IN's history, but especially the pre-territorial, territorial, and early state days.

The collections in Indianapolis are somewhat matched by that of the FHL (Family History Library) of Salt Lake City, UT. They have by far the largest collection of IN genealogical materials outside of IN. The FHL has microfilmed a vast number of IN documents, which they make available through their numerous branch libraries (called Family History Centers, FHC), located all over the US and in many overseas countries. All these materials can be readily located in the catalog of the FHL, which is available at every FHC.

The Allen County Public Library in Ft. Wayne, IN, has a Genealogy Division that puts it in the top few genealogical libraries in the US. Its IN collection is exceptionally good. The Library holds an abundance of books, microfiche, microfilms, computer data bases on CDROMs, journals, and indexes.

Finally, it should not be overlooked that there are some fairly well-stocked regional libraries (RL) in the state of IN. These are generally smaller than the large libraries noted above, but considerably larger than most town and county libraries. Of course, local libraries (LL), that is, county, city, town, and private libraries are sources which are very important to the family history researcher.

The above repositories and their collections and other sources will be treated in detail in Chapter 3. In this chapter the many types of records which are available for IN genealogical research are discussed. Those records which are essentially national or state-wide in scope will be treated in detail. Records which are basically county or city records will be discussed only generally, but a detailed listing of them will be delayed to Chapter 4, where the local records available for each of the 92 IN counties will be given.

---

2. Bible records

During the past 200 years it was customary for families with religious affiliations to keep vital statistics on their members in the family Bible. These records vary widely, but among the items that may be found are names, dates, and places of birth, christening, baptism, marriage, death, and sometimes military service. Although most Bibles containing recorded information probably still remain in private hands, some of the information has been submitted for publication and some has been filed in libraries and archives. Bible records may be found in libraries and archives throughout IN. You should inquire about such records at every possible library and archives in and near your ancestor's county or district, especially the regional libraries (RL) and the local libraries (LL). Sometimes there will be indexes or the records will be arranged alphabetically. RL will be listed in Chapter 3, and LL will be listed under the counties in Chapter 4. You should not overlook the possibility that Bible records may be listed in indexes or in files labelled something other than Bible records. The most likely ones are family records, genealogies, manuscripts, names, surnames. Also do not fail to look in the major card index of each library for the names you are seeking.

There are many published compilations of IN Bible records. Among those you should examine are:
___DAR Chapters in IN, BIBLE RECORDS, or FAMILY AND BIBLE RECORDS, or BIBLE AND CEMETERY RECORDS, and other similar titles, various DAR Chapters, various cities, various dates.
These and other Bible record compilations for IN are listed in:
___FHL, FAMILY HISTORY LIBRARY CATALOG, LOCALITY SECTION, Salt Lake City, UT, latest microfiche and/or computer edition. Look under IN and then under the county of interest.
___C. L. Miller, IN SOURCES FOR GENEALOGICAL RESEARCH IN THE ISL, IHS, Indianapolis, IN, 1984.
___E. K. Kirkham, AN INDEX TO SOME OF THE BIBLE AND FAMILY RECORDS OF THE US, Everton Publishers, Logan, UT, 1980/4, volume 2.

___National Society, DAR, DAR LIBRARY CATALOG, VOLUME 2: STATE AND LOCAL HISTORIES AND RECORDS, The Society, Washington, DC, 1986.
___CARD AND COMPUTER CATALOGS in ISL, IHS, ACPL, RL, and LL.

The Bible record compilations referred to above should be sought in the ISL, IHS, FHL(FHC), ACPL, RL, and LL, and in the DAR Library in Washington, DC. Do not fail to look for vertical files of Bible records in these repositories. Bible records also appear in genealogical periodical articles and in published family genealogies. These two types of records, as well as details on manuscript sources will be discussed in sections 18, 19, 23, and 32 of this chapter.

---

3. Biographies

There are several major national biographical works which contain sketches on nationally-prominent IN personages. There are also numerous good biographical compilations for the state of IN or for sections of it. These volumes list persons who have attained some prominence in the fields of law, agriculture, business, politics, medicine, engineering, science, military, teaching, public service, or philanthropy. There are also many local (county, township, city, town) biographical works, and numerous regional and county histories also contain biographies of leading citizens. In addition, some professional organizations have compiled biographical information on their members. All of these can be of considerable use to genealogical researchers, because they usually carry birth, marriage, and death data, as well as details on children, parents, grandparents, and other ancestors.

Over 500 national biographical compilations have been indexed in a large microfilm/computer set which contains over 6 million entries. This set is available in large libraries, and is added to annually:
___BIOBASE, Gale Research Co., Detroit, MI, latest edition. This database is the successor to M. C. Herbert and B. McNeil, BIOGRAPHY AND GENEALOGY MASTER INDEX, Gale Research Co., Detroit, MI, various dates.
In the IHS, there are surname indexes which cover IN county histories, which contain many biographical sketches. There is an index for each county. Some of them were compiled by the WPA and others by cooperating groups under the IHS.
___ALL NAME INDEXES TO COUNTY HISTORIES, IHS and Historical Records Survey, WPA, Indianapolis, IN, 1938-.

There is also available a microfiche publication which lists over 247 thousand IN names derived from over 525 different published IN historical and biographical sources. A number of these references refer you to biographical information, although many only give the name in some connection with a county.

___J. B. Parker and L. de Platt, MICROFICHE INDIANA BIO-GRAPHICAL INDEX, Genealogical Indexing Associates, West Bountiful, UT, 1983, 16 microfiche. Available at ISL and FHL(FHC).

In the 1930s and 1940s there was an IN association which solicited and compiled biographies on many people in IN:

___Citizens' Historical Association, IN BIOGRAPHIES, The Association, Indianapolis, IN, 1930-49. Biographies of many persons in many IN counties and cities. At ISL and FHL (FHC).

The Works Progress Administrations began in 1938 to compile indexes of persons and firms listed in county histories, atlases, gazetteers, and other sources in Indiana counties. Many of them were completed:

___WPA, INDEXES OF NAMES OF PERSONS AND FIRMS IN INDIANA COUNTIES, The WPA and the ISL, Indianapolis, IN, 1938 ff. At ISL and FHL (FHC).

Over the years, many regional and state biographical compilations have been published for IN or sections of it. Among the most useful of these for your investigations are:

___J. D. Barnhart, IN FROM FRONTIER TO INDUSTRIAL COMMONWEALTH, Lewis Historical Publishing Co., New York, NY, 1954, 4 volumes.

___A. D. Benesch, MEN OF INDIANA IN 1901, Benesch Publishing Co., Indianapolis, IN, 1901.

___BIOGRAPHICAL AND GENEALOGICAL HISTORY OF CASS, MIAMI, HOWARD, AND TIPTON COUNTIES, IN, McDowell Publishing Co., Owensboro, KY, 1974.

___BIOGRAPHICAL AND GENEALOGICAL HISTORY OF WAYNE, FAYETTE, UNION, AND FRANKLIN COUNTIES, IN, McDowell Publishing Co., Owensboro, KY, 1974.

___A BIOGRAPHICAL DIRECTORY OF THE IN GENERAL ASSEMBLY, 1816-1984, IN Historical Bureau, Indianapolis, IN, 1980-84, 2 volumes.

___A BIOGRAPHICAL HISTORY OF EMINENT AND SELF-MADE MEN OF THE STATE OF IN, Western Biographical Publishing Co., Cincinnati, OH, 1880, 2 volumes.

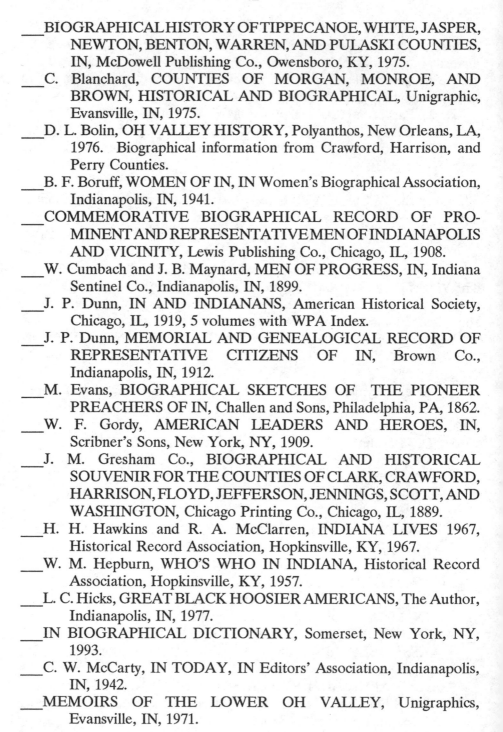

___BIOGRAPHICAL HISTORY OF TIPPECANOE, WHITE, JASPER, NEWTON, BENTON, WARREN, AND PULASKI COUNTIES, IN, McDowell Publishing Co., Owensboro, KY, 1975.

___C. Blanchard, COUNTIES OF MORGAN, MONROE, AND BROWN, HISTORICAL AND BIOGRAPHICAL, Unigraphic, Evansville, IN, 1975.

___D. L. Bolin, OH VALLEY HISTORY, Polyanthos, New Orleans, LA, 1976. Biographical information from Crawford, Harrison, and Perry Counties.

___B. F. Boruff, WOMEN OF IN, IN Women's Biographical Association, Indianapolis, IN, 1941.

___COMMEMORATIVE BIOGRAPHICAL RECORD OF PROMINENT AND REPRESENTATIVE MEN OF INDIANAPOLIS AND VICINITY, Lewis Publishing Co., Chicago, IL, 1908.

___W. Cumbach and J. B. Maynard, MEN OF PROGRESS, IN, Indiana Sentinel Co., Indianapolis, IN, 1899.

___J. P. Dunn, IN AND INDIANANS, American Historical Society, Chicago, IL, 1919, 5 volumes with WPA Index.

___J. P. Dunn, MEMORIAL AND GENEALOGICAL RECORD OF REPRESENTATIVE CITIZENS OF IN, Brown Co., Indianapolis, IN, 1912.

___M. Evans, BIOGRAPHICAL SKETCHES OF THE PIONEER PREACHERS OF IN, Challen and Sons, Philadelphia, PA, 1862.

___W. F. Gordy, AMERICAN LEADERS AND HEROES, IN, Scribner's Sons, New York, NY, 1909.

___J. M. Gresham Co., BIOGRAPHICAL AND HISTORICAL SOUVENIR FOR THE COUNTIES OF CLARK, CRAWFORD, HARRISON, FLOYD, JEFFERSON, JENNINGS, SCOTT, AND WASHINGTON, Chicago Printing Co., Chicago, IL, 1889.

___H. H. Hawkins and R. A. McClarren, INDIANA LIVES 1967, Historical Record Association, Hopkinsville, KY, 1967.

___W. M. Hepburn, WHO'S WHO IN INDIANA, Historical Record Association, Hopkinsville, KY, 1957.

___L. C. Hicks, GREAT BLACK HOOSIER AMERICANS, The Author, Indianapolis, IN, 1977.

___IN BIOGRAPHICAL DICTIONARY, Somerset, New York, NY, 1993.

___C. W. McCarty, IN TODAY, IN Editors' Association, Indianapolis, IN, 1942.

___MEMOIRS OF THE LOWER OH VALLEY, Unigraphics, Evansville, IN, 1971.

___MEMORIAL RECORD OF DISTINGUISHED MEN OF INDIANAPOLIS AND IN, Lewis Publishing Co., Chicago, IL, 1912.

___MEMORIAL RECORD OF NORTHEASTERN IN, Lewis Publishing Co., Chicago, IL, 1896.

___W. D. Nesbit, WHO'S HOOSIER, IN Society of Chicago, Chicago, IL, 1912, 2 volumes.

___PICTORIAL AND BIOGRAPHICAL RECORD OF LAPORTE, PORTER, LAKE, AND STARKE COUNTIES, IN, Goodspeed Publishing Co., Chicago, IL, 1894.

___PICTORIAL AND BIOGRAPHICAL RECORD OF MONT-GOMERY, PARKE, AND FOUNTAIN COUNTIES, IN, Chapman Brothers, Chicago, IL, 1893.

___G. I. Reed, ENCYCLOPEDIA OF BIOGRAPHY OF IN, Century Publishing Co., Chicago, IL, 1895, 2 volumes.

___C. Roll, IN, 150 YEARS OF AMERICAN DEVELOPMENT, Lewis Publishing Co., Chicago, IL, 1931, 5 volumes.

___O. H. Smith, EARLY IN TRIALS AND SKETCHES, Moore, Wilstach, Keys, and Co, Cincinnati, OH, 1858.

___W. H. Smith, THE HISTORY OF THE STATE OF IN, 1763-1897, Blair, Indianapolis, IN, 1897, 2 volumes.

___C. W. Taylor, BIOGRAPHICAL SKETCHES AND REVIEW OF THE BENCH AND BAR OF IN, Bench and Bar Publishing Co., Indianapolis, IN, 1895.

___F. M. Trissal, PUBLIC MEN OF IN, Conkey Co., Hammond, IN, 1922-23, 2 volumes.

___WHO'S WHO IN INDIANA, A BIOGRAPHICAL DICTIONARY, Larkin, Roosevelt, and Larkin, Chicago, IL, 1947.

___W. W. Woollen, BIOGRAPHICAL AND HISTORICAL SKETCHES OF IN, Hammond, IN, 1883.

Most of these volumes will be found in ISL, IHS, ACPL, and FHL(FHC). Those pertinent to various regions will usually be found in RL and larger LL in the area.

In addition to the above national, state, and regional biographical works, there are many local (county, township, district, city, and town) biographical volumes. Further, biographical sketches are more often than not included in county histories. Listings of many of the biographical volumes and county histories are provided in:

___FAMILY HISTORY LIBRARY CATALOG, LOCALITY SECTION, on microfiche and computer, FHL, Salt Lake City, UT, and at every FHC.

___M. J. Kaminkow, US LOCAL HISTORIES IN THE LIBRARY OF
   CONGRESS, Magna Carta Book Co., Baltimore, MD, 1975, 5
   volumes, with SUPPLEMENTS.
___P. W. Filby, A BIBLIOGRAPHY OF AMERICAN COUNTY
   HISTORIES, Genealogical Publishing Co., Baltimore, MD, 1985.
When volumes containing biographical information are available in the
various IN counties, this fact will be noted under the county listings in
Chapter 4. Such volumes will be found in ISL, IHS, ACPL, and
FHL(FHC). Those pertinent to various counties will be found in RL and
LL in the counties. There are also some special biographical collections
and some unpublished compilations in several IN libraries. Do not fail to
inquire in libraries near your ancestor's homeplace. Care should be
exercised in taking the data in biographical sketches too literally.
Remember that your ancestor or some family member supplied the
information, quite often from memory and/or family tradition, and
sometimes from an inventive imagination.

---

4. Birth records   Prior to 1882, a few IN cities kept some
incomplete birth records. These include Fort
Wayne in 1870, Indianapolis in 1872, Logansport
in 1874, and Kokomo in 1875. In 1881, the state
of IN passed a law requiring birth and death
records to be kept in IN counties, cities, and towns, starting in 1882. This
law was largely not enforced, so the records are quite incomplete in some
counties. In 1907, it was mandated by the state that copies of all birth
records be sent to the state capital. Again, enforcement and compliance
were not complete at first, and it was 1915 or 1916 before the records
began to approach being complete. By about 1920, compliance was almost
complete. The birth records available for each IN county are indicated in
the separate county listings in Chapter 4.

The WPA has compiled and indexed many of the available county
birth records for period 1882-1920. They are arranged by the county, and
then under each county are listed alphabetically.
___Historical Records Survey, INDEXES TO BIRTHS, DEATHS,
   MARRIAGES, AND MISCELLANEOUS RECORDS OF IN
   COUNTIES, WPA, Indianapolis, IN, 1938-. Birth data available
   for 68 out of the 92 IN counties.
Counties for which birth indexes are not available include Blackford,
Brown, Crawford, Dearborn, Decatur, Dubois, Fayette, Grant, Jefferson,
Jennings, Lawrence, Marshall, Miami, Noble, Ohio, Randolph, Ripley,

Rush, Scott, Steuben, Switzerland, Tipton, Union, Wabash, and Whitley. These indexes will be found in ISL, IHS, ACPL, and FHL(FHC).

In 1907 the state of IN passed a law requiring state-wide birth registration in addition to the county registration. By 1920 the registrations were running at least 95% complete. These records are in the county or city health departments as well as in the central state repository at Columbus:
___Division of Vital Records, IN State Board of Health, PO Box 1964, Indianapolis, IN, 42606. The Division has indexes.
These records usually contain name of child, place and date of birth, sex, color, name and age and birthplace of father, and maiden name and age and birthplace of mother. In many counties, there were delayed and amended birth registrations, so be sure and seek them out, if you do not find what you want in the regular records.

Prior to the time when IN birth reports come to be almost complete (1908-20), other records may yield dates and places of birth: biographical, cemetery, census, church, death, divorce, marriage, military, mortuary, newspaper, pension, and published. These are all discussed in other sections of this chapter. The finding of birth record articles in genealogical periodicals is also described separately in this chapter.

5. Cemetery records

If you know or suspect that your ancestor was buried in a certain cemetery, the best thing to do is to write to the caretaker of the cemetery, enclose an SASE and $5, and ask if the records show your ancestor. If this fails, other cemeteries in the region can be investigated. Very convenient listings of many IN cemeteries are provided in:
___CEMETERY LOCATOR FILE, ISL, Indianapolis, IN. Card index of cemeteries giving locations of cemeteries and locations of records. Also available at FHL(FHC) on microfilm.
___M. D. Carty, SEARCHING IN INDIANA, ISC Publications, Costa Mesa, CA, 1985.

Should this prove unsuccessful, then the next step is to look into cemetery record collections for your ancestor's county. These have been made by the DAR, the WPA's IN Historical Records Survey, local genealogical and historical societies, and individuals. Much work has been done, and at least some cemeteries in every county have been read and

the data published. Listings of many of the available records will be found
in:

___FAMILY HISTORY LIBRARY CATALOG, LOCALITY SECTION,
FHL, Salt Lake City, UT, latest edition, on both microfiche and
computer. Look under IN and its counties.

___National Society, DAR, DAR LIBRARY CATALOG, VOLUME
TWO: STATE AND LOCAL HISTORIES AND RECORDS,
The Society, Washington, DC, 1986.

When you consult these, you will find that the main sources of IN
cemetery records are the ISL, IHS, ACPL, and FHL(FHC). In addition,
local libraries (LL) in the IN counties often have records of their own
cemeteries. IN regional libraries (RL) and large genealogical libraries
(LGL) outside of IN may also have records.

Several of the larger genealogical periodicals published in IN
contain cemetery listings quite frequently (especially Genealogy, IN
Genealogist, Hoosier Genealogist, Southern IN Genealogical Society
Quarterly, Hoosier Journal of Ancestry, and Tri-State Packet). In addition, many of the local genealogical publications carry cemetery records
from time to time. A useful index which covers many periodicals and
which will locate many of these articles for you is:

___Allen County Public Library, PERIODICAL SOURCE INDEX, The
Library Staff, Fort Wayne, IN, many volumes, 1985-.

There are also some cemetery record compilations which could be of value
to you:

___CEMETERY RECORDS OF IN, Genealogical Society of UT, Salt
Lake City, UT, 1954-64, 6 volumes.

___J. H. Fox, SELECTED GRAVESTONE INSCRIPTIONS IN
ILLINOIS, INDIANA, AND KANSAS, Genealogical Society of
UT, Salt Lake City, UT, 1980.

___VETERANS' GRAVE REGISTRATION FILE, ISA, Indianapolis,
IN. Graves of veterans buried in IN. Covers some cemeteries in
50 of the 92 counties. Also on micrrofilm at ISL.

___DAR of IN, ROSTER OF SOLDIERS AND PATRIOTS OF THE
AMERICAN REVOLUTION BURIED IN INDIANA,
Genealogical Publishing Co., Baltimore, MD, 1968.

___M. R. Waters, REVOLUTIONARY SOLDIERS BURIED IN
INDIANA, Genealogical Publishing Co., Baltimore, MD, 1970.

There are files of veterans' graves in the County Offices in almost all IN
counties. And in some of them, you will also find one or more grave
registration books.

In Chapter 4, those counties for which extensive cemetery records exist in printed or microfilmed form are indicated. Instructions regarding locating the above reference volumes and the records themselves will be presented in Chapter 3. More detailed instructions regarding the finding of cemetery records in genealogical periodical articles are given in a section of this chapter devoted to such periodicals.

6. Census records

Excellent ancestor information is available in six types of census reports which have been accumulated for IN: the IN Territorial Census of 1807 (T), the regular federal censuses (R), the federal farm and ranch censuses (F), the federal manufactures censuses (M), the federal mortality censuses (D for death), and the special 1840 Revolutionary War Pension Census (P).

In 1807 a Census of the IN Territory (T) was taken. The census was meant to list every free white male over 21, but in some cases only the head of the household is given. This enumeration was collected in the existing counties of the Territory: Clark, Dearborn, Knox, and Randolph (now in IL). The data for Clark County were missing, so the voters list has been substituted, and a poll list for Randolph County has also been added. The information is published in:
___R. Fraustein, CENSUS OF IN TERRITORY FOR 1807, IHS, Indianapolis, IN, 1980.
Also useful are several compiled volumes:
___C. M. Franklin, IN TERRITORIAL PIONEER RECORDS, 1801-15, Heritage House, Indianapolis, IN, 1983.
___R. V. Jackson, EARLY IN, Accelerated Indexing Systems, Bountiful, UT, 1980.
Not to be overlooked in the territorial period is a volume of selected records of the IN Territory. The volume gives many names and is indexed.
___C. E. Carter, TERRITORIAL PAPERS OF THE US, VOLUME 7, IN TERRITORY, AMS Press, New York, NY, 1973. Also available as National Archives, TERRITORIAL PAPERS OF THE US, Microfilm M721, The Archives, Washington, DC.
Another set of records which has some use is:
___National Archives, TERRITORIAL PAPERS OF THE US SENATE, 1789-1873, Microfilm M200, The Archives, Washington, DC.

The only 1810 <u>Regular</u> (R) census for IN to survive are the schedules for Exeter and Harrison Townships of Harrison County. They have been published:

___1810 CENSUS FOR HARRISON COUNTY, IN (HARRISON AND EXETER TOWNSHIPS), Hoosier Genealogist, Volume 16 (June 1976) 22-49.

Otherwise, <u>Regular</u> census records (R) are available for almost all IN counties in 1820, 1830, 1840, 1850, 1860, 1870, 1880, 1900, 1910, and 1920. The major exception is that the data for Daviess County in the 1820 census are missing. Please note also that the 1890 census did not survive. The 1840 census and all before it listed the head of the household plus a breakdown of the number of persons in the household according to age and sex brackets. Beginning in 1850 the names of all persons were recorded along with age, sex, real estate, marital, and other information, including the state of birth. With the 1880 census and thereafter, the birthplaces of the mother and father of each person are also shown. Chapter 4 lists the regular census records (R) available for each of the 92 IN counties.

State-wide indexes have been compiled and most have been printed for the 1820, 1830, 1840, 1850, 1860, and 1880 IN regular census records. These volumes are:

___W. C. Heiss, 1820 FEDERAL CENSUS FOR IN, IHS, Indianapolis, IN, 1966. 24,000 names.

___E. M. Cox, 1820 IN FEDERAL CENSUS, The Compiler, Ellensburgh, WA, 1973.

___R. V. Jackson, IN 1820 CENSUS INDEX, Accelerated Indexing Systems, Bountiful, UT, 1976. About 24,000 entries.

___Automated Archives, 1820 IN CENSUS INDEX, CDROM 154, AGLL, Bountiful, UT, 1993.

___IN State Library, INDEX TO THE 1830 FEDERAL POPULATION CENSUS FOR IN, IHS, Indianapolis, IN, 1981.

___R. V. Jackson, IN 1830 CENSUS INDEX, Accelerated Indexing Systems, Bountiful, UT, 1976. About 56,000 entries.

___Automated Archives, 1830 IN CENSUS INDEX, CDROM 148, AGLL, Bountiful, UT, 1993.

___IN State Library, INDEX, 1840 FEDERAL POPULATION CENSUS FOR IN, IHS, Indianapolis, IN, 1975.

___R. V. Jackson, IN 1840 CENSUS INDEX, Accelerated Indexing Systems, Bountiful, UT, 1976.

___Automated Archives, 1840 IN CENSUS INDEX, CDROM 153, AGLL, Bountiful, UT, 1993.

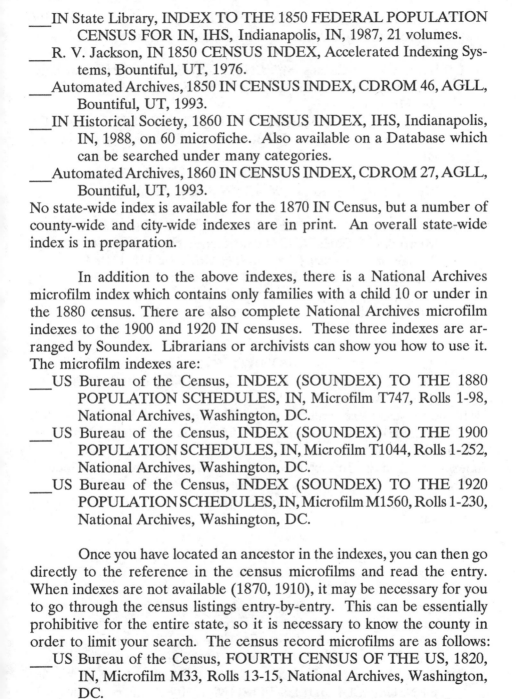

___IN State Library, INDEX TO THE 1850 FEDERAL POPULATION
  CENSUS FOR IN, IHS, Indianapolis, IN, 1987, 21 volumes.

___R. V. Jackson, IN 1850 CENSUS INDEX, Accelerated Indexing Sys-
  tems, Bountiful, UT, 1976.

___Automated Archives, 1850 IN CENSUS INDEX, CDROM 46, AGLL,
  Bountiful, UT, 1993.

___IN Historical Society, 1860 IN CENSUS INDEX, IHS, Indianapolis,
  IN, 1988, on 60 microfiche. Also available on a Database which
  can be searched under many categories.

___Automated Archives, 1860 IN CENSUS INDEX, CDROM 27, AGLL,
  Bountiful, UT, 1993.

No state-wide index is available for the 1870 IN Census, but a number of
county-wide and city-wide indexes are in print. An overall state-wide
index is in preparation.

In addition to the above indexes, there is a National Archives
microfilm index which contains only families with a child 10 or under in
the 1880 census. There are also complete National Archives microfilm
indexes to the 1900 and 1920 IN censuses. These three indexes are arranged by Soundex. Librarians or archivists can show you how to use it.
The microfilm indexes are:

___US Bureau of the Census, INDEX (SOUNDEX) TO THE 1880
  POPULATION SCHEDULES, IN, Microfilm T747, Rolls 1-98,
  National Archives, Washington, DC.

___US Bureau of the Census, INDEX (SOUNDEX) TO THE 1900
  POPULATION SCHEDULES, IN, Microfilm T1044, Rolls 1-252,
  National Archives, Washington, DC.

___US Bureau of the Census, INDEX (SOUNDEX) TO THE 1920
  POPULATION SCHEDULES, IN, Microfilm M1560, Rolls 1-230,
  National Archives, Washington, DC.

Once you have located an ancestor in the indexes, you can then go
directly to the reference in the census microfilms and read the entry.
When indexes are not available (1870, 1910), it may be necessary for you
to go through the census listings entry-by-entry. This can be essentially
prohibitive for the entire state, so it is necessary to know the county in
order to limit your search. The census record microfilms are as follows:

___US Bureau of the Census, FOURTH CENSUS OF THE US, 1820,
  IN, Microfilm M33, Rolls 13-15, National Archives, Washington,
  DC.

___US Bureau of the Census, FIFTH CENSUS OF THE US, 1830, IN,
  Microfilm M19, Rolls 26-32, National Archives, Washington, DC.

___US Bureau of the Census, SIXTH CENSUS OF THE US, 1840, IN, Microfilm M704, Rolls 74-100, National Archives, Washington, DC.

___US Bureau of the Census, SEVENTH CENSUS OF THE US, 1850, IN, Microfilm M432, Rolls 135-181, National Archives, Washington, DC.

___US Bureau of the Census, EIGHTH CENSUS OF THE US, 1860, IN, Microfilm M653, Rolls 242-309, National Archives, Washington, DC.

___US Bureau of the Census, NINTH CENSUS OF THE US, 1870, IN, Microfilm M593, Rolls 296-373, National Archives, Washington, DC.

___US Bureau of the Census, TENTH CENSUS OF THE US, 1880, IN, Microfilm T9, Rolls 263-324, National Archives, Washington, DC.

___US Bureau of the Census, TWELFTH CENSUS OF THE US, 1900, IN, Microfilm T623, Rolls 357-414, National Archives, Washington, DC.

___US Bureau of the Census, THIRTEENTH CENSUS OF THE US, 1910, IN, Microfilm T624, Rolls 338-389, National Archives, Washington, DC.

___US Bureau of the Census, FOURTEENTH CENSUS OF THE US, 1920, IN, Microfilm T625, Rolls 420-475, National Archives, Washington, DC.

Both the census indexes and the census films are available in NA, RBNA, ISL, ACPL, FHL(FHC), and some RL, LGL, and LL. Other LL have the printed or microfiche or computer disk indexes, but not the microfilmed indexes or censuses. In such cases, LL can borrow the microfilm indexes and/or censuses on interlibrary loan from:

___American Genealogical Lending Library, PO Box 329, Bountiful, UT 84011.

Farm and ranch census records (F), also known as agricultural census records, are available for 1850, 1860, 1870, and 1880 for IN. These records list the name of the owner, size of the farm or ranch, value of the property, and other details. If your ancestor was a farmer (many were), it will be worthwhile to seek him in these records. No indexes are available, so it helps to know the county. The records or microfilm copies are available at ISL, FHL(FHC), and ACPL. The records appear in:

___IN State Library, AGRICULTURAL (FARM AND RANCH) CENSUS SCHEDULES FOR IN, 1850-80, on microfilm, ISL, Indianapolis, IN.

These schedules can be very useful because in several census years, particularly 1850, many rural families were omitted in the regular census, but may be found in the farm and ranch schedules.

Manufactures census records (M), also known as industry census records, are available for 1850, 1860, 1870, and 1880. The records list manufacturing firms which produced articles having an annual value of $500 or more. Given in these records are the name of the firm, the owner, the product, the machinery used, and the number of employees. No indexes are available, so a knowledge of the county is helpful. The records or microfilmed copies are at ISL, FHL(FHC), and ACPL. The records appear in:
___IN State Library, MANUFACTURES CENSUS SCHEDULES FOR IN, 1850-80, on microfilm, ISL, Indianapolis, IN.

Mortality census records (D for death) are available for the periods June 01-May 31, 1850, 1860, 1870, and 1880. These records give information on persons who died in the year preceding the 1st of June of each of the above census dates (1850, 1860, 1870, 1880). They are very useful, but are only 60-70% complete. The data contained in the compilations include name, age, sex, occupation, place of birth and other such information. The ISL holds the original schedules along with a card index, and the schedules have been microfilmed. The microfilms are available at ISL, ACPL, and FHC(FHL).
___IN State Library, MORTALITY CENSUS SCHEDULES FOR IN, 1850-80, on microfilm, Luther Co., Indianapolis, IN. Card index and published index in ISL.
The mortality censuses are also recorded and indexed on a CDROM:
___Automated Archives, MORTALITY RECORDS, CDROM 164, AGLL, Bountiful, UT, 1995.
The 1850 mortality data have also been published in an indexed volume:
___L. M. Volkel, 1850 IN MORTALITY SCHEDULE, Ye Olde Genealogie Shoppe, Indianapolis, IN, 1971.

In 1840 a special census of Revolutionary War Pensioners (P) was taken. This compilation was an attempt to list all pension holders, however, there are some omissions and some false entries. The list and an index have been published:
___CENSUS OF PENSIONERS, A GENERAL INDEX FOR REVO-LUTIONARY OR MILITARY SERVICE (1840), Genealogical Publishing Co., Baltimore, MD, 1965.

This volume may be found at ISL, IHS, FHL(FHC), AND ACPL, and in some RL and LL.

<hr/>

7. Church records

<hr/>

Many early IN families were affiliated with a church, many denominations being represented by 1850: Amish, Baptist, Catholic, Christian (Disciples), Episcopal, Friends (Quakers), German Baptist (Dunkers), Jewish, Lutheran, Mennonite, Methodist, Presbyterian, and United Brethren. As of this date of 1850, the major groups in order of decreasing size were Methodist, Baptist, Presbyterian, Christian (Disciples), Friends, Catholic, and Lutheran. Important volumes regarding the denominations in IN are:

___L. C. Rudolph, HOOSIER FAITHS, A HISTORY OF INDIANA'S CHURCHES AND RELIGIOUS GROUPS, IN University Press, Bloomington, IN, 1995.

___Historical Records Survey, A DIRECTORY OF CHURCHES AND RELIGIOUS ORGANIZATIONS IN INDIANA, WPA, Indianapolis, IN, 1941, 3 volumes.

It is well to recognize however, that many early IN settlers had no church affiliation. They were not irreligious, but they were often indifferent to religious organizations.

The records of the churches often prove to be very valuable since they frequently contain information on births, baptisms, marriages, deaths, admissions, dismissals, and reprimands. The data are particularly important for the years before county or state vital records were kept. Unfortunately, records of evangelical Protestant churches tend not to contain birth and death references. Many church records have been copied into books or microfilmed, some have been sent to denominational archives, but many still remain in the individual churches. Several major works and collections list sizable numbers of available church records:

___Historical Records Survey, A DIRECTORY OF CHURCHES AND RELIGIOUS ORGANIZATIONS IN INDIANA, WPA, Indianapolis, IN, 1941, 3 volumes.

___L. C. Rudolph and J. E. Endelman, RELIGION IN INDIANA, A GUIDE TO HISTORICAL SOURCES, IN University Press, Bloomington, IN, 1986. Church repositories are listed on pages 133-186, and congregational histories are listed on pages 189-211.

___FAMILY HISTORY LIBRARY CATALOG, LOCALITY SECTION, FHL, Salt Lake City, UT, latest edition. Look under IN and its counties.

___MANUSCRIPT AND LOCALITY CARD AND COMPUTER CATALOGS, at ISL, IHS, ACPL, and RL.

Use of the above works will convince you that the major sources of church records are the individual churches, ISL, IHS, ACPL, FHL(FHC), RL, and special denominational archives. If you have the good fortune to know your ancestor's church, then you can write directly to the proper church official, enclosing a $5 donation and an SASE, and requesting a search of the records. If you don't know the church and therefore need to look at records of several churches in the county, the above-mentioned books and the collections at the aforementioned repositories should be consulted. LL may have some local records, as is the case for LGL. The RL usually have some records for the area. In Chapter 4, counties which have church records in published or microfilmed form are indicated. Instructions regarding the above referenced volumes and locating the records will be given in Chapter 3. Church records are often published in genealogical periodicals, so instructions for finding these will be given in a section to follow.

If, as is often the case, after exploring the resources mentioned above, you have not located your ancestor's church, you will need to dig deeper. This further searching should involve writing letters (with an SASE) to the LL, the local genealogical society, and/or the local historical society. Names and addresses of these organizations are given under the various counties in Chapter 4. If these procedures still do not yield data, then it might be well for you to contact the headquarters of the denomination you think your ancestor may have belonged to. It is well to remember that English immigrants were usually Episcopalian, Methodist, Quaker, or Congregational, Germans and Swiss were usually Lutheran or Reformed or German Methodist (although those from southern Germany were often Catholic), the Scots-Irish were generally Presbyterian or Quaker, the Dutch were Reformed, the Swedes Lutheran, and the Irish ordinarily Roman Catholic. The denominational headquarters can usually give you a list of the churches of their denomination in a given county, and the dates of their origin. Often they can also direct you to collections of church records.

Some of the major denominations of IN are listed below along with brief historical notes, their denominational and/or historical headquarters, and books which deal with their histories and/or genealogical records.

___(Amish) Broke away from Swiss Mennonites in 1693 under leadership of Jakob Ammann. First came to America in 1727, settling in PA. The largest numbers came from PA into the IN counties of Elkhart and Adams in the period 1830-50. They spread later into neighboring northern counties, and to counties in central and southern IN. Contact: Archives of the Mennonite Church, 1700 South Main St., Goshen, IN 46526. Books: J. A. Hostetler, AMISH SOCIETY, Johns Hopkins Press, Baltimore, MD, 1980; J. A. Hostetler, ANNOTATED BIBLIOGRAPHY OF THE AMISH, Mennonite Publishing House, Scottsdale, PA, 1951; J. C. Wenger, MENNONITES IN INDIANA AND MI, Herald Press, Scottsdale, PA, 1961; E. E. Gingerich, IN AMISH DIRECTORY, ELKHART AND LAGRANGE COUNTIES, Johns Hopkins Press, Baltimore, MD, 1971; D. A. Hilty, IN AMISH DIRECTORY, ADAMS COUNTY AND VICINITY, The Author, Monroe, IN, 1984.

___(Baptist) Originated under leadership of John Smyth, who organized a Baptist Church among English exiles in Holland about 1607. Some of these exiles returned to England and started a Baptist Church there in 1611. The first Baptist Church in the American colonies was formed in Providence, RI, by Roger Williams in 1639. The first Baptist Church in IN met in 1798 in Clark's Grant in the southern part of the state, just across the river from Louisville. There are four major Baptist groups today: American Baptist Churches, Southern Baptist Convention (separated in 1845), - National Baptist Convention USA, and National Baptist Convention of America (separated in 1880), the latter two being predominantly black. Contacts: Franklin College Library, Franklin, IN 46131; American Baptist Churches, PO Box 851, Valley Forge, PA 19482; American Baptist Historical Society, 1100 South Goodman Street, Rochester, NY 14620; Southern Baptist Historical Commission, 901 Commerce Street, Nashville, TN 37203; National Baptist Convention USA Headquarters, 1620 Whites Creek Pike, Nashville, TN 37207. Books: W. T. Stott, IN BAPTIST HISTORY, 1798-1908, Franklin College, Franklin, IN, 1908; W. W. Sweet, RELIGION ON THE AMERICAN FRONTIER, VOL. 1, BAPTISTS, Harper, New York, NY, 1931; R. G. Torbet, A HISTORY OF THE BAPTISTS, Judson Press, Valley Forge, PA, 1973; H. L. McBeth, THE BAPTIST HERITAGE, Broadman Press, Nashville, TN, 1983; ENCY-CLOPEDIA OF SOUTHERN BAPTISTS, Broadman Press, Nashville, TN, 1958, 3 volumes.

___(Brethren or Dunkers) A German pietistic Anabaptist sect founded in 1709 by Alexander Mack in Schwarzenau, Germany. First came to American colonies in 1719, settling at Germantown, PA. The first IN Brethren came in the 1800s and 1810s from PA, OH, NC, and KY. Headquarters: Church of the Brethren, 1451 Dundee Avenue, Elgin, IL 60120; also contact Fellowship of Brethren Genealogists at the same address; Library, Manchester College, College Avenue, North Manchester, IN 46962. Books: H. Holsinger, HISTORY OF THE TUNKERS AND THE BRETHREN CHURCH, Pacific Press, Lathrop, CA, 1901; M. G. Brumbaugh, A HISTORY OF THE GERMAN BAPTIST BRETHREN IN EUROPE AND AMERICA, AMS Press, New York, NY, 1909; O. Winger, HISTORY OF THE CHURCH OF THE BRETHREN IN INDIANA, Brethren Publishing House, Elgin, IL, 1917; S. Bowers, PLANTING THE FAITH IN A NEW LAND, THE HISTORY OF THE CHURCH OF THE BRETHREN IN INDIANA, Church of the Brethren in IN, Indianapolis, IN, 1992; THE BRETHREN ENCYCLOPEDIA, Brethren Encyclopedia, Inc., Philadelphia, PA, 1983-4, 3 volumes.

___(Christian Church-Disciples of Christ) Established largely from a melding of movements started by three Presbyterians, Barton W. Stone (1804) in KY and Thomas and Alexander Campbell (1809) in PA. Within a short time, there were numerous Christian churches in IN. Contact: Disciples of Christ Historical Society, 1101 Nineteenth Avenue, Nashville, TN 37212; Christian Theological Seminary, 1000 West 42nd St., Indianapolis, IN 46208; Books: W. E. Garrison and A. T. DeGroot, THE DISCIPLES OF CHRIST, A HISTORY, Bethany Press, St. Louis, MO, 1948; C. W. Cauble, DISCIPLES OF CHRIST IN INDIANA, Meigs Publ. Co., Indianapolis, IN, 1930.

___(Churches of Christ) Individual churches began to split off from the Christian Church (Disciples) after the 1860s, the movement being essentially complete by about 1900. The Christian Church had been established from a melding of movements started by Barton W. Stone (1804) of KY and by Thomas and Alexander Campbell (1809) of PA. Contact: Harding Graduate School of Religion Library, 1000 Cherry Road, Memphis, TN 38117. Books: W. E. Garrison and A. T. DeGroot, THE DISCIPLES OF CHRIST, A HISTORY, Bethany Press, St. Louis, MO, 1948; A. T. DeGroot, THE GROUNDS OF DIVISIONS AMONG THE DISCIPLES OF CHRIST, The Author, St. Louis, MO, 1940.

___(Congregationalists) Started in England in the early 1600s as a branch of Puritanism, called Separatists. First settled in the colonies in MA in 1620, where they merged with non-Separatist Puritan settlers to form the Congregational Church. In 1931, they merged with other groups to form the Congregational Christian Churches. This group, in turn, merged with the Evangelical and Reformed Church in 1957 to form the United Church of Christ. Contact: Congregational Library, 14 Beacon Street, Boston, MA 02108. Books: W. W. Sweet, RELIGION ON THE AMERICAN FRONTIER, VOL. 3, THE CONGREGATIONALISTS, Harper, New York, NY, 1939-40; G. G. Atkins and F. L. Fagley, HISTORY OF AMERICAN CONGREGATIONALISM, Pilgrim Press, Boston, MA, 1942; W. Walker, THE HISTORY OF THE CONGREGATIONAL CHURCHES IN THE US, American Congregational Historical Society, New York, NY, 1894.

___(Episcopal Church) Developed from the Church of England which split from the Roman Catholic Church in 1534. First brought to the American colonies by English settlers of VA in 1607. Contact: Archives of the Episcopal Church, 815 Second Avenue, New York, NY 10017; Library and Archives of the Church Historical Society, 606 Rathervue Place, Austin, TX 78767; Books: J. M. Booth, HISTORY OF THE EPISCOPAL DIOCESE OF INDIANAPOLIS, 1838-1988, The Diocese, Indianapolis, IN, 1988; THE EPISCOPAL CHURCH ANNUAL, Morehouse, Wilton, CT, latest issue; W. S. Perry, HISTORY OF THE AMERICAN EPISCOPAL CHURCH, 1587-1883, Osgood, Boston, MA, 1885, 2 volumes; R. W. Albright, A HISTORY OF THE PROTESTANT EPISCOPAL CHURCH, Macmillan, New York, NY, 1964.

___(German Methodists) There were two predominant groups of German people who adopted Methodist polity. The first was the United Brethren established by Philip W. Otterbein and Martin Boehm in PA in 1800. The second was the Evangelical Church formed by Jacob Albright in PA in 1803. These two united in 1946 to form the Evangelical United Brethren which in turn, united with the Methodist Church in 1968 to form the United Methodist Church. Contact: Center for Evangelical United Brethren Studies, 1810 Harvard Boulevard, Dayton, OH 45406; Archives and Library, Huntington College, Huntington, IN 46750; Books: A. B. Condo, HISTORY OF THE IN CONFERENCE OF THE CHURCH OF THE UNITED BRETHREN IN CHRIST, The Conference, Huntington, IN, 1926; J. M. Overton, MINISTERS AND CHURCHES

OF THE CENTRAL GERMAN (METHODIST) CONFERENCE, 1835-1907, Heritage House, Thomson, IL, 1975; P. F. Douglass, THE STORY OF GERMAN METHODISM, Methodist Book Concern, New York, NY, 1939.

___(Jewish) Jewish congregations stem back to the Old Testament patriarch Abraham at about 1900 BC. The first established religious community was formed in 1654 in New York, NY. The first IN Jewish association, a burial society, was established in 1849 at Lafayette, a synagogue being formed shortly thereafter. Contact: American Jewish Archives, 3101 Clifton Avenue, Cincinnati, OH 45220; American Jewish Historical Society, 2 Thornton Road, Waltham, MA 02154; Jewish Historical Society of IN, 215 East Berry St., Ft. Wayne, IN 46892. Books: IN JEWISH HISTORY, IN Jewish Historical Society, Ft. Wayne, IN, 1992, and preceding issues; JEWISH ENCYCLOPEDIA, Funk and Wagnalls, New York, NY, 1901-6, 12 volumes; D. Rottenberg, FINDING YOUR FATHERS, Random House, New York, NY, 1977; M. H. Stern, FIRST AMERICAN JEWISH FAMILIES, American Jewish Archives, Cincinnati, OH, 1991.

___(Lutheran) Lutheran church bodies derive from the controversy of Martin Luther with the Roman Catholic Church in the Germanic area in 1521. A Dutch Lutheran Church was formed in New Amsterdam (New York, NY) in the middle 1600s, but most of the early Lutherans came from Germanic areas into Philadelphia and New York, and then moved north, west, and south. Today there are several Lutheran groups, so it may be necessary to contact several agencies. Contact: Lutheran Church MO Synod Archives and Library, 801 De Mun Avenue, St. Louis, MO 63105; Archives of the Lutheran Church in America, 333 Wartburg Place, Dubuque, IA 52001; Lutheran Archives Center, 7301 Germantown Avenue, Philadelphia, PA 19119; Archives of Cooperative Lutheranism, Evangelical Lutheran Church in America, 8765 West Higgins Road, Chicago, IL 60631; Lutheran Church MO Synod, IN District Archives, South Barr St., Ft. Wayne, IN 46802; Lutheran KY-IN Synod Archives, 3733 North Meridian St., Indianapolis, IN 46208; ELCA Archives, 8765 West Higgins Road, Chicago, IL 60631; Books: J. Bodensieck, THE ENCYCLOPEDIA OF THE LUTHERAN CHURCH, Augsburg Publishing House, Minneapolis, MN, 1965; E. L. Luecker, LUTHERAN CYCLOPEDIA, Concordia Press, St. Louis, MO, 1975.

___(Mennonite) This denomination originated in Switzerland under the leadership of Conrad Grebel and Georg Blaurock in 1525. They were originally known as Anabaptists, but took the name Mennonites after their leader Menno Simons who joined them in 1536. Their first settlement in the American colonies was at Germantown, PA, in 1683. Contact: Mennonite Historical Committee, 1700 South Main, Goshen IN 46526; Mennonite General Office, 421 South Second Street, Elkhart, IN 46516. Books: J. C. Wenger, MENNONITES IN INDIANA AND MICHIGAN, Herald Press, Scottsdale, PA, 1961; H. S. Bender and C. H. Smith, THE MENNONITE ENCYCLOPEDIA, Mennonite Brethren Publishing House, Hillsboro, KS, 1955-9, 4 volumes; C. J. Dyck, AN INTRODUCTION TO MENNONITE HISTORY, Herald Press, Scottsdale, PA, 1967.

___(Methodist) The Methodist movement began in the Church of England in the late 1720s under the leadership of John Wesley. In 1784, the group formally separated from the Church of England. Methodist circuit riders came into IN from KY and OH in the late 1790s and early 1800s and congregations were rapidly established. Contact: Archives of IN United Methodism, West Library, DePauw University, Greencastle, IN 46153; General Commission on Archives and History, The United Methodist Church, P.O. Box 127, Madison, NJ 07940; Historical Archives of the Free Methodist Church, 901 College, Winona Lake, IN 46590; Wesleyan Methodist Church Archives, PO Box 2000, Marion, IN 46952. Books: H. L. Heller, IN CONFERENCE OF THE METHODIST CHURCH, 1832-1956, Historical Society of the IN Conference of the Methodist Church, Indianapolis, IN, 1956; J. L. Smith, IN METHODISM, The Author, Valparaiso, IN, 1892; F. C. Holliday, IN METHODISM, Hitchcock and Walden, Cincinnati, OH, 1873; W. J. Walls, AFRICAN METHODIST EPISCOPAL ZION CHURCH, REALITY OF THE BLACK CHURCH, Zion A. M. E. Publishing House, Charlotte, NC, 1974; H. C. Luccock, THE STORY OF METHODISM, Abingdon Press, New York NY, 1949; W. W. Sweet, RELIGION ON THE AMERICAN FRONTIER, VOL. 4, THE METHODISTS, Harper, New York, NY, 1946; B. R. Little, METHODIST UNION CATALOG OF HISTORY, BIOGRAPHY, DISCIPLINES, AND HYMNALS, Association of Methodist Historical Societies, Lake Junaluska, NC, 1967; J. B. Finley, SKETCHES OF WESTERN METHODISM, Arno Press, New York, NY, 1969.

___(Moravian) Moravians had their origins as a community of followers of the Reformer John Hus about 1410 in Bohemia (now the Czech Republic). The faith spread into neighboring Moravia (now the western section of the Slovak Republic), but the members were almost annihilated in the Thirty Years War (1618-48). They first came to the American colonies in 1735, settling in GA, then moving to PA in 1740. Contact: Archives of the Moravian Church, 41 West Locust Street, Bethlehem, PA 18018; Moravian Historical Society, Nazareth, PA 18064. Books: J. E. Hutton, HISTORY OF THE MORAVIAN CHURCH, Moravian Publication Office, London, England, 1909; E. Langton, HISTORY OF THE MORAVIAN CHURCH, Allen and Unwin, London, England, 1955.

___(Mormon or Church of Jesus Christ of Latter-day Saints) Organized in 1830 at Fayette, NY, by Joseph Smith. Contact: Library and Historical Department, CJCLDS, both at 50 East North Temple, Salt Lake City, UT 84150. Books: E. C. Clayton, MEMORIES OF YESTERDAY IN INDIANA, A BRIEF HISTORY OF THE EARLY DAYS OF THE CHURCH OF JESUS CHRIST OF LATTER DAY SAINTS IN INDIANA, The Author, Salt Lake City, UT, 1964; L. J. Arrington and D. Bitton, THE MORMON EXPERIENCE, A HISTORY OF THE LATTER DAY-SAINTS, Random House, New York, NY, 1979; T. F. O'Dea, THE MORMONS, University of Chicago Press, Chicago, IL, 1957; J. Shipps, MORMONISM, THE STORY OF A NEW RELIGIOUS TRADITION, Harper, New York, NY, 1985.

___(Presbyterian) The churches of the Presbyterian or Reformed tradition (as they were and are called in Europe) are Protestant churches governed by boards of ministers and lay persons called elders (presbyters). These churches had their origin by John Calvin in Zurich, Switzerland, during the Reformation in the year 1523. The doctrines and church organization were introduced into Scotland in 1557-60 by John Knox. Although there were some similar churches before, the first clearly Presbyterian congregation in the colonies was probably the one on the Elizabeth River near Norfolk, VA, about 1675. A church was definitely formed at Rehoboth, MD, in 1683, and the first presbytery (association) dates back to 1706 in Philadelphia. Presbyterians came to IN only in small numbers prior to about 1815, establishing their first church in Clark County in 1805. Contact: Duggan Library, Hanover College, PO Box 287, Hanover, IN 47243; American Home Missionary Society, Amistad Research Center, Tilton Hall, Tulane University, New Orleans, LA 70118; Presbyterian Historical Association, Presbyterian Church USA, 425 Lombard Street, Philadelphia, PA 19147; Historical Center, Presbyterian Church in

America, 12330 Conway Road, St. Louis, MO 63141. Books: L. C. Rudolph, HOOSIER ZION, THE PRESBYTERIANS IN EARLY INDIANA, Yale University Press, New Haven, CT, 1963; H. A. Edson, CONTRIBUTIONS TO THE EARLY HISTORY OF THE PRESBYTERIAN CHURCH IN INDIANA, The Author, Indianapolis, IN, 1898; W. W. Sweet, RELIGION ON THE AMERICAN FRONTIER, VOL. 2, THE PRESBY-TERIANS, Harper, New York, NY, 1936; L. A. Loetscher, A BRIEF HISTORY OF THE PRESBYTERIANS, Westminster Press, Philadelphia, PA, 1978; W. L. Lingle, PRESBYTERIANS, THEIR HISTORY AND BELIEFS, John Knox Press, Richmond, VA, 1960; UNION CATALOG OF PRESBYTERIAN MANU-SCRIPTS, Presbyterian Library Association, Philadelphia, PA, 1964.

___(Quakers or Religious Society of Friends) These people trace their origin back to George Fox who began making converts in 1647 in the midlands of England. Quakers soon began showing up in the American colonies. The first Quaker yearly meeting in the colonies was organized in 1661 in Newport, RI, by the many Friends who had come to RI. The first Monthly Quaker meeting in IN came together in Wayne County in 1809. Contact: Lilly Library, Earlham College Archives, Richmond, IN 47374. Books: W. Heiss, ABSTRACTS OF THE RECORDS OF THE SOCIETY OF FRIENDS IN INDIANA, IHS, Indianapolis, IN, 1962-75, 7 volumes; W. W. Hinshaw, ENCYCLOPEDIA OF AMERICAN QUAKER GENEALOGY, IN QUAKER RECORDS, Genea-logical Publishing Co., Baltimore, MD, 1973, volume 7; E. T. Elliott, QUAKERS IN THE AMERICAN FRONTIER, Friends United Press, Richmond, IN, 1969; W. Heiss and L. S. Mote, EARLY SETTLEMENT OF FRIENDS IN THE MIAMI VALLEY, Woolman Press, Indianapolis, IN, 1961.

___(Roman Catholic) The Roman Catholic Church traces its origins back to Peter, an apostle of Jesus and traditionally the first Bishop of Rome, approximately 55-64 AD. The first coming of Catholics to the American English colonies was to St. Marys, MD, in 1634. They came into the IN country in the 1670s, and a church was founded at Vincennes in 1749 by the French. The number of Catholics declined following the British victory in the French and Indian War, and did not begin to rise again until the 1830s. IN Catholic records 1749-1917 have been microfilmed, and are available at ISL, IHS, and FHL(FHC). Contact the Catholic dioceses of IN: Indianapolis/Vincennes, Fort Wayne/South Bend,

Lafayette, and Evansville. Addresses in the telephone books. Books: C. Blanchard, HISTORY OF THE CATHOLIC CHURCH IN INDIANA, Bowen and Co., Logansport, IN, 1898, 2 volumes; T. T. McAvoy, THE CATHOLIC CHURCH IN INDIANA, 1789-1834, AMS Press, New York, NY, 1967; J. P. Dolan, THE AMERICAN CATHOLIC EXPERIENCE, A HISTORY FROM COLONIAL TIMES TO THE PRESENT, Doubleday, New York, NY, 1985; THE NEW CATHOLIC ENCYCLOPEDIA, McGraw-Hill, New York, NY, 1967, 15 volumes, with supplementary volumes published after.

___(Shakers) This fellowship, more correctly the United Society of Believers in Christ's Second Coming, was founded in 1772 in Manchester, England, by Ann Lee. She and some of her followers came to Watervliet, NY, in 1776. Contact: Western Reserve Historical Society Library, 10825 East Boulevard, Cleveland, OH 44106. Books: E. A. Andrews, THE PEOPLE CALLED SHAKERS, Dover Publications, New York, NY, 1953; M. F. Melcher, THE SHAKER ADVENTURE, Oxford University Press, London, England, 1960.

___(Unitarian-Universalist) In 1779, John Murray became the pastor of the first Universalist Church in the US at Gloucester, MA. Many other churches in New England and PA soon joined them. The first Unitarian Church in the US was established by Joseph Priestly in 1796 in Philadelphia. By the early 1800s, many Congregational churches were joining the movement, and in 1825 a separate denomination was formed. In 1961, the Unitarians and the Universalists united to form the Unitarian-Universalist Association. Contact: Archives of the Unitarian-Universalist Association, 25 Beacon Street, Boston, MA 02108. Books: C. L. Scott, THE UNIVERSALIST CHURCH OF AMERICA, A SHORT HISTORY, Universalist Historical Society, Boston, MA, 1957; G. W. Cooke, UNITARIANISM IN AMERICA, American Unitarian Association, Boston, MA, 1906.

Many IN city and county histories contain histories of churches. These city and county histories are discussed in section 9 of this chapter. Numerous church records have also been published in genealogical periodicals. Indexes are generally available for these periodicals, which makes searching them for church records very convenient. The periodicals and their indexes will be treated in a later section. The books referred to above can be located at ISL, IHS, and ACPL, with some being available at FHL(FHC) and in some RL and LL. Look up the county, the church name, and the denominational name in the card and/or computer catalogs in these repositories.

8. City directories

During the 19th century many larger cities in the US began publishing city directories. These volumes usually appeared erratically at first, but then began to come out annually a little later on. They list heads of households and workers plus their addresses and occupations. In addition, there will usually be city officials, church addresses, associations, hospitals, banks, libraries, cemeteries, clubs, unions, schools, and other such helpful data. The earliest series of directories (starting before 1860) in IN are:

___Evansville, 1858-
___Fort Wayne, 1858-
___Indianapolis, 1855-
___Jeffersonville, 1860-
___Lafayette, 1858-
___Lawrenceburgh, 1859-

___Logansport, 1859-
___Madison, 1859-
___New Albany, 1836-
___Richmond, 1857-
___Shelbyville, 1860-
___Terre Haute, 1858-

After about 1865, many of these towns and cities published a city directory each year. In general, the smaller cities and towns of IN did not begin regular publication until later in the 19th or in the 20th century. Many of the directories are available in ISL, IHS, ACPL, and FHL(FHC). RL and LL also usually have collections pertaining to their own cities.

The telephone was invented in 1876-7, underwent rapid development, and became widespread fairly quickly. By the late years of the century telephone directories were coming into existence. Older issues can often be found in LL, and as the years go on, they have proved to be ever more valuable genealogical sources.

9. City and county histories

Histories for many IN counties and numerous cities have been published. These volumes usually contain biographical data on leading citizens, details about early settlers, histories of organizations, businesses, trades, and churches, and often list clergymen, lawyers, physicians, teachers, governmental officials, farmers, military men, and other groups. Three works which list many of these histories are:
___M. J. Kaminkow, US LOCAL HISTORIES IN THE LIBRARY OF CONGRESS, Magna Carta, Baltimore, MD, 1975, 5 volumes, index in the 5th volume.

___P. W. Filby, A BIBLIOGRAPHY OF COUNTY HISTORIES IN 50
STATES, Genealogical Publishing Co., Baltimore, MD, 1985.
___FAMILY HISTORY LIBRARY CATALOG, LOCALITY SECTION,
in either microform or computer, FHL, Salt Lake City, UT, latest
edition. Look under state, then under county, then city or town.
Also at every FHC.
Most of the IN volumes in these bibliographies can be found in ISL, IHS,
and ACPL. Many are available at FHL or through FHC, and some are
usually in LGL. RL and LL are likely to have those relating to their
particular areas.

Two useful sets of indexes to many of the county histories of IN
are available. In the IHS, there are surname indexes which cover IN
county histories. There is an index for each county. Some of them were
compiled by the WPA and others by cooperating groups under the IHS.
___ALL NAME INDEXES TO COUNTY HISTORIES, IHS and
Historical Records Survey, WPA, Indianapolis, IN, 1938-.
There is also available a microfiche publication which lists over 247
thousand IN names derived from over 525 different published IN
historical and biographical sources.
___J. B. Parker and L. de Platt, MICROFICHE INDIANA BIO-
GRAPHICAL INDEX, Genealogical Indexing Associates, West
Bountiful, UT, 1983, 16 microfiche. Available at ISL and
FHL(FHC).
In Chapter 4 you will find listed under the counties various recommended
county histories. Also there will be an indication under each county for
which city histories are available.

10. Court records

Among the most unexplored genealogical source
materials are the court records of the state of IN
and of the IN counties. They are often exceptionally valuable, giving information that is
obtainable no where else. It is, therefore, of
great importance that you carefully examine all available court documents.
A good treatments of the court system of IN is available:
___L. J. Monks, COURTS AND LAWYERS OF IN, Indianapolis, IN,
1916, 3 volumes.

There are two minor difficulties that need to be recognized if you
are not to miss court data. The first is that there were several types of
courts, some no longer exist, some replaced others, some had their names
changed, often their jurisdictions overlapped, and further, the exact court

situation sometimes varies from county to county. You are likely to find records of the following courts:

___County Courts of Common Pleas (1790-1813, 1853-73): handled civil cases, criminal cases, equity matters, guardianships, insanity matters, naturalizations, and probates (1790-1813).

___County Courts of Quarter Sessions (1790-1805): handled civil, criminal, and probate matters.

___County Circuit Courts (1790-present): handled coroner's actions, major criminal matters, equity cases, insanity matters, marriages, naturalizations, and probates (1813-29, 1853-).

___County Probate Courts (1790-1805, 1829-52): probates. Note that in 1853 county Probate Courts were terminated and jurisdiction was transferred to the Circuit Court. There were two exceptions: Marion and St. Joseph Counties. The Probate Courts in these counties were not abolished and have continued.

___County Orphans' Court (1795-1805); guardianships, probates.

___County Superior Courts (1909-present): handled civil cases, criminal cases, and naturalizations.

___State Supreme Court (1817-present): appeals.

___State Court of Appeals (1891-present): appeals.

___US Federal District Courts (approximately 1816-present)

___US Federal Circuit Courts (approximately 1816-1911)

The second difficulty is that the records of the different courts appear in record books, file cabinets, and filing boxes with various titles and labels. These titles and labels do not always describe everything in the volumes, and records of various types may be mixed up or they may all appear in a single set of books. This latter is especially true in earlier years. Fortunately, there is a simple rule that avoids all these difficulties: look for your ancestor in all available court records, regardless of what the label-lings on the books, cabinets, files, and boxes happen to be.

In certain kinds of court matters (such as trials, estates, wills, and others), the record books will refer to folders which contain detailed documents concerning the matters. The folders are usually filed in the court house (CH) and must not be overlooked because they are often gold mines of information. In the county of your interest, you may find records dealing with proceedings of the various courts (records, minutes, dockets, enrollments, registers, orders), with land (deeds, entries, land grants, mortgages, trust deeds, surveys, ranges, plats, roads), with probate matters (wills, estate, administrators, executors, inventories, settlements, sales, guardians, orphans, insolvent estates, bastardy, apprentices, insanity), with vital records (birth, death, marriage, divorce), and with taxation (tax, bonds, appropriations, delinquent taxes). In most cases there will not be records with all these titles, but several of these items will appear in one type of book, cabinet, file, or box. If all of this seems complicated, do not worry. All you need to do is to remember the rules: examine all court records, be on the lookout for references to folders, ask about them and then examine them also.

First, we will discuss the county records. The original record books, boxes, cabinets, files, and folders are in the county court houses (CH). Microfilms and transcripts (published and manuscript) of many of the books have been made, but only a very few of the boxes, files, folders, and cabinet contents have been copied. Many of the microfilmed and transcribed records are available at ISL, IHS, and ACPL. Many are in FHL and are available through FHC. Some of the transcribed materials are to be found in RL but only a few of the microfilms. A few LGL have some of the transcribed records. LL may have transcribed records for the local area. Listings of many of the microfilms available at ISL, IHS, ACPL, and FHL(FHC) are shown in:
___FAMILY HISTORY LIBRARY CATALOG, LOCALITY SECTION,
     FHL, Salt Lake City, UT, latest microfiche and computer editions.
     Look under IN and the counties.
Chapter 3 discusses the process of obtaining these records, and Chapter 4 lists those available for each of the 92 IN counties.

Not only were there county-based courts, there were ones with regional and state-wide jurisdiction. The records of many of these are available in original, microfilm, or published form. Included among the most promising of these sources for genealogists are:
___State Supreme Court (1817-present): appeals. See inventories,
     indexes, and microfilms in ISA.
___State Court of Appeals (1891-present): appeals. See inventories,
     indexes, and microfilms in ISA.
Further, there is a name index to cases which were appealed from a lower IN court to a higher one:
___IN DIGEST, West Publ. Co., St. Paul, MN, 1953-, 27 volumes.

Finally, the federal and territorial court records must not be overlooked. Many of the records of the US Federal District and Circuit Courts for IN (approximately 1803-1962) are available at the Chicago Branch of the National Archives, 7358 South Pulaski Road, Chicago, IL 60629 [Phone 1-(312)-581-7816]. Northwest Territorial records (for 1787-1801) and IN Territorial records (for 1804-16), including some court records, are available at the National Archives in Washington, DC in Record Group 59. A somewhat helpful inventory is:

___W. B. Griffin, PRELIMINARY INVENTORY OF RECORDS OF THE US COURTS FOR THE DISTRICT OF IN, National Archives and Records Service, Washington, DC, 1967.

11. DAR records

The Daughters of the American Revolution (DAR), in their quest for the lines linking them to their Revolutionary War ancestors, have gathered and published many volumes of records of genealogical pertinence. The IN chapters of the organization have provided many volumes of county records (chiefly court, deed, marriage, probate, tax, will), Bible records, cemetery records, and family records. Copies of most of the books or microfilms of most of them are available at the DAR Library in Washington, ISL, IHS, ACPL, FHL, and through FHC. Copies of some are in RL and LGL, and materials of local interest will often be found in LL. Chapter 3 tells you how to locate these records, and in Chapter 4, these records are included in the listings for the various IN counties.

There are several excellent catalog volumes to the many records that the DAR members have compiled:

___National Society, DAR, DAR LIBRARY CATALOG, VOLUME 1: FAMILY HISTORIES AND GENEALOGIES, VOLUME 2: STATE AND LOCAL HISTORIES AND RECORDS, The Society, Washington, DC, 1982/6.

Those counties for which there are DAR compilations will be so indicated in Chapter 4. Look into these DAR volumes for materials on your IN ancestor(s).

12. Death records

Prior to 1882, a few IN cities kept some incomplete death records. These include Logansport starting in 1874, Ft. Wayne in 1871, Kokomo in 1875, and Indianapolis in 1872. In 1881, the state of IN passed a law requiring birth and death records to be kept in IN counties, cities, and towns, starting in 1882. This law was largely not enforced, so the records are quite incomplete in some counties. In 1899, it was mandated by the state that copies of all death records be sent to the state capital, beginning in 1900. Enforcement and compliance were not complete at first, and it was 1915 or 1916 before the records began to approach being complete. By about 1920, compliance was almost complete. The death records available for each IN county are indicated in the separate county listings in Chapter 4.

The WPA has compiled and indexed many of the available county birth records for period 1882-1920. They are arranged by the county, and then under each county are listed alphabetically.

___Historical Records Survey, INDEXES TO BIRTHS, DEATHS, MARRIAGES, AND MISCELLANEOUS RECORDS OF IN COUNTIES, WPA, Indianapolis, IN, 1938-. Death data available for 68 out of the 92 IN counties.

Counties for which death indexes were not transcribed include Blackford, Brown, Crawford, Dearborn, Decatur, Dubois, Fayette, Grant, Jefferson, Jennings, Lawrence, Marshall, Miami, Noble, Ohio, Randolph, Ripley, Rush, Scott, Steuben, Switzerland, Tipton, Union, Wabash, and Whitley. These indexes will be found in ISL, IHS, ACPL, and FHL(FHC). More recently, other groups or individuals have compiled death indexes for some of the missed counties, and most counties have indexes of their own.

In 1899 the state of IN passed a law requiring state-wide birth registration in addition to the county registration, starting in 1900. By 1920, registrations were running at least 95% complete. These records are in the county or city health departments as well as in the central state repository at Columbus:

___Division of Vital Records, State Board of Health, PO Box 1964, Indianapolis, IN, 42606. The Division has indexes.

These records usually contain name of the deceased with age, birthplace, sex, occupation, and marital status, date and cause of the death, name of spouse, names and birthplaces of parents, name of the person giving the information, physician's signature, funeral director, place of burial, and date of the certificate.

Prior to the time when IN death reports came to be almost complete (1908-20), other records may yield dates and places of death: biographical, cemetery, census, church, death, divorce, marriage, military, mortuary, newspaper, pension, and published. These are all discussed in other sections of this chapter. The finding of death record articles in genealogical periodicals is also described separately in this chapter.

13. Divorce records

From 1795-1800 divorces in the area which is now IN are by the General court and the Circuit court of the Northwest Territory. The General Court of the IN Territory granted divorces from 1800-1817, except for one divorce that was given by the Legislature in 1808. From 1817-52, IN divorces were taken care of by the General Assembly. Sometimes the Assembly granted the divorce, and sometimes it gave permission for the county Circuit Court to do so. A compilation of these divorces has been published:

___M. E. E. Newhard, DIVORCES GRANTED BY THE IN GENERAL ASSEMBLY PRIOR TO 1852, The Compiler, Harland, IN, 1981.

From 1853-forward divorces have been handled in each county by the Circuit Court, although other county courts were sometimes active in this capacity. Even so, the records are usually found in the office of the Clerk of the Circuit Court, where indexes are generally to be found. In chapter 4, the various divorce records available for the IN counties are given.

14. Emigration and immigration records

Early settlement in IN (1787-1810) involved the Scots-Irish and some Scottish who left from KY, and the back country of VA, NC, and PA, and came to the area which is now southern IN. They settled along the OH River and the Lower Wabash River. Shortly thereafter, they were followed by people of German derivation who came from the same general areas. The southern third of IN was thus settled chiefly from the upland southeast of the US. As central IN began to open up (about 1812-15), some people came from this area, but more entered IN from the east, namely from OH, PA, MD, NJ, and DE. These were of Scots-Irish, German, and English extraction, and they were joined by people moving north from southern IN. The last area to be settled, namely northern IN, was opened up in the period 1817-26. The principal early settlers were from northern OH, PA, NY, the New England States, and NJ. That is, they were from the northern tier of states. As before, they were joined by people coming north from central and southern IN.

These streams of entrants continued for quite some years. There were also some notable groups who came into IN in the years following. One group were the Quakers who came from South and North Carolina in the 1820s and 1830s. Among their reasons for departure was a strong anti-slavery position. Several surges of overseas Germans came into IN during the time frame of 1836-60, most of them coming directly from their landings in New York, Philadelphia, and Baltimore. They were in a large measure escaping the military turbulence of the times. The several Irish famines during 1830-60, coupled with the need for labor on the roads, canals, and railroads brought many Irish to IN during these times. After about 1870, the above foreign immigrants to IN were joined by Italians, Slavs, Jews, Polish, Ukrainians, and Slovaks, who usually settled in the northern part of the state. After the turn of the century, more of all the above plus many more ethnic groups were attracted to the industrial cities of northern IN.

The movement of population into IN can be readily seen by examination of the statistics provided by the censuses of the latter half of the 19th century. Numbers of people are expressed in thousands (K). In 1850, the birth places of IN people who had been born outside of IN were as follows:

120K(OH), 68K(KY), 44K(PA), 41K(VA), 33K(NC)

In 1860:

171K(OH), 68K(KY), 66K(Germany), 57K(PA), 37K(VA)

In 1870:

189K(OH), 78K(Germany), 67K(KY), 57K(PA), 42K(British/Irish)

In 1880:

185K(OH), 81K(Germany), 61K(KY), 57K(PA), 27K(NY), 27K(Ireland)

In 1890:

164K(OH), 85K(Germany), 66K(KY), 40K(PA), 31K(IL)

In 1900:

178K(OH), 78K(KY), 74K(Germany), 58K(IL), 40K(PA)

Now, let us turn to view those living in other states which were born in IN. This will show you the pattern of migration out of IN in 1850:

30K(IL), 20K(IA), 13K(MO)

In 1860:

62K(IL), 57K(IA), 30K(MO), 9K(KS), 9K(WI)

In 1870:

86K(IL), 64K(IA), 51K(MO), 31K(KS), 17K(OH), 12K(KY)

In 1880:

91K(IL), 77K(KS), 60K(MO), 59K(IA), 27K(OH), 20K(NE)

In 1890:

98K(KS), 96K(IL), 71K(MO), 51K(IA), 40K(NE), 36K(OH)

In 1900:

128K(IL), 75K(KS), 71K(MO), 52K(OH), 48K(IA), 30K(MI), 29K(KY), 29K(NE)

In addition to IN histories which have been previously mentioned, there are several other books which will give you information on the above topics:

___J. D. Barnhart and D. F. Carmody, IN FROM FRONTIER TO INDUSTRIAL COMMONWEALTH, Lewis Historical Publishing Co., New York, NY, 1954, volume 1, pages 161ff.

___R. C. Buley, THE OLD NORTHWEST, PIONEER PERIOD, 1815-40, IN University Press, Bloomington, IN, 1951, 2 volumes.

___W. M. Cockrum, HISTORY OF IN.....THE EARLY SETTLERS, Oakland City Journal, Oakland City, IN, 1907.

___W. A. Fritsch, GERMAN SETTLERS AND GERMAN SETTLEMENT IN INDIANA, The Author, Evansville, IN, 1915.

___W. Heiss, IN SOURCE BOOK,, VOL. 3, IHS, Indianapolis, IN, 1982. See article on foreign immigration.

___L. McDonald, NEGRO MIGRATION INTO IN, 1800-60, The Author, Bloomington, IN, 1945.

___C. Moore, THE NORTHWEST UNDER THREE FLAGS, 1635-1796, Harper and Brothers, New York, NY, 1900.

___S. S. Sprague, KENTUCKIANS IN OH AND IN, Genealogical Publishing Co., Baltimore, MD, 1986.

___R. M. Taylor, Jr., and others, IN: A NEW HISTORICAL GUIDE, IHS, Indianapolis, IN, 1989.

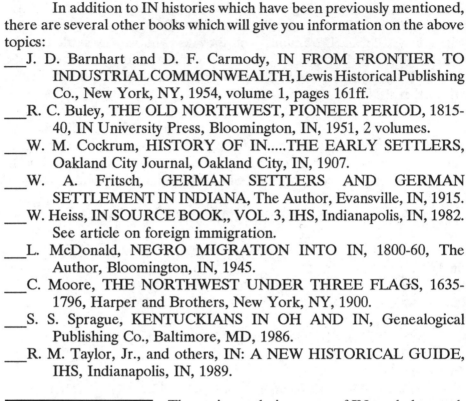

15. Ethnic records

The various ethnic groups of IN tended to each be largely affiliated with a particular religious persuasion. The English tended to be Congregational, Episcopalian, and Quaker. Many of these turned Methodist or Baptist or Christian later. Blacks tended to be Baptist or Methodist. Early Germans were Lutheran, Brethren, Mennonite, Moravian, and Reformed, with many later Germans being Catholic. The Scots-Irish and the Scots were chiefly Presbyterian, and the Irish were usually Catholic. The immigrants from eastern and southern Europe tended to be Catholic if they were from the western parts of these areas and Orthodox if they were from the eastern parts. Hence, for many of these groups, ethic information and connections are closely allied with their religious affiliations. Therefore, for all but the blacks, please see the previous section on church records.

Even though slavery was prohibited by the Northwest Ordinance of 1787, the IN territorial government allowed slaves to be brought in. A law passed in 1816 forbid slavery, but permitted previous slaves to be held in bondage. In 1820, slavery under any condition was prohibited. Some of the people of IN, especially Quakers, participated in the Underground Railroad, and assisted slaves from the south to escape to Canada through IN. In the early days of statehood, not many free blacks came into IN, but a number began entering as time went on. By 1850, there were over 11,000, most of them having come from KY, NC, TN, and VA. In 1851, the state of IN prohibited any more free blacks from settling in the state, forbid free blacks to vote, serve in the military, attend white schools, or testify against a white person. After the Civil War, blacks came into IN, but were discriminated against. In the 1940s, many blacks migrated from the south into northern IN, where they took up work in the industrial cities.

Among the historical, reference, and source materials for blacks in IN are the following volumes which will get you started if you have interest in this ethnic group.
___J. W. Lyda, THE NEGRO HISTORY OF IN, The Author, Terre Haute, IN, 1953.
___L. McDonald, NEGRO MIGRATION INTO IN, 1800-60, The Author, Bloomington, IN, 1945.
___C. D. Robbins, IN NEGRO REGISTERS, 1852-65, Heritage Books, Bowie, MD, 1994. Registers of blacks in fifteen IN counties.
___E. L. Thornbrough, THE NEGRO IN INDIANA, IN Historical Bureau, Indianapolis, IN, 1957.
___C. B. Witcher, BIBLIOGRAPHY OF SOURCES FOR BLACK FAMILY HISTORY IN THE ALLEN COUNTY PUBLIC LIBRARY GENEALOGY DEPARTMENT, The Library, Ft. Wayne, IN, 1986.

The last of the Native Americans to leave IN, namely those in the northwestern region, left in 1846. For investigations of the Native American groups in Indiana, a beginning can be made by the use of the following volumes:
___J. B. Dillion, THE NATIONAL DECLINE OF THE MIAMI INDIANS, IN State Historical Society, Indianapolis, IN, 1897.
___S. Rafert, AMERICAN INDIAN GENEALOGICAL RESEARCH IN THE MIDWEST, RESOURCES AND PERSPECTIVES, National Genealogical Society Quarterly 76 (1988) 212.
___S. Rafert, THE HIDDEN COMMUNITY, THE MIAMI INDIANS OF IN, 1846-1940, The Author, Indianapolis, IN, 1982.
___C. B. Witcher, BIBLIOGRAPHY OF SOURCES FOR NATIVE AMERICAN FAMILY HISTORY IN THE ALLEN COUNTY

PUBLIC LIBRARY GENEALOGY DEPARTMENT, The
Library, Ft. Wayne, IN, 1988.

16. Gazetteers, atlases, and maps

A gazetteer is a volume which lists geographical names (towns, settlements, rivers, streams, hills, mountains, crossroads, villages, districts), locates them, and sometimes gives a few details concerning them. Several such volumes or similar volumes which list IN place names which could be of help to you include:

___J. Scott, THE IN GAZETTEER, 1826, Indianapolis, IN, 1954.

___E. Chamberlaine, THE IN GAZETTEER, The Author, Indianapolis, IN, 1849.

___G. W. Hawes, IN STATE GAZETTEER AND BUSINESS DIRECTORY, 1858/9 and 1859/60, Hawes and Co., Indianapolis, IN, 1860/61, 2 volumes.

___NEW TOPOGRAPHICAL ATLAS AND GAZETTEER OF IN, 1871, Unigraphics, Inc., Evansville, IN, 1975.

___R. L. Polk, IN STATE GAZETTEER AND BUSINESS DIRECTORY, 1890-91, Bookmark, Knightstown, IN, 1978.

___R. L. Baker and M. Carmony, IN PLACE NAMES, IN University Press, Bloomington, IN, 1975.

___IN, HER COUNTIES, HER TOWNSHIPS, AND HER TOWNS, The Researchers, Indianapolis, IN, 1979.

___F. R. Abate, editor, OMNI GAZETTEER OF THE USA, Omnigraphics, Detroit, MI, 1991, see IN listings.

Numerous early atlases (collections of maps) are available for IN, for its counties, and for some of its larger cities. Many of these are listed in:

___C. E. LeGear, US ATLASES, Library of Congress, Washington, DC, 1950-3, 2 volumes.

Among the state volumes and the county/state compilations are:

___L. A. Brown, EARLY MAPS OF THE OH VALLEY, 1673-1783, University of Pittsburgh Press, Pittsburgh, PA, 1959.

___J. H. Long and S. L. Hansen, HISTORICAL ATLAS AND CHRONOLOGY OF COUNTY BOUNDARIES, 1788-1980, Newberry Library, Chicago, IL, 1984.

___W. Thorndale and W. Dollarhide, MAP GUIDE TO THE US FEDERAL CENSUSES, IN, 1790-1920, Bellingham, WA, 1984.

___NEW TOPOGRAPHICAL ATLAS AND GAZETTEER OF IN, Asher, Adams, and Higgins, New York, NY, 1871.

___ILLUSTRATED HISTORICAL ATLAS OF THE STATE OF IN, Baskin, Forster, and Co., Chicago, IL, 1876, with D. E. Gradeless, INDEX TO PLACES, The Author, Racine, WI, 1974.

___BOWEN'S IN STATE ATLAS, Bowen and Co., Indianapolis, IN, 1917.

___G. Pence and N. C. Armstrong, IN BOUNDARIES, TERRITORIAL, STATE, AND COUNTY, IHS, Indianapolis, IN, 1967.

___O. D. Morrison, IN HOOSIER STATE, NEW HISTORICAL ATLAS, The Author, Athens, OH, 1958.

Those counties for which atlases are available are indicated in Chapter 4. The counties which had atlases published before 1900 and the dates of their earliest atlases are: Allen 1898, Bartholomew 1879, Boone 1878, Carroll 1874, Cass 1878, Clinton 1878, Daviess 1888, Dearborn 1875, Decatur 1882, DeKalb 1880, Delaware 1887, Elkhart 1874, Fayette 1875, Franklin 1882, Fulton 1883, Gibson 1881, Grant 1877, Greene 1879, Hamilton 1880, Hancock 1887, Harrison 1882, Hendricks 1878, Henry 1893, Howard 1877, Huntington 1879, Jay 1881, Jennings 1884, Johnson 1881, Knox 1880, Kosciusko 1879, Lagrange 1874, LaPorte 1874, Lawrence 1879, Marion 1889, Martin 1892, Miami 1877, Montgomery 1878, Noble 1874, Ohio 1883, Parke 1874, Pike 1881, Porter 1876, Putnam 1879, Randolph 1874, Ripley 1883, Rush 1879, St. Joseph 1875, Scott 1889, Shelby 1880, Spencer 1879, Steuben 1880, Sullivan 1899, Switzerland 1883, Tippecanoe 1878, Union 1884, Vanderburg 1880, Vigo 1874, Wabash 1875, Warren 1877, Warrick 1880, Washington 1878, Wayne 1874, Wells 1881, and White 1896. In the ISL, there are name and firm indexes to IN county histories and atlases:

___ISL, COUNTY HISTORY AND ATLAS INDEXES, The Library, Indianapolis, IN.

ISL, IHS, ACPL, and FHL(FHC) have many of the above materials. Some RL have some of them, and LL are likely to have those of the counties in which they are located. There are good to excellent IN map collections in ISL (Indianapolis), IN University (Bloomington), IN State University (Terre Haute), and the University of Notre Dame (Notre Dame). The special indexes in each of these places should be consulted. These collections contain state maps, county maps for practically every county (some quite early), considerable numbers of city maps, and a few for towns.

Especially valuable are landowner maps. These are maps which show the lands of a county with the names of the owners written on them.

Most of these maps date between 1860-1900 and are available for 41 IN counties. Such maps are listed in:

___R. W. Stephenson, LAND OWNERSHIP MAPS, Library of Congress, Washington, DC, 1967. [41 IN counties have such maps.] Available at Library of Congress and on microfiche at ACPL.

Very good detail maps of IN are available at reasonable prices from the US Geological Survey. Each of these maps shows only a portion of a county and therefore a great deal of detail can be shown. Write to the address below and request the Index to Topographic Maps of IN. Or call the indicated number. Then order the maps pertaining to your ancestor's area. These maps show roads, streams, cemeteries, settlements, and churches. Such maps will aid you greatly if your ancestor lived in a rural area and you desire to visit the property and the surrounding region.

___US Geological Survey, 503 National Center, 12201 Sunrise Valley Drive, Reston, VA 22092. Call 1-800-USA-MAPS for the IN Index to Topographic Maps.

Another source of detailed county maps is the IN Department of Conservation. They can provide you with individual maps of the IN counties showing roads, cities, streams, railroads, and other features. Order them from:

___IN Department of Conservation, State Office Building, Indianapolis, IN 46204.

---

17. Genealogical compilations and indexes

For the state of IN there are a number of books which are essentially compilations and/or indexes of state-wide or regional genealogical information. Some of the volumes are mentioned under other headings in this chapter: Biographies, County histories, DAR records, Regional publications. Others of this general sort which can possibly be useful to you include:

___R. Dorrel, PIONEER ANCESTORS OF MEMBERS OF THE SOCIETY OF IN PIONEERS, IHS, Indianapolis, IN, 1983. 7500 listings.

___C. M. Franklin, IN TERRITORIAL PIONEER RECORDS, 1801-20, Heritage House, Indianapolis, IN, 1983/5, 2 volumes. Over 3500 names.

___W. Heiss and others, IN SOURCE BOOK, GENEALOGICAL MATERIAL FROM THE HOOSIER GENEALOGIST, IHS, Indianapolis, IN, 1961/90, 7 volumes. First 3 volumes indexed in

INDEX, IN SOURCE BOOKS, IHS, Indianapolis, IN, 1983. About 175,000 names.

___K. G. Lindsay, HOOSIER FAMILY ARCHIVES, Kenma Publishing Co., Evansville, IN, 1977-, several volumes.

___B. L. McCay, IN ANCESTORS INDEX, Roth, Riverdale, GA, 1976-77, 2 volumes. About 10,000 names from articles in the Indianapolis Sunday Star.

___E. R. Means, HOOSIER ANCESTORS INDEX, Indianapolis Star, Indianapolis, IN, 1965/70, 2 volumes.

___D. L. Riker, GENEALOGICAL SOURCES, REPRINTED FROM THE GENEALOGY SECTION, IN MAGAZINE OF HISTORY, IHS, Indianapolis, IN, 1979.

___Southern IN Genealogical Society, FAMILY GROUP SHEETS, The Society, New Albany, IN, 1982, 4 volumes.

___B. S. Wolfe, HOOSIER GENEALOGIST INDEX, Ye Olde Genealogie Shoppe, Indianapolis, IN, 1984.

___B. S. Wolfe, IN MAGAZINE OF HISTORY, INDEX TO GENEALOGICAL GLEANINGS, 1902-82, Ye Olde Genealogie Shoppe, Indianapolis, IN, 1984.

---

18. Genealogical periodicals

Many genealogical periodicals have been or are being published in IN. These journals or newsletters contain genealogies, local histories, genealogical records, family queries and answers, book reviews, and other pertinent local information. If you had an IN ancestor, you will find it of great value to subscribe to one or more of the state-wide periodicals, as well as to any periodicals published in the region or county where he/she lived. Among the more important previous or present IN statewide and regional periodicals are:

___HOOSIER GENEALOGIST, published by IHS, Indiananpolis, IN, quarterly, 1961-. See W. Heiss, INDIANA SOURCE BOOK, IHS, Indianapolis, IN, 1961/90, 7 volumes, with INDEX TO VOLUMES 1-3, for abstracts.

___IN MAGAZINE OF HISTORY, IHS, IN University Department of History, Bloomington, IN, quarterly, 1904-. See D. L. Riker, GENEALOGICAL SOURCES, REPRINTED FROM THE GENEALOGY SECTION, IN MAGAZINE OF HISTORY, IHS, Indianapolis, IN, 1979.

___GENEALOGY, published by IHS, Indianapolis, IN, 1973-.

___IN GENEALOGIST, published by the IN Genealogical Society, Ft. Wayne, IN.

___IN GENEALOGICAL SOCIETY NEWSLETTER, published by the IN Genealogical Society, Ft. Wayne, IN.

___HOOSIER JOURNAL OF ANCESTRY, published by N. K. Sexton, Little York, IN, 1969-72, 1977-, specializes in southeastern IN.

___IN GENEALOGICAL INFORMER, M. E. E. Newhard, Harlan, IN, monthly, 1979-82.

___SOUTHERN IN GENEALOGICAL SOCIETY QUARTERLY, published by Southern IN Genealogical Society, New Albany, IN, quarterly,. Also publishes SOUTHERN IN GENEALOGICAL SOCIETY NEWSLETTER.

___SYCAMORE LEAVES, published by the Wabash Valley Genealogical Society, Terre Haute, IN, 1971-.

___THE TRI-STATE PACKET, published by the Tri-State Genealogy Society, Evansville, IN, quarterly, 1977-.

___HOOSIER CONNECTION, published by Central West IN Genealogical Society, Greencastle, IN, quarrterly, 1981-.

In addition to the above statewide and regional periodicals, many county, and some city and private historical and genealogical organizations publish periodicals (newsletters, quarterlies, monthlies, journals, yearbooks) which can be of exceptional value to you if you are forebear hunting in their areas. Those societies which issue periodicals and/or record compilations are indicated in the county listings of Chapter 4. Most of these publications are in the ISL and at ACPL. Many are available at FHL(FHC) and RL, some are in LGL, and those of various local regions are likely to be found in LL.

Not only do articles pertaining to IN genealogy appear in these IN publications, they also are printed in other genealogical periodicals. Fortunately, indexes to the major genealogical periodicals (including those from IN) are available:

___For periodicals published 1847-1985, then annually 1986-present, consult Allen County Public Library Foundation, PERIODICAL SOURCE INDEX, The Foundation, Fort Wayne, IN, 1986-.

These index volumes will be found in ISL, ACPL, and FHL(FHC), most RL, most LGL, and a few LL. In them you should consult all IN listings under the county names which concern you and all listings under the family names you are seeking.

19. Genealogical and historical societies	In the state of IN various societies for the study of genealogy, the accumulation of data, and the publication of the materials have been

organized. These societies are listed in Chapter 4 under the names of the IN counties in which they have their headquarters. Many of them publish regular journals and/or newsletters containing the data which they have gathered, queries from their members, and book reviews. They are indicated in Chapter 4. The local members of such societies are generally well informed about the genealogical resources of their regions, and often can offer considerable help to non-residents who had ancestors in the area. It is thus advisable for you to join the societies in your ancestor's county as well as the IN Genealogical Society (PO Box 10507, Ft. Wayne, IN 46852) and the Genealogy Division of the IN Historical Society (315 West Ohio St., Indianapolis, IN 46202). All correspondence with societies should be accompanied by an SASE. Detailed listings of them are provided by

___E. P. Bentley, THE GENEALOGIST'S ADDRESS BOOK, Genealogical Publishing Co., Baltimore, MD, latest edition.

Historical societies are often also of interest to genealogists. In addition to the IN Historical Society, there are many city, county, and regional historical societies in IN. These organizations along with their addresses are listed in the reference volumes named below. Some of these societies have strong genealogical interests (as does the IHS), some deal with genealogical interests in addition to their historical pursuits, and some have essentially no interest in genealogy. Even if they do not carry out much genealogy as such, their work will be of considerable interest to you since it deals with the historical circumstances through which your ancestor lived. It is often well for you to dispatch an SASE and an inquiry to one or more asking about membership, genealogical interest, and publications. Most of these valuable organizations are named in these very detailed compilations:

___DIRECTORY OF HISTORICAL SOCIETIES AND AGENCIES IN THE US AND CANADA, American Association for State and Local History, Nashville, TN, latest edition.

___E. P. Bentley, THE GENEALOGIST'S ADDRESS BOOK, Genealogical Publishing Co., Baltimore, MD, latest edition.

20. Land records

One of the most important types of genealogical records are those which deal with land. This is because IN for many years was predominantly an agricultural state. In addition, land was up until the 20th century (the 1900s) widely available and quite inexpensive. These factors meant that the vast majority of IN people owned land, and therefore their names appear in land records. The land was first granted by the government to private individuals or groups, and thereafter the land records were locally kept. These latter records (deed, entry, mortgage, settler, survey, tax) for the 92 IN counties are indicated in Chapter 4 along with the dates of availability. In most cases, the originals are in the CH, but transcripts and/or microfilm copies of many of them are to be found in ISL, ACPL, and FHL, and are available through FHC. Some transcribed land records are available in RL and LGL, and transcribed copies and some microfilms for individual counties are often available in the LL of the counties.

In addition to the county records, there were a large number of early land grants made to the first settlers in various areas of the state. To understand the granting of lands by the government to its first owners, it is necessary to recognize that the area which makes up IN was divided into 7 major regions for the original granting of land. These regions are centered around land offices which began to operate at the following dates in the following regions:

1800	Adjacent South IN (Cincinnati, OH)
1804	Southwest IN (Vincennes)
1807	Southeast IN (Jeffersonville)
1819	East central IN (Brookville, moved to Indianapolis 1825)
1820	West central IN (Terre Haute, moved to Crawfordsville 1828)
1823	Northeast IN (Ft. Wayne)
1833	Northwest IN (LaPorte, moved to Winamac 1839)

Remember that land grants are for the first disposition of the land from the federal government to an individual owner. Thereafter the county records (see above paragraph) must be consulted for changes in land ownership. The original land grant records for IN are widely dispersed and are available as follows:

___Original land-entry case files, NA, Washington, DC.

___Original federal land record books and registers, 1807-76, ISA, Indianapolis, IN. Also available on microfilm at ISA, ACPL, and FHL (FHC). Not all are indexed.

___Original patents, tract books, and plats, Bureau of Land Management, Springfield, VA.

___Original applications to purchase and registers of cash certificates and sales, 1808-76, National Archives Regional Branch, Great Lakes Region, Chicago, IL. Arranged chronologically by land office. Not indexed.

Your first step in seeking the land grant of an ancestor is to use some major indexes which lead to many of the original grantees in IN:

___US House of Representatives, LAND CLAIMS, VINCENNES DISTRICT, IHS, Indianapolis, IN, 1983.

___L. Lux, THE VINCENNES DONATION LANDS, IHS, Indianapolis, IN, 1949. Lists settlers and land claims before 1800 in this area.

___W. Clark, PLAT BOOK OF CLARK'S GRANT IN CLARK COUNTY, 1789-1810, Manuscript in ISL, Indianapolis, IN.

___S. K. Mikesell, EARLY SETTLERS IN INDIANA'S GORE, 1803-20, Heritage Books, Bowie, MD, 1995. Records from entry tract books and county deed books.

___M. R. Waters, IN LAND ENTRIES, The Bookmark, Knightstown, IN, 1948, 2 volumes. Land entries for Cincinnati (1801-40) and Vincennes (1807-77).

___J. C. Cowen, JEFFERSONVILLE LAND ENTRIES, 1808-18, McDowell Publications, Utica, KY, 1984.

___J. C. Cowen, CRAWFORDSVILLE LAND ENTRIES, 1820-30, The Author, Indianapolis, IN, 1985.

___J. C. Cowen, IN ORIGINAL LAND RECORDS, BROOKVILLE-INDIANAPOLIS, 1820-31, The Author, Indianapolis, IN, 1986.

___AMERICAN STATE PAPERS, PUBLIC LANDS, Gales and Seaton, Washington, DC, 1832-61, 7 volumes; indexed in P. W. McMullen, GRASSROOTS OF AMERICA, Gendex Corporation, Salt Lake City, UT, 1972.

___Bureau of Land Management, GLO AUTOMATED RECORDS AND INDEX TO PATENTS, GRANTS, AND WARRANTS IN INDIANA, The Bureau, 7450 Boston Blvd., Springfield, VA 22153. Almost 188,000 documents. On CDROM or write to have the index searched.

___C. N. Smith, FEDERAL LAND SERIES, American Library Association, Chicago, IL, 1972/73/80/82, 4 volumes.

___F. C. Ainsworth, PRIVATE LAND CLAIMS, IL, IN, MI, AND WI, The Author, Natchitoches, LA, 1981.

The information obtained from these indexes will permit records to be obtained from the various repositories mentioned in the previous paragraph. The books mentioned in this section on land records are available in ISL, ACPL, FHL, and are obtainable through FHC. They are also to be found, or at least some of them, in RL and LGL. In addition a few of the larger LL have them.

Following the first granting of land to the original purchaser by the US government, subsequent land transfers and other land-related records are kept in the counties. Included are deeds, mortgages, tax records, civil land cases, and indexes. Listings of those available for the 92 IN counties will be given in Chapter 4. In most counties, there are also some records relating to the original US grants to the first owners. Many of these county-based records are available on microfilm and/or in books at ISL, ACPL, and FHL (FHC).

21. Manuscripts

The most valuable sources of manuscripts from the state of IN are the ISL and IHS, both in Indianapolis. There are also collections, some small, some moderate sized, in LL, local museums, and local historical societies. Their holdings can include records of religious, educational, patriotic, business, social, civil, professional, governmental, and political organizations; documents, letters, memoirs, notes, and papers of early settlers, politicians, ministers, business men, educators, physicians, dentists, lawyers, judges, and farmers; records of churches, cemeteries, mortuaries, schools, corporations, and industries; works of artists, musicians, writers, sculptors, photographers, and architects; and records, papers, letters, and reminiscences of participants in the various wars, as well as records of various military organizations and campaigns.

Many of these repositories are listed in the following volumes, some of which give brief descriptions of their holdings:

__US Library of Congress, THE NATIONAL UNION CATALOG OF MANUSCRIPT COLLECTIONS, The Library, Washington, DC, issued annually 1959-. Both cumulative indexes and annual indexes. Check your ancestor's county, and then under the heading Genealogy.

__E. Altman and others, INDEX TO PERSONAL NAMES IN THE NATIONAL UNION CATALOG OF MANUSCRIPT COLLECTIONS, 1959-84, Chadwyck-Healey, Arlington, VA, 1988, 2 volumes. Check your ancestor's name.

__E. Altman and others, INDEX TO SUBJECTS AND FIRMS IN THE NATIONAL UNION CATALOG OF MANUSCRIPT COLLECTIONS, 1959-84, Chadwyck-Healey, Arlington, VA, 1995, 3 volumes. Check your ancestor's locality.

__US National Historical Publications and Records Commission, DIRECTORY OF ARCHIVES AND MANUSCRIPT REPOSITORIES IN THE US, The Commission, Oryx Press, New York, NY, 1988.

There are also some special volumes which describe and/or catalog the IN manuscript holdings in various important repositories.

___ The Society of IN Archivists, IN ARCHIVAL AND HISTORICAL REPOSITORIES, The Society, Indianapolis, IN, 1994.

___ P. Brockman, E. Brockman, and P. Brockman, A GUIDE TO MANUSCRIPT COLLECTIONS OF THE IHS AND THE ISL, IHS, Indianapolis, IN, 1986.

___ D. E. Thompson, PRELIMINARY CHECKLIST OF ARCHIVES AND MANUSCRIPTS IN INDIANA REPOSITORIES, IHS, Indianapolis, IN, 1980.

___ W. B. Griffin, PRELIMINARY INVENTORY OF RECORDS OF THE US COURTS FOR THE DISTRICT OF IN, National Archives and Records Service, Washington, DC, 1967.

___ J. L. Harper, A GUIDE TO THE DRAPER MANUSCRIPTS, WI State Historical Society, Madison, WI, 1982. See IN references.

Numerous other manuscripts are listed in the manuscript card catalogs and in special indexes provided at IHS, ISL, and other archives, libraries, and museums in IN. There are also good manuscript collections in some RL and in some of the college and other university libraries of IN. In the county listings in Chapter 4, the important manuscript repositories will be noted.

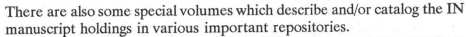

22. Marriage records

From its beginning, each IN county has kept marriage records. Since 1958, copies of these marriage records have been filed in Indianapolis on a statewide basis. The state office has overall state indexes for the period from 1958 on. This index is kept at:

___ Division of Vital Records, State Board of Health, 1330 West Michigan St., Indianapolis, IN 46207.

Prior to 1958 marriage records were collected by the counties, where the originals remain in the County Clerk's Office (or in the office of the clerk of the court where the ceremony was performed). Up to 1882, the records consist largely of registers of marriage returns, very few licenses having survived. The registers show only the names of the bride and groom, the date of the return, and the officiating person. A parent's name appears only when the bride or groom is under age. The registers are generally incomplete, and some contain errors, especially spelling errors. After 1882, the records give the names of the bride and groom, and often the age, birth date, and birth place of each, the names of the parents of each, and any previous marriage of each. Further information after 1882 may be given in a set of records books called Marriage Supplements. It is important to note that Friends (Quakers) did not have to obtain a marriage license from 1820 to 1940, their marriages being recorded in church registers.

A number of aids are available for searching out IN marriage records:

___ISL, STATEWIDE INDEX OF MARRIAGES BEFORE 1850, ISL, Indianapolis, IN. Dearborn County not included. Most Quakers not included.

___Family History Library, INTERNATIONAL GENEALOGICAL INDEX, IN SECTION, FHL, Salt Lake City, UT. Available on microfiche and/or computer at every FHC, and at several LGL. Lists many marriages.

___J. R. Dodd and N. L. Moyes, IN MARRIAGES, EARLY TO 1825, Precision Indexing, 1991. Over 27,000 names.

___W. Heiss and others, IN SOURCE BOOK, GENEALOGICAL MATERIAL FROM THE HOOSIER GENEALOGIST, IHS, Indianapolis, IN, 1961/90, 7 volumes. First 3 volumes indexed in INDEX, IN SOURCE BOOKS, IHS, Indianapolis, IN, 1983. Many marriage records.

___N. R. Murray, IN SURNAME INDEX, COMPUTER INDEXED MARRIAGE RECORDS, Hunting for Bears, Hammond, LA, 1987.

___Automated Archives, MARRIAGE RECORDS, MID 1700s THROUGH LATE 1800s, CDROM-002, AGLL, Boutiful, UT, 1993. Contains many IN entries.

___Automated Archives, IL AND IN MARRIAGE RECORDS, CDROM-228, AGLL, Bountiful, UT, 1995. Contains IN records 1802-50.

___Researchers of Indianapolis, IN MARRIAGES THROUGH 1820 IN THE COUNTIES OF WASHINGTON, JEFFERSON, CLARK, SCOTT, JACKSON, JENNINGS, SWITZERLAND, AND RIPLEY, The Researchers, Indianapolis, IN, 1981.

___C. A. Ridlen, IN COUNTY MARRIAGES, IN EARLY RETURNS, 1821-38, Ye Olde Genealogie Shoppe, Indianapolis, IN, 1977. Records from Bartholomeew, Boone, Decatur, Hancock, Henry, Johnson, Marion, Morgan, Richardson, and Shelby Counties.

The IN WPA has compiled indexes for marriages in 68 of the 92 IN counties during the approximate time span 1850-1920. They have also provided Marriage Supplement Books for 26 counties.

___Historical Records Survey, INDEXES TO BIRTHS, DEATHS, MAR-
RIAGES, AND MISCELLANEOUS RECORDS OF IN
COUNTIES, WPA of IN, Indianapolis, IN, 1937/40. Marriage
records for 62 IN counties, marriage supplements for 26.
Available at ISL, ACPL, and FHL (FHC).
Other persons and agencies have indexed some of the other county
marriages.

Microfilm copies of many IN marriage records are available at ISL
and FHL, and are therefore obtainable through FHC. Some microfilms
are available for individual counties in their LL. Lists of records and
microfilms available for the various counties are given in:
___Family History Library, FAMILY HISTORY LIBRARY CATALOG,
LOCALITY SECTION, FHL, Salt Lake City, UT, latest edition.
On microfiche and/or computer in each FHC. Look under the
relevant county.
The marriage records that are available for the various IN counties will be
listed under the counties in Chapter 4. Instructions for locating the
records and microfilms of them will be given in Chapter 3.

Other records which often yield marriage dates and places include
biographical, cemetery, church, mortuary, newspaper, obituary, pension,
and published. All of these are discussed in other sections of this chapter.
In addition, the location of marriage data in genealogical periodicals has
been described in section 18.

**23. Military records:
Revolutionary War**

The Revolutionary War was fought
before IN became a state, that is, in
the years 1775-83. Since the area was
quite sparsely populated during these
years, very few, if any, Indianans actu-
ally fought in the Revolution. After
the War, however, many veterans came into the IN country as part of a
general westward migration. There are three sets of records relating to
this War in which data on your ancestor could appear: service records,
pension records, and bounty land records. To search out all these
records, write the following address and request copies of NATF Form
80:
___Military Service records (NNCC), Washington, DC 20408.
When the forms come, fill them out with as much information on your
ancestor as you know, check the record request box on one for military
service, the pension box on another, and the bounty land record box on

another, attach a note asking for all records, and mail the forms off. The Military Service Records staff will examine their indexes to Revolutionary War soldiers and naval personnel, will try to find your ancestor, then, if they do, will copy and send you his records, along with a bill for their services. The staff is very busy and your reply may take a month or longer. If you live in certain areas of the US, there are quicker alternatives than this route to the military records. The next paragraph will detail these.

Microfilms of the Revolutionary War indexes (M860, 58 rolls, M879, 1 roll), microfilms of Revolutionary War records (M881, 1097 rolls, M880, 4 rolls), and microfilms of pension and bounty land applications (M804, 2670 rolls) are available at the National Archives (Washington, DC), Regional Branches of the National Archives (Waltham, MA; New York, NY; Philadelphia, PA; East Point, GA; Chicago, IL; Kansas City, MO; Ft. Worth, TX; Denver, CO; San Bruno, CA; Laguna Niguel, CA; Seattle, WA), ACPL, and FHL (Salt Lake City, UT). You may look at the indexes in these locations and also read the records. The indexes and the record microfilms may also be ordered through FHC and by your local library from AGLL (PO Box 329, Bountiful, UT 84011).

There are also several printed national sources which you should consult regarding your Revolutionary War ancestor:
___F. J. Metcalf et al., INDEX TO REVOLUTIONARY WAR PENSION [AND BOUNTY LAND] APPLICATIONS, National Genealogical Society, Washington, DC, 1966.
___National Society of the DAR, DAR PATRIOT INDEX, The Society, Washington, DC, latest edition with supplements.
___War Department, REVOLUTIONARY WAR PENSIONERS OF 1818, Genealogical Publishing Co., Baltimore, MD, 1959.
___War Department, PENSION ROLL OF 1835, Genealogical Publishing Co., Baltimore, MD, 1968, 4 volumes.
___US Department of State, A CENSUS OF PENSIONERS FOR REVOLUTIONARY OR MILITARY SERVICE TAKEN IN 1840, Genealogical Publishing Co., Baltimore, MD, 1974.
___National Society of the DAR, INDEX TO THE ROLLS OF HONOR, (ANCESTOR'S INDEX) IN THE LINEAGE BOOKS, Genealogical Publishing Co., Baltimore, MD, 1972, 2 volumes.
___J. Pierce, REGISTER OF CERTIFICATES TO US OFFICERS AND SOLDIERS OF THE CONTINENTAL ARMY UNDER THE ACT OF 1783, Genealogical Publishing Co., Baltimore, MD, 1973.

___F. Rider, AMERICAN GENEALOGICAL INDEX, Godfrey Memorial Library, Middletown, CT, 1942-52, 43 volumes, and AMERICAN GENEALOGICAL-BIOGRAPHICAL INDEX, Godfrey Memorial Library, Middletown, CT, 1952-, in process, over 190 volumes so far.

In addition, several printed IN sources for your search are in existence. Among the better ones are:

___R. M. Sutton, GEORGE ROGERS CLARK AND THE CAMPAIGN IN THE WEST: THE FIVE MAJOR DOCUMENTS, IN Magazine of History 76 (1980) 335. List of Clark's soldiers who were granted land in the Clark Grant.

___A. L. Funk, THE REVOLUTIONARY WAR ERA IN INDIANA, ALFCO Publishers, Corydon, IN, 1975. List of soldiers who received land in Clark's Grant.

___E. O'Byrne, ROSTER OF SOLDIERS AND PATRIOTS OF THE REVOLUTIONARY WAR BURIED IN INDIANA, DAR of IN, Brookville, IN, 1938/66/80, 3 volumes.

___Mrs. T. M. Egan, A ROSTER OF REVOLUTIONARY ANCESTORS OF THE IN DAR, DAR of IN, Indianapolis, IN, 1976.

___R. M. Waters, REVOLUTIONARY SOLDIERS BURIED IN INDIANA, Genealogical Publishing Co., Baltimore, MD, 1970.

___B. S. Wolfe, INDEX TO REVOLUTIONARY SOLDIERS OF IN AND OTHER PATRIOTS, Ye Olde Genealogie Shoppe, Indianapolis, IN, 1983.

___Sons of the American Revolution, IN MEMBERSHIP ROSTER AND FEATURES OF THE IN SOCIETY OF THE SONS OF THE AMERICAN REVOLUTION, The Sons, Indianapolis, IN, 1973/74/78.

___P. L. Hatcher, ABSTRACT OF GRAVES OF REVOLUTIONARY PATRIOTS, Pioneer Heritage Press, Dallas, TX, 1987, 4 volumes.

Also do not fail to examine:

___IN VETERANS' GRAVE REGISTRATION FILE, ISA, Indianapolis, IN. Incomplete listing of graves of veterans in 50 of the 92 IN counties. Incomplete. Also at on microfilm at ISL and FHL (FHC).

Most of the reference works listed above are in ISL, ACPL, and FHL(FHC). Some of them are in RL and LGL.

Numerous other Revolutionary War records sources are listed in the following work which goes into considerable detail and is recommended to all researchers who had Revolutionary War ancestors:

___Geo. K. Schweitzer, REVOLUTIONARY WAR GENEALOGY, The
Author, 407 Ascot Court, Knoxville, TN 37923, 1996.

Several sources are available for IN militia which served between
the Revolutionary period and the War of 1812:
___National Archives, INDEX TO COMPILED SERVICE RECORDS
OF VOLUNTEER SOLDIERS WHO SERVED FROM 1784
TO 1811, Microfilm M694, The Archives, Washington, DC, leads
to National Archives, COMPILED SERVICE RECORDS OF
VOLUNTEER SOLDIERS WHO SERVED FROM 1784 TO
1811, Microfilm M905, The Archives, Washington, DC, 32 rolls,
with Roll 22 giving IN militia.
___National Archives, MILITIA IN THE BATTLE OF TIPPECANOE
(1811), photocopies of records in the National Archives, with
index, ISA, Indianapolis, IN, 1939.
___W. Heiss, INDIANA SOURCE BOOK, VOLUME 3, IHS, Indianap-
olis, IN, 1982, pages 12-18.   Indianans in the Battle of
Tippecanoe.
___SOME EARLY IN TERRITORIAL MILITIA RECORDS, Hoosier
Genealogist 27(1987), No. 2.
___C. E. Carter, TERRITORIAL PAPERS OF THE US, VOLUME 7,
IN TERRITORY, AMS Press, New York, NY, 1973.   Also
available as National Archives, TERRITORIAL PAPERS OF
THE US, Microfilm M721, The Archives, Washington, DC. Some
lists of militiamen.

24. Military records: 1812-48

Over 3600 soldiers from IN Territory
saw active service in the War of
1812, which was fought 1812-5. As
was the case with the Revolutionary
War, three types of records should
be sought: military service, pension, and bounty land.   The National
Archives has original service records, pension records, and bounty land
records, plus indexes of all three.   These indexes are as follows:
___US Department of War, INDEX TO COMPILED SERVICE
RECORDS OF VOLUNTEER SOLDIERS WHO SERVED
DURING THE WAR OF 1812, National Archives, Washington,
DC, Microfilm M602, 234 rolls.
___US Veterans Administration, INDEX TO WAR OF 1812 PENSION
APPLICATION FILES, National Archives, Washington, DC,
Microfilm M313, 102 rolls.

___US Bureau of Land Management, WAR OF 1812 MILITARY BOUNTY LAND WARRANTS, National Archives, Washington, DC, Microfilm M848, 14 rolls, with indexes on the first roll.

You can either have the National Archives look into the indexes, or if they are easily available, you can do it. They are located at NA, NARB, FHL(FHC), and some LGL. If you find your ancestor, or if you want the NA to look for him, write the following and request several copies of NATF Form 80:

___Military Service Records (NNCC), Washington, DC 20408.

Upon receiving them, fill three out, giving your ancestor's name and state, as much other pertinent data as you can, check the request box for military service on one, the pension box on another, and the bounty land record box on the third, attach a note asking for all records, then mail them back. There are also several nationally-applicable books which could be of assistance to you:

___F. I. Ordway, Jr., REGISTER OF THE GENERAL SOCIETY OF THE WAR OF 1812, The Society, Washington, DC, 1972.

___E. S. Galvin, 1812 ANCESTOR INDEX, National Society of US Daughters of 1812, Washington, DC, 1970.

___C. S. Peterson, KNOWN MILITARY DEAD DURING THE WAR OF 1812, The Author, Baltimore, MD, 1955.

In addition, there are materials relating specifically to IN. The following can be quite helpful:

___C. M. Franklin, IN WAR OF 1812 SOLDIERS - MILITIA, Ye Olde Genealogie Shoppe, Indianapolis, IN, 1984.

___CARD INDEX OF OFFICERS COMMISSIONED IN THE INDIANA STATE MILITIA, 1811-51, ISA, Indianapolis, IN.

___IN VETERANS' GRAVE REGISTRATION FILE, ISA, Indianapolis, IN. Incomplete listing of graves of veterans in 50 of the 92 IN counties. Also at on microfilm at ISL and FHL (FHC).

ISL, ACPL, and FHL(FHC) have many of the above books (both the national and IN), and those held by FHL can be borrowed through FHC. The nationally-oriented books are likely to be found in many LGL, and some of the national and the IN volume will be found in RL. Finally, do not overlook records that might be in the counties, most notably discharge and grave records.

Many other War of 1812 record sources are given in the following work which goes into considerable detail for tracing your ancestors who served in this war:

___Geo. K. Schweitzer, WAR OF 1812 GENEALOGY, The Author, 407 Ascot Court, Knoxville, TN 37923, 1995.

During the Indian Wars period (1817-98), IN personnel were involved in several conflicts. National Archives again has military records, pension records, and bounty land records, plus indexes to all three. NATF Form 80 should be used in accordance with the above instructions to obtain records. Also some IN counties have records on the Wars. These are indicated under the counties in Chapter 4. The Black Hawk War of 1832 was notable in Indiana because it was fought just to the northwest of the state. Muster rolls for the various IN companies that were involved have been published in:

___W. Heiss, INDIANA SOURCE BOOK, VOLUME 3, IHS, Indianapolis, IN, 1982.

And a card file of participants in some of the actions of the War is:

___IHS, IN BLACK HAWK WAR MILITIA INDEX, MAY-JULY, 1832, IHS, Indianapolis, IN. Gives name, rank, unit, and some enlistment data.

The Mexican War was fought 1846-8, with over 5000 IN soldiers and navy personnel participating. NATF Form 80 should be employed to obtain military service, pension, and bounty land records from the National Archives. Published sources include:

___O. Perry, IN Adjutant General's Office, INDIANA IN THE MEXICAN WAR, Burford, Indianapolis, IN, 1908. Regimental rosters.

___W. H. Robarts, MEXICAN WAR VETERANS: A COMPLETE ROSTER, 1846-8, Washington, DC, 1887.

___C. S. Peterson, KNOWN MILITARY DEAD DURING THE MEXICAN WAR, The Author, Baltimore, MD, 1957.

These source materials should be sought in places such as ISL, ISA, ACPL, FHL, LGL, and may be borrowed through FHC.

---

25. Military records: Civil War

There are several major keys to the well-over 208,000 Civil War veterans of the state of IN:

___W. H. H. Terrell, REPORT OF THE ADJUTANT GENERAL OF THE STATE OF IN, The Office of the Adjutant General, Indianapolis, IN, 1865-69, 8 volumes. Index at ISA. Also on microfilm at FHL.

___INDEX TO COMPILED SERVICE RECORDS OF VOLUNTEER UNION SOLDIERS WHO SERVED IN ORGANIZATIONS FROM THE STATE OF IN, National Archives Microfilm M540, Washington, DC, 86 rolls of microfilm.

The indexes should be looked into for your ancestor's name. Upon finding him, you will discover listed alongside his name his regiment, battalion, or ship, as well as his company. This information is what is needed to locate the detailed records. The above indexes should be sought at ISL, ACPL, and FHL. They are available through FHC or the microfilms may be borrowed on interlibrary loan from:

___American Genealogical Lending Library, PO Box 244, Bountiful, UT 84010.

Once you know your ancestor's military unit, you can write the following address for several copies of NATF Form 80:

___Military Service Records (NNCC), Washington, DC 20408.

When your forms come, fill them out, giving as much data as you can, especially all the information from the above indexes. Then check the military service box on one form and the pension record box on another, ask for all records, and mail the forms back. In a few weeks you will receive a notice of military record data and/or pension data along with a bill.

In addition, there are several state sources which will be useful to investigate:

___CARD FILE OF IN CIVIL WAR VOLUNTEERS, ISA, Indianapolis, IN. Gives name, rank, military unit, dates of enlistment and muster, place of muster, age, birthplace, occupation, and physical description.

___CARD FILE OF THE IN LEGION (STATE MILITIA DURING THE CIVIL WAR), ISA, Indianapolis, IN.

___CARD FILE OF CIVIL WAR SUBSTITUTES, ISA, Indianapolis, IN.

___CARD FILE OF VETERANS' GRAVES REGISTRATIONS, ISA, Indianapolis, IN. Covers only 51 of the 92 IN Counties.

___VETERANS' ENROLLMENTS OF 1886, 1890, AND 1894, ISA, Indianapolis, IN. A series of books arranged by township, then county. Give the veteran's name, military unit, state, and current health information.

___REGISTER OF VISITORS TO THE NATIONAL ENCAMPMENT OF THE GAR AT INDIANAPOLIS, 1893, The GAR, Indianapolis, IN, 1893, 39 volumes. Gives name, military unit, and residence.

___THE UNION ARMY, Volume 3, Madison, WI, 1908, pp. 110-207. Histories of IN Union regiments.

___F. H. Dyer, A COMPENDIUM OF THE WAR OF THE REBEL-LION, National Historical Society, Dayton, OH, 1979, pp. 131-40, 1103-58. IN Union regimental histories.

___W. L. Phillips, INDEX TO PENSIONERS OF 1883, Heritage Books, Bowie, MD, 1987.

___A. Turner, GUIDE TO IN CIVIL WAR MANUSCRIPTS, IN Civil War Centennial Commission, Indianapolis, IN, 1965.

The books listed above and several other similar books are available at ISL, ACPL, and FHL(FHC).

If you care to go into considerable detail in researching your IN Civil War ancestor, this book will be of considerable help:

___Geo. K. Schweitzer, CIVIL WAR GENEALOGY, The Author, 407 Ascot Court, Knoxville, TN 37923, 1989.

This work treats local, state, and national records, service and pension records, regimental and naval histories, enlistment rosters, hospital records, court-martial reports, burial registers, national cemeteries, gravestone allotments, amnesties, pardons, state militias, discharge papers, officer biographies, prisons, prisoners, battle sites, maps, relics, weapons, museums, monuments, memorials, deserters, black soldiers, Indian soldiers, and many other topics.

Some militia records for the period 1872-96 are available in ISA:

___CARD FILE OF INDIANA MILITIA, 1872-99, ISA, Indianapolis, IN.

There is in the National Archives an index to the service records of the Spanish-American War. This index is also available at RBNA. Again a properly filled out and submitted NATF Form 80 will bring you both military service and pension records. It is also possible that you will find the following materials useful:

___J. K. Gore, RECORD OF INDIANA VOLUNTEERS IN THE SPANISH-AMERICAN WAR, 1898-99, IN Adjutant General's Office, Indianapolis, IN, 1900.

___MICROFILM OF IN SPANISH-AMERICAN WAR VOLUNTEERS REGISTRATION CARDS, ISA, Indianapolis, IN. Gives name, military unit, age, birthplace, muster in and muster out dates, physical description, occupation.

Some records for World War I and subsequent wars may be obtained from:

___National Personnel Records Center, GSA (Military Records), 9700
Page Blvd., St. Louis, MO 63132.
There is also a 4-volumed publication on IN World War I participants:
___IN Adjutant General's Office, WORLD WAR I VETERANS LIST,
The Office, Indianapolis, IN, 1918.

26. Mortuary records

Very few IN mortuary records have been transcribed or microfilmed. This means that you must write directly to the mortuaries which you know or suspect were involved in burying your ancestor. Sometimes the death certificate will name the mortuary; sometimes it is the only one nearby; sometimes you will have to write several in order to ascertain which one might have done the funeral arrangements. Mortuaries for IN with their addresses are listed in the following volume:

___C. O. Kates, editor, THE AMERICAN BLUE BOOK OF FUNER-
AL DIRECTORS, Kates-Boylston Publications, New York, NY,
latest issue.
This reference book will usually be found in the offices of most mortuaries. In all correspondence with mortuaries be sure to enclose an SASE.

27. Naturalization records

Before IN became a state (1816), it was part of the IN Territory (1800-16), and before that part of the Northwest Territory (1787-1800). During 1776-1789, the original states instituted naturalization regulations and/or procedures applying to their own areas. These requirements usually specified a period of residence, an oath of allegiance, and sometimes a confession of Protestant religion, all to be taken in a court of law. In 1790, the US Congress passed a naturalization act, followed in 1802 by a more comprehensive act. Although there were many modifying laws, the basic citizenship requirement until 1906 was that an alien to become a citizen, must live in the US 5 years, must file a declaration of intent, must wait two years, must then petition for naturalization, and finally take an oath of loyalty before a circuit or district court of the US, a supreme or district court of a territory, or any court of record of a state. The declaration of intent and the petition and oath-taking could occur in different courts. Following June 1906, about the same procedure was employed, but records and court actions were centralized by the US government. For this post-1906 period, write to the

following address for a Form G-641, which you can use to request records:
___Immigration and Naturalization Service, 425 I St., Washington, DC 20536.

Prior to June 1906, the naturalization process could have taken place in a US, state, or local court. This often makes locating the records a fairly difficult process. What it means is that all possible court records must be gone through in the quest. Fortunately, a very useful index for the early period of IN has been compiled:
___AN INDEX TO INDIANA NATURALIZATION RECORDS IN VARIOUS ORDER BOOKS OF THE 92 LOCAL COURTS PRIOR TO 1907, IHS, Indianapolis, IN, 1981.
Please be careful to note that this compilation by no means contains all the naturalizations for this time period, but it does contain the majority. The most likely IN courts for naturalizations are the county Courts of Common Pleas before 1816, the county Circuit Courts 1816-1909, the Court of Common Pleas 1848-52, and the Court of Probate Causes 1829-52. However, other courts must not be overlooked. The records are generally filed under headings such as declaration of intent, first papers, second papers, petitions, naturalization records, court journal, and court minutes. From 1790, children under 21 years were automatically naturalized with the parent. And until 1922, a wife was automatically naturalized along with the husband. During and after the Civil War, foreigners who had served in the military could become citizens simply by petition.

Naturalization records for many IN counties are on microfilm at ISL and FHL(FHC). Most of these are noted under the pertinent counties in Chapter 4. Others need to be sought in the counties and in the WPA compilations which were made for a number of the counties. County naturalization records are also to be found in genealogical journals. Many of these articles are indexed in the following publication:
___For periodicals published 1847-1985, then annually 1986-present, consult Allen County Public Library Foundation, PERIODICAL SOURCE INDEX, The Foundation, Fort Wayne, In, 1986-.
Numerous records of the US Federal District and Circuit Courts for IN (approximately 1803-1962) are available at the Chicago Branch of the National Archives, 7358 South Pulaski Road, Chicago, IL 60629 [Phone 1-(312)-581-7816]. Northwest Territorial records (for 1787-1801) and IN Territorial records (for 1804-16), including some court records, are available at the National Archives in Washington, DC in Record Group 59.

28. Newspaper records

Newspaper publication began in the Northwest Territory with the appearance of the CENTINEL OF THE NORTH-WESTERN TERRITORY in Cincinnati in 1793. The first newspaper published in the IN Territory was the IN GAZETTE which originated in Vincennes in 1804. A number of original and microfilmed newspapers are available for towns, cities, and counties of IN. These records are likely to contain information on births, deaths, marriages, anniversaries, divorces, family reunions, land sales, legal notices, ads of professionals and businesses, and local news. The largest IN collections are to be found in ISL and at IN University in Bloomington, both originals and microfilms being included. Available IN newspapers and their locations will be found listed in:

___C. S. Brigham, HISTORY AND BIBLIOGRAPHY OF AMERICAN NEWSPAPERS, 1690-1820, American Antiquarian Society, Worcester, MA, 1947, 1961, 2 volumes.

___W. Gregory, AMERICAN NEWSPAPERS, 1821-1936, H. W. Wilson Co., New York, NY, 1937.

___Library of Congress, NEWSPAPERS IN MICROFILM, US Library of Congress, Washington, DC, 1973; Supplements, 1978, 1979, etc.

___J. W. Miller, IN NEWSPAPER BIBLIOGRAPHY, IHS, Indianapolis, IN, 1982. Locations of over 8000 IN newspapers during 1804-1980.

FHL, FHC, and RL have some IN newspapers. Very few IN newspapers have been indexed. A few LL may have newspaper indexes, so it is always important to inquire. Newspapers should also be sought in the offices of County Recorders, because Indiana in 1852 started requiring them to keep newspapers published within their borders. Compliance was spotty and some newspapers were lost.

Not to be overlooked are the newsletters and denominational newspapers of the various religious groups in IN. Many were published over considerable periods of time. These may be located in ISL and IHS. Newspaper abstracts also appear in genealogical journals. The periodical indexes mentioned in the previous section should be used to locate these useful materials.

29. Published genealogies

There are a large number of index volumes and microfilm indexes which list published genealogies at the national level. Among the larger ones which you might examine are:

___FHL and FHC, FAMILY HISTORY LIBRARY CATALOG, Surname index.

___F. Rider, AMERICAN GENEALOGICAL INDEX, Godfrey Memorial Library, Middletown, CT, 1942-52, 48 volumes (millions of references).

___F. Rider, AMERICAN GENEALOGICAL AND BIOGRAPHICAL INDEX, Godfrey Memorial Library, Middletown, CT, 1952-, over 190 volumes (millions of references).

___The Newberry Library, THE GENEALOGICAL INDEX OF THE NEWBERRY LIBRARY, G. K. Hall, Boston, MA, 1960, 4 volumes (500,000 names).

___The New York Public Library, DICTIONARY CATALOG OF THE LOCAL HISTORY AND GENEALOGY DIVISION OF THE NEW YORK PUBLIC LIBRARY, G. K. Hall, Boston, MA, 1974, 20 volumes (318,000 entries).

___M. J. Kaminkow, GENEALOGIES IN THE LIBRARY OF CONGRESS, Magna Carta, Baltimore, MD, 1976-86. (25,000 references). Also see GENEALOGIES CATALOGED BY THE LIBRARY OF CONGRESS SINCE 1986, Library of Congress, Washington, DC, 1991.

___M. J. Kaminkow, COMPLEMENT TO GENEALOGIES IN THE LIBRARY OF CONGRESS, Magna Carta, Baltimore, MD, 1981.

___J. Munsell's Sons, INDEX TO AMERICAN GENEALOGIES, 1771-1908, reprint, Genealogical Publishing Co., Baltimore, MD, 1967 (60,000 references).

The first index is available at FHL and all FHC. At least some of the rest are held by ISL, ACPL, FHL, FHC, most RL, and some LGL.

For the state of IN, the above volumes are likely to be of help since most of them (with the exception those by Kaminkow) are largely eastern and northern oriented. Even better sources of published genealogies of Indianans are the Card Catalog, the special indexes, and the special alphabetical files in ISL and ACPL. Surname listings in card catalogs, special surname indexes, and family record files in RL and LL should not be overlooked.

30. Regional publications

In addition to national, state, and local publications, there are also numerous regional publications which should not be overlooked by any IN researcher. For the most part, these are volumes which are basically historical in character, but are likely to carry much genealogical information, sometimes incidentally, sometimes as addenda. They vary greatly in accuracy and coverage, so it is well the treat the data cautiously. In general, they cover specific regions which are made up of many or a few IN counties. In deciding which ones of these books to search for your forebears, you will need to make good use of the historical detail and the maps of Chapter 1.

The following works are ones which should prove useful to you if one or more deal with geographical areas of concern to you:

___T. E. Ball, NORTHWESTERN IN FROM 1800 TO 1900, Donohue and Henneberry, Chicago, IL, 1900. Lake, Porter, LaPorte, Pulaski, Starke, White, Newton, and Jasper Counties.

___H. W. Beckwith, HISTORY OF THE WABASH VALLEY, Bookmark, Knightstown, IN, 1978.

___BIOGRAPHICAL AND GENEALOGICAL HISTORY OF CASS, MIAMI, HOWARD, AND TIPTON COUNTIES, McDowell Publications, Owensboro, KY, 1974, with INDEX by B. S. Wolfe, 1979.

___BIOGRAPHICAL AND GENEALOGICAL HISTORY OF WAYNE, FAYETTE, UNION, AND FRANKLIN COUNTIES, McDowell Publications, Owensboro, KY, 1974.

___BIOGRAPHICAL AND HISTORICAL SOUVENIR FOR THE COUNTIES OF CLARK, CRAWFORD, FLOYD, HARRISON, JEFFERSON, SCOTT, AND WASHINGTON, Unigraphic, Evansville, IN, 1974, with INDEX by B. L. McKay, 1970.

___C. Blanchard, COUNTIES OF MORGAN, MONROE, AND BROWN, HISTORICAL AND BIOGRAPHICAL, Unigraphic, Evansville, IN, 1975.

___D. L. Bolin, OHIO VALLEY HISTORY, Polyanthos, New Orleans, LA, 1976. Includes biographical and genealogical information from Crawford, Harrison, and Perry Counties.

___W. Fritsch, GERMAN SETTLERS AND SETTLMENTS IN INDIANA, A Press, Greenville, SC, 1915.

___HISTORY OF MORGAN, MONROE, AND BROWN COUNTIES, McDowell Publications, Owensboro, KY, 1968.

___HISTORY OF THE COUNTIES OF WARREN, BENTON, JASPER, AND NEWTON, McDowell Publications, Owensboro, KY, 1973.

___HISTORY OF WARRICK, SPENCER, AND PERRY COUNTIES, McDowell Publications, Owensboro, KY, 1965.

___Indianapolis Public Library, A CONSOLIDATED INDEX TO 32 HISTORIES OF INDIANAPOLIS AND IN, The Library, Indianapolis, IN, 1939.

___MEMORIAL RECORD OF DISTINGUISHED MEN OF INDIANAPOLIS AND IN, Lewis Publ. Co., Chicago, IL, 1912.

___MEMORIAL RECORD OF NORTHEASTERN IN, Lewis Publishing Co., Chicago, IL, 1896.

___PICTORIAL AND BIOGRAPHICAL RECORD OF LAPORTE, PORTER, LAKE, AND STARKE COUNTIES, IN, Goodspeed Publishing Co., Chicago, IL, 1894.

___PICTORIAL AND BIOGRAPHICAL RECORD OF MONTGOMERY, PARKE, AND FOUNTAIN COUNTIES, IN, Chapman Brothers, Chicago, IL, 1893.

___M. E. Wood, FRENCH IMPRINT OF THE HEART OF AMERICA, HISTORICAL VIGNETTES OF 110 FRENCH-RELATED LOCALITIES IN INDIANA AND THE OHIO VALLEY, Unigraphic, Evansville, IN, 1976.

Most of these volumes will be found in ISL, IHS, ACPL, and FHL(FHC). Those pertinent to various regions will usually be found in RL and larger LL in the area.

---

31. Tax lists

Practically every IN county from the year 1817 collected tax from its residents annually. Records of assessments and of those from whom tax was collected were kept, and fortunately, some of these assessment and tax lists have survived, especially those from 1842 onward. Sometimes the tax lists are very simple, giving only the names of the taxpayers; at other times the lists also give the amount of property, its value, and its location. At still other times there are also tax records of taxes on personal property. The original tax records are in the CH, and there are microfilm copies of many of them in the CH, the ISL, and the FHL(FHC). The tax lists available for the 92 IN counties are listed in Chapter 4. These are extremely valuable records, because when the tax records exist for long periods of time (as sometimes they do), you can have a year-by-year accounting of your ancestor. The tax records often give indirect indications of death of a landowner, death of his widow, and distribution of the land to sons and daughters.

In addition to the original and microfilmed tax records, there are a few books which contain many tax records, especially the earlier ones:

___J. E. Darlington, IN TAX LISTS, 1835-48, The Author, Indianapolis, IN, 1990, 2 volumes.

There are quite a number of tax lists which have been published in genealogical journals. They may be located by looking in the following genealogical periodical indexes:

___For periodicals published 1847-1985, then annually 1986-present, consult Allen County Public Library Foundation, PERIODICAL SOURCE INDEX, The Foundation, Fort Wayne, In, 1986-.

During and shortly after the Civil War, there were federal tax assessments on IN people. Some of these records are in the Chicago Branch of the National Archives:

___Internal Revenue Service, TAX ASSESSMENT LISTS, 1867-73, Record Group 58, Chicago Branch, National Archives, Chicago, IL.

32. Wills and probate records

When a person died leaving any property (the estate), it was necessary for the authorities in the county of residence to see that this property was properly distributed. If a will had been written (testate), its wishes were carried out; if no will was left (intestate), the law indicated to whom distribution had to be made. Throughout the distribution process, many records had to be kept. From 1790-1805, probate matters were managed by the Probate and Orphans' Courts, from 1806-13 by the Court of Common Pleas, from 1814-29 by the Circuit Court, from 1829-52 by the Probate Court, from 1853-73 by the Court of Common Pleas, and thereafter by the Circuit Court. This is an oversimplified scheme, because in a number of counties other courts concurrently handled some of the probate matters, and the dates given above are approximate. In the various IN counties, the probate records can usually be found in the records of the Circuit Court. Exceptions to this are (1) in Marion, St. Joseph, and Vanderburgh Counties they are in the Probate Court, (2) in Allen, Hendricks, and Madison Counties they are in the Superior Court, and (3) in Bartholomew, Elkhart, Grant, Lake, LaPorte, and Porter Counties they are in both the Circuit and the Superior Courts.

Many sorts of records may be found in probate proceedings: accounts, administrator, appearance, appraisal, bonds, claims and allowances, executor, estate, fees, final records, guardian, inventories, letters testamentary, orders, partitions, sales, will, and perhaps others. In addition to the books containing the above sorts of records, there were usually estate papers in which the numerous detailed loose records pertaining to the estates were filed. The books carry references to the papers so that they can be found in the boxes or cabinets where they are filed. All of these records are quite valuable genealogically, because they generally mention the wife or husband, the children, and the spouses of the children. They may also mention the exact date of death, but if not, they indicate the approximate date. The records thereby serve, as very few others do, to solidly connect the generations. An unmarried woman or a widow could make a will, but a married woman required her husband's permission.

The original books and estate papers of loose records are in the CH, usually with accompanying indexes. ISL and the FHL(FHC) have microfilm copies of many of the books. And ISL and ACPL have transcripts of a number of the books. A few transcripts are also available in RL, LGL, and LL. Very few of the loose records have been microfilmed or transcribed. Listed in Chapter 4 are the will and probate records available in the IN counties. In seeking records of this type, you need to realize that all books with any of the key words (accounts, administrator, appearance, appraisal, bonds, claims and allowances, executor, estate, fees, final records, guardian, inventories, letters testamentary, orders, partitions, sales, will) need to be examined. Remember that quite often, especially in earlier years, estate records are mixed in with the regular court records. Further, the titles on books may not be precise. For example, a book labelled simply Wills may also contain settlements, inventories, and sales. Or a book labelled Settlements may contain wills, executors, administrators, and inventories. Records of other courts should also be investigated because disputes over inherited land may appear there.

A very useful index to IN wills before 1881 is:
__C. M. Franklin, INDEX TO IN WILLS THROUGH 1880, Heritage House, Indianapolis, IN, 1987, 9 volumes.
Please be careful to note that this index does not list estates of intestates (persons who did not make wills).

33. WPA works

The Works Progress Administration (WPA) of the federal government established the IN Historical Records Survey in 1936. The purpose of the IN Survey was to inventory state, county, municipal, and church records of historical importance. In 1939, supervision of the project was taken over by the IN Historical Bureau and the ISL. The Survey ended in 1942, and the unpublished inventories were deposited in the ISL. The data which the WPA

Historical Records Survey accumulated are often very useful to genealogists because they indicate where many records were located in the period 1936-42. They, therefore, can alert you to what was available, and can give you clues as to where to start in your search for them. Remember that many of the items to which these works refer remain where they were in 1936-42, but some have been moved to other depositories.

Among the materials which could be of assistance to you are the following. Many of them are incomplete and there are errors in them, some worse than others:

___WPA of IN, INDEXES OF BIRTH AND DEATH RECORDS IN INDIANA COUNTIES FOR THE YEARS 1882-1920, The WPA, Indianapolis, IN, 1937-41. Available for only 68 of the 92 counties. See separate listings under the counties in Chapter 4. Available in ISL, ACPL, and FHL(FHC).

___WPA of IN, INDEXES OF MARRIAGE RECORDS IN INDIANA COUNTIES FOR THE YEARS 1850-1920, The WPA, Indianapolis, IN, 1937-41. Available for only 68 of the 92 counties. See separate listings under the counties in Chapter 4. Available in ISL and FHL(FHC).

___WPA IN Historical Records Survey, INDEXES TO IN COUNTY HISTORIES, The Survey, Indianapolis, IN, 1938-41. Done by the WPA for the counties Adams through Madison. Completed for all counties by IHS. Available in ISL, IHS, ACPL, and FHL(FHC).

___WPA IN Historical Records Survey, INVENTORIES OF (OR GUIDES TO) THE COUNTY ARCHIVES OF IN, The Survey, Indianapolis, IN, 1937-42. Available for each county. Some are typeset, and some are typewritten. Each volume gives a historical sketch of the county and a list of the types of available county records. In ISL and FHL(FHC).

___WPA IN Historical Records Survey, A GUIDE TO THE PUBLIC VITAL STATISTICS RECORDS IN INDIANA, The Survey, Indianapolis, IN, 1941. In ISL, ACPL.

___WPA IN Historical Records Survey, MICROFILMS OF COUNTY RECORDS, The Survey, Indianapolis, IN, 1937-42. Some records microfilmed for the following counties: Allen, Clark, Dearborn, Floyd, Franklin, Gibson, Harrison, Jefferson, Jennings, Knox Perry, Scott, Spencer, Warrick, and Washington. In ISL, ACPL, and FHL(FHC).

___WPA IN Historical Records Survey, TRANSCRIPTS OF VARIOUS
IN COUNTY RECORDS, The Survey, Indianapolis, IN, 1937-42.
Some records transcribed in each of 79 counties. In ISL.

LIST OF ABBREVIATIONS

ACPL	=	Allen County Public Library, Ft. Wayne, IN
AGLL	=	American Genealogical Lending Library, Bountiful, UT
CH	=	Courthouse(s)
D	=	Mortality (death) census(es)
DAR	=	Daughters of the American Revolution
F	=	Farm and ranch census(es)
FHC	=	Family History Center(s)
FHL	=	Family History Library, Salt Lake City, UT
IN	=	Indiana
IHS	=	IN Historical Society, Indianapolis, IN
ISA	=	IN State Archives, Indianapolis, IN
ISL	=	IN State Library, Indianapolis, IN
LGL	=	Large genealogical library(ies)
LL	=	Local library(ies)
M	=	Manufactures census(es)
NA	=	National Archives, Washington, DC
P	=	Revolutionary War pension census
R	=	Regular federal census(es)
RBNA	=	Regional Branches of the National Archives
RL	=	Regional library(ies)
T	=	Territorial census(es)

Chapter 3

RECORD LOCATIONS

━━━━━━━━━━━━━━━━━━━━

1. Introduction

━━━━━━━━━━━━━━━━━━━━

The purpose of this chapter is to describe for you the major genealogical record repositories for IN records. These repositories are of two major types, libraries and archives. In general, libraries hold materials which have been published in printed, typescript, photocopied, computerized, and microfilm (microcard, microfiche) forms. Archives, on the other hand, are repositories for original records, largely in manuscript (hand-written) form, but also often as microfilm copies. Usually, libraries will have some original materials, and archives will have some published materials, but the predominant character of each is as indicated. When visiting and making use of the materials of repositories, there are several rules which almost all of them have. (1) You are required to check all overcoats, brief cases, and packages. (2) You are required to present some identification and to sign a register or fill out a form. (3) There is to be no smoking, no eating, no loud talk, and the use of pencils only. (4) All materials are to be handled with extreme care, with no injury to or defacing of any of them. (5) Materials are usually not to be returned to the stacks or drawers from which they came, but are to be returned to designated carts, tables, or shelves. (6) Upon leaving you should submit all materials for inspection and/or pass through security devices.

Libraries and archives have finding aids to facilitate locating the records which they hold. These aids are usually alphabetically arranged lists or indexes according to names or locations or subjects or authors or titles, or combinations of these, or they may be by dates. They consist of computer catalogs, card catalogs, microform catalogs, printed catalogs, typed catalogs and lists, various indexes, inventories, calendars, and tables of contents. In using these aids, especially computer, card, and microform catalogs, they must be searched in as many ways as possible to ensure that you extract everything from them. These ways are by name, by location, by subject, by author, by title, and sometimes by date. Sometimes certain catalogs are arranged by only one or two of these categories, but otherwise be sure and search them for all that are applicable. To help you to recall these categories, remember the word SLANT, with S standing for subject, L for location, A for author, N for name, and T for title. This is not, however, the order in which they should be searched for the maximum efficiency. They should be searched N-L-S-A-T. First, search the catalog for N(name), that is, for the surnames of all your IN forebears. Second, search the catalog for L(location), that is, look under all places where your ancestor lived (Northwest Territory, IN Territory, IN state, region, county, city, town, village), but especially the county, city, and town. Examine every entry in order to make sure you miss nothing. Third, look under appropriate S(subject) headings, such as the titles related to the sections in Chapter 2 [Bible, biography, birth, cemetery, census, church denomination, church name, court, Daughters of the American Revolution, death, divorce, emigration, ethnic group name (such as Germans, Huguenots, Irish), genealogy, historical records, immigration, marriage, US-history-Revolutionary War, US-history-War of 1812, US-history-Civil War, naturalization, newspaper, pensions, tax, will], but never neglecting these [biography, deeds, epitaphs, family records, genealogy, registers of births etc., wills]. Then finally, look under A(author) and/or T(title) for books mentioned in the sections of Chapter 2 which you need to examine.

When you locate references in finding aids to materials you need to examine, you will usually find that a numbered or alphabetized or combined code accompanies the listing. This is the access code which you should copy down, since it tells you where the material is located. For books it will usually be a code which refers to shelf positions. For microfilms, it usually refers to drawers and reel numbers. For manuscripts, it usually refers to folders, files, or boxes. In some repositories, the materials will be out on shelves or in cabinets to which you have access. In other repositories you will need to give the librarian or archivist a call slip on which you have written the title and code for the material so that it can be retrieved for you. In the microfilm (microfiche) areas of repositories you will find microfilm (microfiche) readers which attendants can help you with, if necessary.

Never leave a library or archives without discussing your research with a librarian or archivist. These people are trained specialists who know their collections and the ways for getting into them. And they can often suggest innovative approaches to locating data relating to your progenitors. They also can usually guide you to other finding aids. When you do discuss your work with librarians and archivists, please remember that they are busy people with considerable demands on their time. So be brief, get to the point, and don't bore them with irrelevant detail. They will appreciate this, and you and others will get more and better service from them.

In general, you cannot expect to do much of your genealogy by corresponding with libraries and archives. The reason is that the hard-working professionals who run these repositories have little time to give to answering mail. This is because of the heavy demands of serving the institutions which employ them, of maintaining the collection, and of taking care of patrons who visit them. Some simply cannot reply to mail requests. Others will answer one brief question which can be quickly looked up in a finding aid, but none of them can do even brief research for you. If you do write them, make your letter very brief, get right to the point, enclose an SASE, and be prepared to wait. Repositories will generally not recommend researchers you can hire, but they will some-times provide you with a list of researchers. Such a list will bear no warranty from the repository, and they in no way have any responsibility toward either you or the researcher, because they are not in the business of certifying searchers.

As mentioned at the beginning of Chapter 2, there are several record repositories in IN which will be of immense value in your genealogical research. The best collections of IN materials are to be found in the following repositories:

__(ISL) IN State Library, 140 North Senate Avenue, Indianapolis, IN 46204-2296. Telephone: 1-317-232-3689. Published national, territorial, state, county, municipal, and private records for IN. Especially Rooms B50, 206, 210, 250, 253.

__(ISA) IN State Archives, Room 117, 140 North Senate Avenue, Indianapolis, IN 46204-2296. Telephone: 1-317-232-3660. Original, microfilmed, and published IN state governmental and some selected local governmental records.

__(IHS) IN Historical Society Library, Third Floor, 315 West Ohio Street, Indianapolis, IN 46202-3299. Telephone: 1-317-232-1879. Published records and manuscript materials relating to IN.

__(FHL) Family History Library, Genealogical Library of the Church of Jesus Christ of Latter-day Saints, 35 North West Temple, Salt Lake City, UT 84150. Microfilmed and published national, state, county, municipal, and private records.

__(FHC) Family History Center(s), over 1700 of them, located all over the world. They are local branch affiliates of the Family History Library (FHL). They can be found in most major US cities, in-cluding 9 in IN. Most of the microfilmed national, state, county, municipal, and private records held by the FHL can be borrowed through the FHC.

___(ACPL) Allen County Public Library, Genealogical Department, 900 Webster Street, Fort Wayne, IN 46802. Published and micro-filmed national, state, county, municipal, and private records.

___(CPL) Cincinnati Public Library, Library Square, 800 Vine Street, Cincinnati, OH 45202. Many major IN holdings.

___(RL) Regional Libraries in IN which hold larger genealogical collections than are usually held by most local libraries. Published and some microfilmed national, state, regional, county, and local private records.

___(LL) Local Libraries in the cities and towns of the IN counties. These include county, city, town, and private libraries. Published county, city, and local private records.

___(LR) Local Repositories which have special types of records in counties, cities, and towns : historical societies, genealogical societies, record archives and institutes, museums, cemetery offices, organizations, mortuaries, and newspaper offices.

___(CH) County Court Houses in the county seats of the 92 IN counties. Original and microfilmed county records.

Records which are national (federal) and those which are state-wide in scope have been treated in detail in Chapter 2. The locations of the records have also been given. Records which are basically county-wide in scope were treated generally in Chapter 2, and detailed listings of those available will be given in Chapter 4.

Most of the original county records referred to in Chapter 2 and partially listed under the counties in Chapter 4 are stored in the court houses. The court houses are located in the county seats which are listed along with their zip codes in Chapter 4. The original records ordinarily consist of variously-labelled books (usually handwritten), files with file folders in them, and boxes with large envelopes or file folders in them. The records are generally stored in the offices of various county officials, or in the case of older records they may be found in special storage vaults. In many instances, they are readily accessible. In a few cases, they are put away so that they are very difficult to get out and use. The records which will most likely be found in the county court houses include the following, these categories being taken largely from the WPA inventories:

___Auditor: county commissioner minutes, personal tax, poll tax, property tax, township assessors' budget records

___County Clerk: adoptions, bonds, circuit court records, court of common pleas records, divorces, estray records, guardianships,

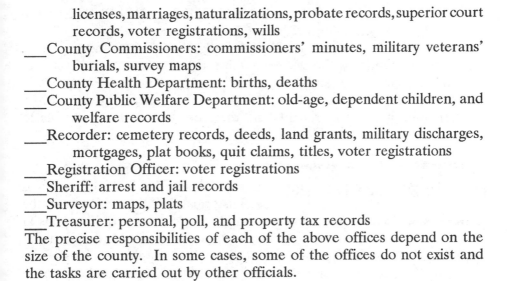

licenses, marriages, naturalizations, probate records, superior court records, voter registrations, wills
___County Commissioners: commissioners' minutes, military veterans' burials, survey maps
___County Health Department: births, deaths
___County Public Welfare Department: old-age, dependent children, and welfare records
___Recorder: cemetery records, deeds, land grants, military discharges, mortgages, plat books, quit claims, titles, voter registrations
___Registration Officer: voter registrations
___Sheriff: arrest and jail records
___Surveyor: maps, plats
___Treasurer: personal, poll, and property tax records

The precise responsibilities of each of the above offices depend on the size of the county. In some cases, some of the offices do not exist and the tasks are carried out by other officials.

Once you have located the county in which your ancestor lived, it is usually not a good idea to go there first. It is best to explore the microfilmed, transcribed, and published copies of the records at some central repository such as ISL-ISA-IHS, ACPL, and FHL(FHC). (ISL-ISA-IHS are hyphenated to remind you that all three may be visited together since all are in Indianapolis.) This is because it is the business of these repositories to make the records available to you, but the primary task of the county officials and employees at the court houses is to conduct the record keeping task as an aid to regulating the society and keeping the law. Therefore, it is best not to encroach upon their time and their good graces until you have done as much work elsewhere as possible. Many of the major record books have been microfilmed or transcribed so you can go through them nicely at ISL-ISA-IHS, ACPL, and FHL(FHC). Or you can hire a researcher to do the investigating for you if a trip is not workable or would be too expensive. Most of the contents of the case files, however, have not been copied. Hence, after doing work at ISL-ISA-IHS, ACPL, and FHL(FHC) you then need to make a trip to the county (LL, LR, CH), or hire a researcher to do so for you. In general, you will find the people there very helpful and cooperative, and often they will make photocopies for you or will give you access to a copying machine. It is usually best to visit the LL before going to the CH, and do not forget the many other possible LR in the counties.

Researchers who are near ISL-ISA-IHS, ACPL, FHL, FHC, or the CH in the various counties will be listed in:

___G. B. Everton, Jr., editor, GENEALOGICAL HELPER, Everton
    Publishers, Logan, UT, latest Jul-Aug issue.
In addition, staff members at ISL-ISA-IHS, ACPL, FHL, and the LL in
the various counties will often send you a list of researchers if you will
dispatch a request and an SASE to them. Do not write the officials in
the CH for researcher recommendations since they generally deem this a
matter to be handled by the LL and therefore are ordinarily unable to
help you.

----

2. The IN State Library (ISL)

The IN State Library (ISL) is located in the IN State Library and
Historical Building which is in the
midst of downtown Indianapolis at
140 North Senate Avenue, India-
napolis, IN 46204-2296. The Genealogy Section telephone number is 1-
317-232-3689, and its open hours are 8:00 am to 4:30 pm Monday through
Friday, plus 8:30 am to 4:00 pm Saturday only for the months of
September-through May. It is important that you recognize that the
opening times may change, so do not fail to call before you go. Several
convenient, but a bit expensive, parking lots are nearby. There are a
number of hotels within walking distance of the ISL. Included are the
following:
___The Canterbury Hotel, 123 S. Illinois St., Zip 46225, Telephone 1-317-
    634-3000.
___Courtyard by Marriott - Downtown, 501 W. Washington St., Zip
    46204, Telephone 1-317-635-4443.
___Crowne Plaza Union Station, 1234 W. Louisiana St., Zip 46206,
    Telephone 1-317-631-2221.
___Days Inn Downtown, 401 E. Washington St., Zip 46204, Telephone 1-
    317-637-6464.
___Embassy Suites Hotel - Downtown, 110 W. Washington St., Zip
    46204, Telephone 1-317-236-1800.
___Hyatt Regency Indianapolis, One S. Capitol Ave., Zip 46204,
    Telephone 1-317-632-1234.
___Omni Severin Hotel, 40 W. Jackson Place, Zip 46225, Telephone 1-
    317-634-6664.
___Ramada Plaza Hotel, 31 W. Ohio St., Zip 46204, Telephone 1-317-
    635-2000.
___The Westin Hotel Indianapolis, 50 S. Capitol Ave., Zip 46204,
    Telephone 1-317-262-8100.

The ISL consists of several divisions with the following two being of chief interest to family researchers: (Room 206) The Reference and Government Services Division, and (Room 210) The Indiana Division. This latter Division, the Indiana Division, has three sub-Sections: (Room 250) The Genealogy Section, (Room 253) The Manuscripts Section, and (Room B50) The Newspaper Section. Your initial task will be to make a brief visit to all of these rooms and to identify the finding aids in each. These finding aids will permit you to locate all records in the ISL which are pertinent to your ancestor search.

When you go in the Main Entrance of the IN State Library and Historical Building, you will find yourself facing a flight of wide stairs leading to the Second Floor. Go up these stairs, and at the top, you will be in a Lobby containing a central desk and a back wall lined with card file cabinets. These cabinets contain:

___(L-1) LC Card Catalog (items obtained 1966-75), on the left,

___(L-2) DEC Card Catalog (items obtained 1825-1966), in the center,

___(L-3) IN Card Catalog, on the right, and

___(L-4) IN County Card Catalog, on the far right.

On a table in the lobby, you will also observe the ISL On-Line Computer Catalog:

___(C-5) ISL On-Line Computer Catalog (items obtained after 1975 plus
        many obtained before).

For a thorough search of tthe holdings of the ISL, all five of these catalogs and a catalog in the Genealogy Section must be employed.

On the left of the Lobby is Room 206, which houses the Reference and Services Division of the ISL. Probably their most important holding for genealogical purposes are national and international biographical works and indexes. There are also national and world atlases and a vast collection of US governmental documents, including the 12-volumed US Serial Set Index. These books index 14,000 volumes of Federal governmental records. Most of the other material in Room 206 is not ordinarily useful to ancestor hunters. The staff in this Division can assist in locating any general historical or geographical publications and periodicals.

On the right of the Lobby is Room 210, which is the Indiana Division. The personnel here manage IN state documents and publications, IN histories (territorial, state, regional, county, township, city, rivers, river valleys, railroads, canals), IN city and county directories, IN biographical works (state, regional, local, professional), IN maps, gazetteers, and atlases, many IN periodicals, and a sizeable picture collection. These items may be located by using the five catalogs listed above (L-1, L-2, L-3, L-4, C-5). The ISL On-Line Computer Catalog (C-5) is also located in the Indiana Division room. The major finding aids in Room 210 are:

___(C-5) ISL On-Line Computer Catalog,

___(I-6) Biography Card Index, contains data from many IN histories, atlases, and other similar biographical sources,

___(I-7) Indianapolis Newspaper Index, 1898-forward,

___(I-8) Picture Collection Card Index.

Just behind the Indiana Division is the Manuscript Section in Room 253. Its manuscripts are indexed in the Section's major finding aids, two books and a card index:

___(M-9) E. Pumroy and P. Brockman, A GUIDE TO MANUSCRIPT COLLECTIONS OF THE IHS AND THE ISL, IHS, Indianapolis, IN, 1986. Incomplete, be sure and use the card index,

___(M-10) Manuscripts Card Index, and

___(M-11) A. Turner, GUIDE TO IN CIVIL WAR MANUSCRIPTS, IN Civil War Centennial Commission, Indianapolis, IN, 1965.

In the basement (take elevator 2 flights down) in Room B50 is the Newspaper Section of the Indiana Division. The large collection of original and microfilmed newspapers is detailed and the papers are located in three finding aids, a book and two looseleaf guidebooks:

___(N-12) J. W. Miller, IN NEWSPAPER BIBLIOGRAPHY, IHS, Indianapolis, IN, 1982,

___(N-13) Newspaper Holdings Guidebook, by county, and

___(N-14) Guidebook to Newspaper Indexes, by county.

The last section to be visited is the most important one, namely the Genealogy Section in Room 250, located behind the Reference and Government Services Division (Room 206). When you walk in, you will see an information desk on your left. Just beyond it is an area with lockers for the storing of your coat, briefcase, packages, and other items. Straight ahead you will see work tables and walls with books and file cabinets. Off on your far right is the entrance to the Microfilm Reader Room, and within it the Microfilm Request Counter. Immediately to your right, you will observe several card cabinets containing valuable card indexes:

___(G-15) Card Index to IN Marriages Through 1850,

___(G-16) Card Index to the 1850 IN Census,

___(G-17) Card Index to the 1820 and 1830 IN Censuses,

___(G-18) Main Genealogy Card Catalog, to all published materials prior to 1976, all microfilms, and all pamphlet and family history files, (for military records search under US-History--[Name of War]), and

___(C-5) ISL On-Line Computer Catalog, to published materials after 1975, some published materials before that, some microfilms, and some loose file materials.

Card cabinets with useful card indexes are also located on your immediate left:

___(G-19) Card Index to IN Enrollments of Soldiers, Their Widows, and Orphans, 1886,

___(G-20) Card Index to the 1850, 1860, 1870, and 1880 Mortality Census Schedules,

___(G-21) IN DAR Bible Records Index,

___(G-22) IN Cemetery Locator File, by county,

___(G-23) Heraldry Card Index, and

___(G-24) DAR Lineage Book Card Index.

Over in the far left corner are the IN county record indexes and record volumes published by the WPA, the DAR, various organizations, and different individuals:

___(G-25) IN County Record, History, and Atlas Indexes.

And in the center of the far wall are IN census indexes:

___(G-26) IN Census Indexes, 1820-60, 1880, 1900, 1920.

Now that you have viewed the major finding aids of the ISL, here is a proposed order of use to ensure that you do not overlook any pertinent source. Remember that libraries and archives can be searched by recalling SLANT (S for subject, L for locality, A for author, N for name, and T for title). The best order is N (name) first, the L (locality) second, and then S (subject), A (author), and T (title). So, you should first examine those resources which provide large listings of surnames. Then, you should examine those finding aids which will lead you to other available records which might contain data on your ancestor. These will be chiefly finding aids which list records under your ancestor's locality (county, city, IN). So, your first search is for your ancestor's name in those of the following name indexes which you judge to be pertinent:

___(G-26) IN Census Indexes.

___(G-18) Main Genealogy Card Catalog.

___(C-5) ISL On-Line Computer Catalog.

___(G-25) IN County Record, History, and Atlas Indexes.

___(I-6) Biography Card Index.

___(G-15) Card Index to IN Marriages Through 1850.

___(G-19) Card Index to Enrollments of Soldiers, Their Widows, and Orphans, 1886.

___(G-20) Card Index to 1850, 1860, 1870, 1880 Mortality Censuses

___(G-21) IN DAR Bible Record Index.

___(G-24) DAR Lineage Book Card Index.

___(L-1) LC Card Catalog, 1966-75.

___(L-2) DEC Card Catalog, 1825-1966.

___(L-3) IN Card Catalog.

___(I-7) Indianapolis Newspaper Index, 1898-forward.

___(M-9) Pumroy and Brockman, GUIDE TO MANUSCRIPT COL-LECTIONS.

___(M-10) Manuscripts Card Index.

___(M-11) Turner, GUIDE TO IN CIVIL WAR MANUSCRIPTS.

Your next or second step is to examine a number of finding aids to locate other records which might give data on your ancestor. This means searching the following finding aids for the localities in which your ancestor lived. Look at every card or item listed under your ancestor's county, town, and/or city. Then you should make your way carefully through all the many listings under the state of IN to see if any are pertinent. These are the finding aids to use:

___(C-5) ISL On-Line Computer Catalog,

___(G-18) Main Genealogy Card Catalog,

___(L-3) IN Card Catalog,

___(L-4) IN County Card Catalog,

___(L-1) LC Card Catalog,

___(L-2) DEC Card Catalog,

___(G-22) IN Cemetery Locator File,

___(G-25) IN County Record, History, and Atlas Indexes.

___(M-9) Pumroy and Brockman, A GUIDE TO MANUSCRIPT COLLECTIONS OF THE IHS AND THE ISL,

___(M-10) Manuscripts Card Index,

___(M-11) Turner, GUIDE TO IN CIVIL WAR MANUSCRIPTS,

___(N-12) Miller, IN NEWSPAPER BIBLIOGRAPHY,

___(N-13) Newspaper Holdings Guidebook, by county, and

___(N-14) Guidebook to Newspaper Indexes, by county.

Now you are ready to take the third and the fourth steps to complete your coverage of the ISL resources. The third step is to check the appropriate items for any specialized subjects under which you think you might find information on your forebear. The headings of sections in

Chapter 2 will suggest some of these subjects (atlas, Bible, biography, birth, cemetery, church, city directory, city history, county history, court, DAR, death, deed, divorce, ethnic, family history, gazetteer, genealogical periodical, genealogy, map, land, marriage, military, mortuary, naturalization, newspaper abstracts, probate, regional histories, registers of births, tax, and will). Examples of others might be millwrights, Germans, Methodist Episcopal Church, epitaphs, War of 1812, underground railroad. The items that should be checked are:

___(C-5) ISL On-Line Computer Catalog,
___(G-18) Main Genealogy Card Catalog,
___(L-3) IN Card Catalog,
___(L-4) IN County Card Catalog,
___(L-1) LC Card Catalog,
___(L-2) DEC Card Catalog,
___(G-22) IN Cemetery Locator File,
___(G-25) IN County Record, History, and Atlas Indexes.
___(M-9) Pumroy and Brockman, A GUIDE TO MANUSCRIPT COLLECTIONS OF THE IHS AND THE ISL,
___(M-10) Manuscripts Card Index,
___(M-11) Turner, GUIDE TO IN CIVIL WAR MANUSCRIPTS,

Fourth, do the author and title checking. Look carefully at the large number of books and other items that are listed in the many sections of Chapter 2. As you find books and other items which you have not seen, locate them in the computer and card catalogs (C-5, G-18, L-3, L-4, L-1) by author and/or title.

Do not fail to discuss your research with one of the competent staff of the ISL, especially those in the Genealogy Section. Be brief, because their time is valuable. You will find that they will be able to save you much time and considerable effort. Remember, however, that they cannot do your work for you, they can only give you guidance.

3. The IN State Archives (ISA)

The IN State Archives (ISA) is located in the same building as the ISL. The ISA occupies Room 117. All the material concerning parking and nearby hotels is the same as that given in the previous section of this chapter. The times for the ISA are 8:00am - 4:30pm, Monday through Friday. But times can change, so be sure to check by calling them at 1-317-232-3660.

The ISA has an unbelievably large volume of records. Much of this is inventoried in finding aids, and some of it is indexed. Listed below are some of the principal finding aids and records which the staff can make available to you and help you use. You should go to work in the ISA only after you have made thorough use of the resources of the ISL. When you enter Room 117, report to the attendant at the registration desk just to the right. Ask the attendant to summon an Archivist who will assist you with the finding aids, indexes, and records in which you are interested. The Archivist will also often be able to recommend other pertinent materials to you. Among the finding aids, indexes, and records in which you might be interested are the following. The first group consists of military materials:

___Microfilms of Muster Rolls of the Battle of Tippecanoe in 1811,
___Card Index of IN Soldiers in the War of 1812,
___IN State Militia Officer Card Index, 1812-51,
___Card Index of IN State Militia in the Black Hawk War of 1832,
___Index to Indianans in the Mexican War,
___Microfilms of Mexican War Records,
___Civil War Regiments by County of Origin,
___Listing of Civil War Substitutes, alphabetical by name of person hiring
    the substitute,
___Lists of IN African-American Recruits, 1864-65,
___Microfilms of IN Civil War Participants and Records,
___Microfilms of Civil War Regimental Histories,
___Records of the Grand Army of the Republic (GAR),
___Card Index to IN Men in the Veteran's Reserve Corps,
___Card Index of Union Soldiers Buried in Indiana,
___Card Index of IN Militia, 1877-96,
___Microfilms of IN Legion (Civil War Militia, 1861-65) and National
    Guard Records (1880-1917),
___Microfilms of the Veterans' Enrollment of 1886,
___Inventory of State Soldiers' Homes Records,
___Microfilms of Spanish-American War Records,
___Microfilms of World War I Service, Draft, and Address Records,
___Microfilms of World War II Discharge and Casualty Records, and
___Microfilms of Korean War Records.

Another sizeable set of finding aids, indexes, and records is those dealing with land. Among the more important are:

___Inventory of Plat and Field Notes, by county,
___Vincennes Land Office Tract Book Index, by name,
___Inventory of State Land Records,

___Microfilms of IN Agricultural Censuses, 1850/60/70/80,
___Microfilms of US Surveyor General Records,
___Microfilms of US Land Office Records,
___Ft. Wayne Land Office Entry Index, by name,
___LaPorte-Winamac Land Office Entry Index, by name,

There are also numerous miscellaneous governmental finding aids, indexes, and records:
___Index to Territorial Manuscripts, by name and by subject,
___Inventory of Court Case Files for the Northwest Territory and the IN Territory, 1791-1816,
___Inventory of General Court Papers for the Northwest Territory and the IN Territory, 1791-1820,
___IN Legislative Records, Senate and House,
___Card Index of Records of Dissolved IN Corporations, Charities, and Organizations,
___Card Index Inventory of State Agency Records, by agency; important listings for genealogists are Adjutant General, Appellate Court, Auditor of State, Corrections Department, General Assembly, Health Board of IN, Mental Health Administration, Secretary of State, Supreme Court, and Veterans' Affairs,
___Microfilms of State Agency Records,
___Microfilms of State Prison Records,
___Card Index of County Records,
___Microfilms of County Records,
___Card Index of Newspapers, by county,
___Inventory of County Vital Records,
___Microfilms of IN Manufactures Censuses, 1820, 1850, 1860, 1870, 1880, and
___Microfilms of IN Social Statistics Censuses, 1850, 1860, 1870.

Finally, we come to the two most valuable finding aids in the ISA:
___The Archivists of the ISA. They know much about the collections that is not in print. All materials must be and should be accessed through them, since they can almost always give you further information and assistance.
___The WPA Name Index. A 660,000-card file of names found in land office, court, military, treasury, and numerous other ISA records relating to the period prior to 1851. Access to this valuable index is only by request to an Archivist. Do not overlook it.

---

4. The IN Historical Society (IHS)

As are the ISL and the ISA, the IN Historical Society is located in the IN State Library and Historical Building which is in the midst of downtown Indianapolis. The official entrance is 315 West Ohio Street, Indianapolis, IN 46202-3299, which is just around the corner from the ISL-ISA entrance. The telephone number is 1-317-232-1879. The IN Historical Society's Library (IHS) will be found in Room 365 on the third floor. All the material concerning parking and nearby hotels is the same as that given in the second section back in this chapter. The times for the IHS are 8:00am - 4:30pm, Monday through Friday, and 8:30am - 4:00pm on Saturday only from Labor Day to Memorial Day. But times can change, so be sure to check by calling them.

The library of the IN Historical Society is very rich in all sorts of publications and manuscript materials relating to the history of IN, its government, its regions, its counties, its cities, its industries, its agriculture, its schools, its transportation facilities, its culture, and its people. Many of the works referenced in Chapter 2 will be found in its collection. When you enter Room 365, you will be asked to leave your brief case, overcoat, purses, and all electronic devices in the lockers located just outside the door. Upon returning to the room, you will see a desk on your right where you will be given a set of regulations and a registration card. Take a seat, read the regulations, fill out the registration card, and hand it to the attendant along with a photographic ID. Only paper and pencil should be brought into the Library.

The major finding aids which will give you access to the IHS holdings are located to the left and to the right of the door. On the left, you will see:

___Main Card Catalog, IHS, lists printed, microform, manuscript, and map materials. Includes books, periodicals, newspapers, pamphlets, maps. Strong holdings in early IN, early exploration, Civil War regimental histories, and county histories.

To the right, you will find:

___Manuscript Catalog, IHS. Good holdings for early settlers, Civil War, and Indian conflicts. Entries lead to manuscripts, guides to manuscripts, and inventories of manuscripts.

___Browsing Catalog, a shelf list of the holdings of the IHS arranged in order in which they appear on the shelf. Useful for looking for materials which relate to the same subject.

___Chronological Catalog, lists printed materials by publication date.

___Catch Reference Catalog, items from a wide variety of miscellaneous sources. Must not be overlooked.

All of the above catalogs are to be searched by all of these categories which are applicable: name, location (IN, region, county, township, city), subject, author, title. When you locate items you wish to examine, you will find that some of the more widely-used ones are on open shelves in the library. Other less-employed items will need to be requested by filling out a library material request form and handing it to the attendant at the reference desk. The IHS plans to move nearby in 1998. This means that the finding aids will be essentially the same, but their arrangement may differ.

---

5. The Allen County Public Library (ACPL)

The Allen County Public Library (ACPL) has the second largest genealogical collection in the US. The holdings include almost 190,000 printed works and over 220,000 rolls of microfilm or packs of microfiche. These represent genealogical indexes, family histories, federal and state censuses, city directories, federal passenger lists, federal and state military records, local histories, major genealogical reference works, state and private collections of microfilmed records, manuscript collections, maps, native American records, African-American records, Canadian records, British records, German records, periodicals, computer data bases, FHL indexes and catalogs, videos, and a comprehensive index to the most important genealogical periodicals. Their IN collection is very strong. Many of the materials mentioned in Chapter 2 will be found there. The facility is located at 900 Webster Street, Ft. Wayne, IN 46802, and the telephone number is 1-(219)-424-7241, Ext. 3315. The hours are 9am-9pm Monday-Thursday, 9am-6pm Friday-Saturday, and 1pm-6pm Sunday. Hours vary in the summer and they are subject to change, so if you are planning to go, telephone and inquire about the times. Parking is available in several commercial lots a block away from the ACPL.

Nearby places to stay when working at the ACPL include the Fort Wayne Hilton (1020 South Calhoun Street, Telephone: 1-219-420-1100), and the Holiday Inn Downtown (300 East Washington Boulevard, Telephone: 1-219-422-5511). They often have a special Discover-Your-Roots rate which you should ask for.

After entering the library, proceed to the second floor where the Genealogy Department is located. Register at the entrance, then take a look to your left, and then a second look straight ahead. To your left you will see a sizable room, with a second room behind, and a third room beyond that. The second room is the microtext reader and copier room and also contains the International Genealogical Index (IGI) on microfiche.

___(M-1)International Genealogical Index, microfiche edition.

The third room, just beyond the second room, is the microtext (microfilm, microfiche, microcard) storage room containing many cabinets of microtext materials. Also just to the left of the door to this room is a set of cabinets containing the following microtext catalogs:

___(M-2) Military Microtext Records,

___(M-3) Passenger List Microtext Records,

___(M-4) Family Histories on Microtext,

___(M-5) African-American Microtext Materials,

___(M-6) Native American Microtext Materials,

___(M-7) Census Schedules on Microtext, and 1880/1900/1910/1920 Census Indexes (for IN only 1880/1900/1920),

___(M-8) State Records on Microtext.

The references in these catalogs identify the cabinets in which the microtexts may be found. When you locate microtext materials that you want to view, take note of the storage cabinet listed on the card, proceed to the storage cabinet, remove the microtext, then take it into the adjoining room and view it on one of the readers. After you are through, return it to the top of the storage cabinet. Do not replace it in the cabinet.

In the first room to the left of the entranceway, you will see a large number of card cabinets on the left wall. These cabinets contain:

___(L-1) Main Card Catalog, but does not refer to microtext materials. Search it by name, location (IN, region, county, township, city), subject, author, title.

When you locate items you wish to examine, you will find that some of the more widely-used ones are on open shelves in the library. Other less-employed items will need to be requested by filling out a library material request form and placing it in a tray on top of a cabinet near the entrance to the room. Against the back wall of this first room to the left of the entrance are bookshelves containing:

___(L-2) IN Census Indexes, 1820/30/40/50/60. Search by name.

Along the left wall of this room is the library's shelf list which lists the books in the library in the order in which they appear on the shelves:

___(L-3) ACPL Shelf List. Very useful for browsing, that is for seeing what volumes relate to a given county or what family histories there are under a given surname.

On an island at the entrance to this first room to the left are the very valuable Periodical Source Index and a reference list of the periodicals cited in it:

___(L-4) Periodical Source Index (PERSI), with list of cited periodicals. Search by name and location.

Walk down through these three rooms and locate every one of the finding aids, M-1 through L-4.

Now, return to the entrance to the Genealogy Department, and look straight ahead into a large room. On your immediate right will be the service desk. Then continuing along the right wall notice a table with several computers on it. These are stations of the:

___(C-1) ACPL On-Line Computer Catalog. Search by name, location (IN, region, county, township, city), subject, author, title. Catalog is incomplete.

Next to the computers are copiers, and beyond them two small side rooms in which genealogical record CDROMs and computers for reading them are located.

___(C-2) Computer Centers for CDROMs. All those mentioned in Chapter 2 are available here.

Then back in the far right corner will be found computer stations for using an extensive CDROM genealogical reference set:

___(C-3) The Family History Library's Family Search CDROM Set consisting of International Genealogical Index (IGI), Ancestral File (careful!), Family History Library Catalog (FHLC), and Social Security Death Index. See Section 7 of this chapter for detailed search instructions.

All along the back wall of this room are bookstacks bearing major state reference volumes (including IN) and bound genealogical periodicals. Then beginning in the far left corner and moving toward you, these items will be found:

___(C-4) Fort Wayne city directories,

___(C-5) Allen County materials,

___(C-6) Canadian materials,

___(C-7) Heraldry sources,

___(C-8) International reference works,

___(C-9) Quaker records, and

___(C-10) Rider's GENEALOGICAL BIOGRAPHICAL INDEX.

To make a thorough search of the ACPL for your IN ancestor, the following procedure can be used. First, search all the appropriate ones of the above finding aids for the name. Every finding aid and set mentioned above contains name listings: C-1, L-1, L-2 and M-7, M-1, C-3, L-4, C-10, C-9, L-3, C-2, M-2, M-4, M-5, M-6, M-3, M-8, C-4, C-5, C-6, C-7, C-8. Then search the pertinent finding aids for location (county, township, city, IN): C-1, L-1, C-3, L-4, L-3, C-2, M-2, M-8, C-9. Then search applicable finding aids for subjects which might yield information: C-1, L-1, C-3, L-4, M-5, M-6, M-8, C-7, C-8. The headings of sections in Chapter 2 will suggest some subjects that you will find rewarding. And finally, search for materials mentioned in Chapter 2 (books, treatises, indexes, microforms, CDROMs) which you believe will be useful.

---

6. The Public Library of Cincinnati (PLC)

The Public Library of Cincinnati (PLC) is a well-stocked genealogical library which has excellent IN material. The library is located at Library Square, 800 Vine Street, Cincinnati, OH 45202, and its telephone number is 1-(513)-369-6900. The hours are 9am-9pm Monday-Friday, and 9am-6pm Saturday. The library is closed on Sundays. Hours may change, so call about them before you pay the PLC a visit. Nearby hotels include the Cincinnati Terrace Hilton, 15 West Sixth Street, Zip 45202 [Phone 1-(513)-381-4000], the Clarion Hotel, 141 West Sixth Street, Zip 45202 [Phone 1-(513)-352-2100], the Hyatt Regency, 151 West Fifth Street, Zip 45202 [Phone 1-(513)-579-1234], and the Omni Netherland Plaza, 35 West Fifth Street, Zip 45202 [Phone 1-(513)-421-9100].

Most of the genealogically-pertinent materials in the PLC are to be found in the History Department, which is located on the 1st Floor South of the library. Among its abundant holdings are atlases, biographical works, census indexes and microfilms, city directories, gazetteers, genealogical periodicals and indexes, genealogies, guide books, histories, the International Genealogical Index, maps, military records, passenger lists, newspapers, and many books of compiled records. The major finding aids in the library are:

___Main Card Catalog (search by name, locality, subject, author, title),
___CINCH Computer Catalog (search by name, locality, subject, author, title),
___Local History Index (search by name and subject),
___Local Newspaper Indexes (search by name and subject),

___Genealogy Index (search by name),
___Newspaper Holdings List (search by town, city, and county).
These should all be searched according to the search technique described
in Paragraph 2 of Section 1 of this chapter. You will remember that this
involves SLANT: N = name, L = location, S = subject, A = author, and
T = title. When you find items of interest to your search, they may be
requested at the History Desk by submitting a carefully filled-out call slip.

7. The Family History Library and its Branch Family History Centers (FHL/FHC)

The largest genealogical library in the world is the Family History Library of the Genealogical Society of UT (FHL). This library, which holds almost two million rolls of microfilm, almost 400,000 microfiche, plus a vast number of books, is located at 50 East North Temple St., Salt Lake City, UT 84150. The basic keys to the library are composed of six indexes. (1) The International Genealogical Index, (2) The Surname Index in the FHL Catalog, (3) Listings of the Indexes to the Family Group Records Collection, (4) The Ancestral File, (5) The Social Security Death Index, and (6) The Locality Index in the FHL Catalog. In addition to the main library, the Society maintains a large number of Branches called Family History Centers (FHC) all over the US. Each of these branches has microfiche and computer copies of the International Genealogical Index, the Surname Index, the Index to the Family Group Records Collection, the Ancestral File, the Social Security Death Index, and the Locality Index. In addition each FHC has a supply of forms for borrowing microfilm copies of the records from the main library. This means that the astonishingly large holdings of the FHL are available through each of its numerous FHC branches.

The FHC in or near IN are as follows:
___Bloomington FHC, 2411 East Second Street.
___Cincinnati FHC, 5505 Bosworth Place, Cincinnati, OH.
___Evansville FHC, 519 East Olmstead Avenue.
___Fort Wayne FHC, 5401 Saint Joe Road.
___Indianapolis FHC, 900 East Stop 11 Road.
___Louisville FHC, 1000 Hurstbourne Lane, Louisville, KY.
___New Albany FHC, 1534 State Run Road.
___Noblesville FHC, 777 Sunblest Boulevard.
___South Bend FHC, 3050 Edison Road.
___Terre Haute FHC, 1845 North Center.

___West Lafayette FHC, 3224 Jasper Street.

Other FHC are to be found in the cities listed below. They may be located by looking in the local telephone directory under the listing CHURCH OF JESUS CHRIST OF LATTER-DAY SAINTS-GENE-ALOGY LIBRARY or in the Yellow Pages under CHURCHES-LATTER-DAY SAINTS.

___In AL: Bessemer, Birmingham, Dothan, Huntsville, Mobile, Montgomery, Tuscaloosa, in AK: Anchorage, Fairbanks, Juneau, Ketchikan, Kotzebue, Sitka, Sodotna, Wasilla, in AZ: Benson, Buckeye, Camp Verde, Casa Grande, Cottonwood, Eagar, Flagstaff, Glendale, Globe, Holbrook, Kingman, Mesa, Nogales, Page, Payson, Peoria, Phoenix, Prescott, Safford, Scottsdale, Show Low, Sierra Vista, Snowflake, St. David, St. Johns, Tucson, Winslow, Yuma, in AR: Fort Smith, Jacksonville, Little Rock, Rogers,

___In CA (Bay Area): Antioch, Concord, Fairfield, Los Altos, Menlo Park, Napa, Oakland, San Bruno, San Jose, Santa Clara, Santa Cruz, Santa Rosa, In CA (Central): Auburn, Clovis, Davis (Woodland), El Dorado (Placerville), Fresno, Hanford, Merced, Modesto, Monterey (Seaside), Placerville, Sacramento, Seaside, Stockton, Turlock, Visalia, Woodland, In CA (Los Angeles County): Burbank, Canoga Park, Carson, Cerritos, Chatsworth (North Ridge), Covina, Glendale, Granada Hills, Hacienda Heights, Huntington Park, La Crescenta, Lancaster, Long Beach (Los Alamitos), Los Angeles, Monterey Park, Northridge, Norwalk, Palmdale, Palos Verdes (Rancho Palos Verdes), Pasadena, Torrance (Carson), Valencia, Van Nuys, Whittier, In CA (Northern): Anderson, Chico, Eureka, Grass Valley, Gridley, Mt. Shasta, Quincy, Redding, Susanville, Ukiah, Yuba City, In CA (Southern, except Los Angeles): Alpine, Anaheim, Bakersfield, Barstow, Blythe, Buena Park, Camarillo, Carlsbad, Corona, Cypress (Buena Park), El Cajon (Alpine), Escondido, Fontana, Garden Grove (Westminster), Hemet, Huntington Beach, Jurupa (Riverside), Los Alamitos, Mission Viejo, Moorpark, Moreno Valley, Needles, Newbury Park, Orange, Palm Desert, Palm Springs (Palm Desert), Poway (San Diego), Redlands, Ridgecrest, Riverside, San Bernardino, San Diego, San Luis Obispo, Santa Barbara, Santa Maria, Simi Valley, Thousand Oaks (Moorpark), Upland, Ventura, Victorville, Vista, Westminster,

___In CO: Alamosa, Arvada, Aurora, Boulder, Colorado Springs, Columbine, Cortez, Craig, Denver, Durango, Fort Collins, Frisco, Grand Junction, Greeley, La Jara, Littleton, Louisville, Manassa,

Meeker, Montrose, Longmont, Northglenn, Paonia, Pueblo, in CT: Bloomfield, Hartford, Madison, New Canaan, New Haven, Waterford, Woodbridge, in DC: Kensington, MD, in DE: Newark, Wilmington, in FL: Boca Raton, Cocoa, Ft. Lauderdale, Ft. Myers, Gainesville, Hialeah, Homestead, Jacksonville, Lake City, Lake Mary, Lakeland, Miami, Orange Park, Orlando, Palm City, Panama City, Pensacola, Plantation, Rockledge, St. Petersburg, Tallahassee, Tampa, West Palm Beach, Winterhaven, in GA: Atlanta, Augusta, Brunswick, Columbus, Douglas, Gainesville, Jonesboro, Macon, Marietta, Powder Springs, Roswell, Savannah, Tucker, in HI: Hilo, Honolulu, Kaneohe, Kauai, Kona, Laie, Lihue, Miliani, Waipahu,

___In ID: Basalt, Blackfoot, Boise, Burley, Caldwell, Carey, Coeur D'Alene, Driggs, Emmett, Firth, Hailey, Idaho Falls, Iona, Lewiston, McCammon, Malad, Meridian, Montpelier, Moore, Mountain Home, Nampa, Pocatello, Paris, Preston, Rexburg, Rigby, Salmon, Sandpoint, Shelley, Soda Springs, Twin Falls, Weiser, in IL: Champaign, Chicago Heights, Fairview Heights, Nauvoo, Peoria, Rockford, Schaumburg, Wilmette, in IN: Bloomington, Evansville, Fort Wayne, Indianapolis, New Albany, Noblesville, South Bend, Terre Haute, West Lafayette, in IA: Ames, Cedar Rapids, Davenport, Sioux City, West Des Moines, in KS: Dodge City, Olathe, Salina, Topeka, Wichita, in KY: Hopkinsville, Lexington, Louisville, Martin, Paducah, in LA: Alexandria, Baton Rouge, Denham Springs, Monroe, Metairie, New Orleans, Shreveport, Slidell,

___In ME: Augusta, Bangor, Cape Elizabeth, Caribou, Farmingdale, Portland, in MD: Annapolis, Baltimore, Ellicott City, Frederick, Kensington, Lutherville, in MA: Boston, Foxboro, Tyngsboro, Weston, Worcester, in MI: Ann Arbor, Bloomfield Hills, East Lansing, Escanaba, Grand Blanc, Grand Rapids, Hastings, Kalamazoo, Lansing, Ludington, Marquette, Midland, Muskegon, Traverse City, Westland, in MN: Anoka, Duluth, Minneapolis, Rochester, St. Paul, in MS: Clinton, Columbus, Gulfport, Hattiesburg, in MO: Cape Girardeau, Columbia, Farmington, Frontenac, Hazelwood, Independence, Joplin, Kansas City, Liberty, Springfield, St. Joseph, St. Louis, in MT: Billings, Bozeman, Butte, Glasgow, Glendive, Great Falls, Havre, Helena, Kalispell, Missoula, Stevensville, in NE: Grand Island, Lincoln, Omaha, Papillion,

___In NV: Elko, Ely, Henderson, LaHonton Valley, Las Vegas, Logandale, Mesquite, Reno, Tonapah, Winnemucca, in NH: Concord,

Exeter, Nashua, Portsmouth, in <u>NJ</u>: Caldwell, Dherry Hill, East Brunswick, Morristown, North Caldwell, in <u>NM</u>: Albuquerque, Carlsbad, Farmington, Gallup, Grants, Las Cruces, Santa Fe, Silver City, in <u>NY</u>: Albany, Buffalo, Ithaca, Jamestown, Lake Placid, Liverpool, Loudonville, New York City, Pittsford, Plainview, Queens, Rochester, Scarsdale, Syracuse, Vestal, Williamsville, Yorktown, in <u>NC</u>: Asheville, Charlotte, Durham, Fayetteville, Goldsboro, Greensboro, Hickory, Kinston, Raleigh, Skyland, Wilmington, Winston-Salem, in <u>ND</u>: Bismarck, Fargo, Minot, in <u>OH</u>: Akron, Cincinnati, Cleveland, Columbus, Dayton, Dublin, Fairborn, Kirtland, Perrysburg, Reynoldsburg, Tallmadge, Toledo, Westlake, Winterville,

In <u>OK</u>: Lawton, Muskogee, Norman, Oklahoma City, Stillwater, Tulsa, in <u>OR</u>: Beaverton, Bend, Brookings, Central Point, Coos Bay, Corvallis, Eugene, Grants Pass, Gresham, Hermiston, Hillsboro, Keizer, Klamath Falls, LaGrande, Lake Oswego, Lebanon, Minnville, Medford, Newport, Nyssa, Ontario, Oregon City, Portland, Prineville, Roseburg, Salem, Sandy, The Dallas, in <u>PA</u>: Altoona, Broomall, Clarks Summit, Erie, Kane, Philadelphia(Broomall), Pittsburgh, Reading, Scranton(Clarks Summit), State College(Altoona), York, in <u>RI</u>: Providence, Warwick, in <u>SC</u>: Charleston, Columbia, Florence, Greenville, North Augusts, in <u>SD</u>: Gettysburg, Rapid City, Rosebud, Sioux Falls, in <u>TN</u>: Chattanooga, Franklin, Kingsport, Knoxville, Madison, Memphis, Nashville, in <u>TX</u>: Abilene, Amarillo, Austin, Bay City, Beaumont, Bryan, Conroe, Corpus Christi, Dallas, Denton, Duncanville, El Paso, Ft. Worth, Friendswood, Harlingen, Houston, Hurst, Katy, Kileen, Kingwood, Longview, Lubbock, McAllen, Odessa, Orange, Pasadena, Plano, Port Arthur, Richland Hills, San Antonio, Sugarland,

In <u>UT</u>: American Fork, Altamont, Beaver, Blanding, Bloomington, Bluffdale, Bountiful, Brigham City, Canyon Rim, Castle Dale, Cedar City, Delta, Duchesne, Escalante, Farmington, Ferron, Fillmore, Granger, Heber, Helper, Highland, Holladay, Hunter, Huntington, Hurricane, Hyrum, Kanab, Kaysville, Kearns, Laketown, Layton, Lehi, Loa, Logan, Magna, Manti, Mapleton, Midway, Moab, Monticello, Moroni, Mt. Pleasant, Murray, Nephi, Ogden, Orem, Panguitch, Parowan, Pleasant Grove, Price, Provo, Richfield, Riverton, Roosevelt, Rose Park, Salt Lake City, Sandy, Santaquin, South Jordan, Springville, St. George, Syracuse, Tooele, Trementon, Tropic, Vernal, Wellington, Wendover, West Jordan, West Valley City, in <u>VA</u>: Annandale, Bassett, Charlottesville, Chesapeake, Dale City, Falls Church, Fredericksburg, Hamilton, Martinsville, McLean, Newport News, Norfolk, Oakton, Pembroke, Richmond, Roanoke, Salem, Virginia Beach, Waynesboro, Winchester, in VT: Berlin, Montpelier,

___ In WA: Auburn, Bellevue, Bellingham, Bremerton, Centralia, Colville, Edmonds, Ellensburg, Elma, Ephrata, Everett, Federal Way, Ferndale, Lake Stevens, Longview, Lynnwood, Marysville, Moses Lake, Mt. Vernon, North Bend, Olympia, Othello, Port Angeles, Pullman, Puyallup, Quincy, Renton, Richland, Seattle, Silverdale, Spokane, Sumner, Tacoma, Vancouver, Walla Walla, Wenatchee, Yakima, in WV: Charleston, Fairmont, Huntington, in WI: Appleton, Eau Clair, Hales Corner, Madison, Milwaukee, Shawano, Wausau, in WY: Afton, Casper, Cheyenne, Cody, Gillette, Green River, Jackson Hole, Kemmerer, Laramie, Lovell, Lyman, Rawlins, Riverton, Rock Springs, Sheridan, Urie, Worland.

The FHL is constantly adding new branches so this list will probably be out-of-date by the time you read it. An SASE and a $2 fee to the FHL (address in first paragraph above) will bring you an up-to-date listing of FHC.

When you go to FHL or FHC, first ask for the IN International Genealogical Index and examine it for the name of your ancestor, then if you are at FHL, request the record. If you are at FHC, ask them to borrow the microfilm containing the record from FHL. The cost is only a few dollars, and when your microfilm arrives (usually 4 to 6 weeks), you will be notified so that you can return and examine it. Second, ask for the Surname Catalog. Examine it for the surname of your ancestor. If you think any of the references relate to your ancestral line, and if you are at FHL, request the record. If you are at FHC, ask them to borrow the record for you. Third, ask for the Listings of Indexes to the Family Group Records Collection which will be found in the Author/Title Section of the FHL Catalog. There are several listings, so be sure you see them all. Locate the microfilm number which applies to the index of the surname you are seeking. If you are at FHL, request the microfilm. If you are at FHC, ask them to borrow the microfilm for you. When it comes, examine the microfilm to see if any records of your surname are indicated. If so, obtain them and see if they are pertinent.

Fourth, ask for the Ancestral File and look up the name you are seeking. If it is there, you will be led to sources of information, either people who are working on the line, or records pertaining to the line. Be careful with the material in this file, because in some of the cases, there appears to be no documentation. Fifth, if you are seeking a person who died after 1937, request the Social Security Death Index and look her/him up in it. Sixth, ask for the IN Locality Catalog. Examine all listings under the main heading of INDIANA. Then examine all listings under the subheading of the county you are interested in. These county listings will follow the listings for the state of IN. Toward the end of the county listings, there are listed materials relating to cities and towns in the county. Be sure not to overlook them. If you are at FHL, you can request the materials which are of interest to you. If you are at FHC, you may have the librarian borrow them for you. A large number of the records referred to in Chapter 2 and those listed under the counties in Chapter 4 will be found in the IN locality catalog.

The FHL and each FHC also have a set of Combined Census Indexes. These indexes are overall collections of censuses and other records for various time periods. Set 1 covers all colonies and states 1607-1819, Set 2 covers all states 1820-9, Set 3 covers all states 1830-9, Set 4 covers all states 1840-9, Set 5 covers the southern states 1850-9, Set 6 covers the northern states 1850-9, Set 7 covers the midwestern and western states 1850-9, Set 7A covers all the states 1850-9, and further sets cover various groups of states 1860 and after. Additional details concerning the records in FHL and FHC along with instructions for finding and using them will be found in:

___J. Cerny and W. Elliott, THE LIBRARY, A GUIDE TO THE LDS FAMILY HISTORY LIBRARY, Ancestry Publishing, Salt Lake City, UT, 1988.

___J. C. Parker, GOING TO SALT LAKE CITY TO DO FAMILY HISTORY RESEARCH, Marietta Publishing Co., Turlock, CA, latest edition.

8. The National Archives (NA)

The National Archives and Records Service (NA), located at Pennsylvania Avenue and 8th Street, Washington, DC 20408, is the central national repository for federal records, many being of importance to IN genealogical research. The NA does not concern itself with colonial records (pre-1776), state, county, city, or town records. Among the most important NA records which pertain to IN are the following:

___Census records: Federal census records for IN Territory and IN 1807, 1810 (for only 2 townships in Harrison County), 1820 (Daviess County missing), 1830-80, 1900-20, see Section 6, Chapter 2

___Non-population census schedules: farm, manufacture, and mortality records for IN, 1850-80, see Section 6, Chapter 2

___Military records: Service, bounty land, pension, claims records, and indexes for the Revolution, War of 1812, Mexican War, Civil War, Spanish-American War, see Sections 23-25, Chapter 2

___Land records: Land warrant applications, land warrant redemptions, land sales, surveys, land grants for IN, 1789-, records are in ISL, ISA, NA, Bureau of Land Management in Springfield, VA, and the Chicago Branch of the NA, see Section 20, Chapter 2

___Naturalization records: For US District and Circuit Courts in IN, records are in the Chicago Branch of the NA

___Federal District and Circuit Court records: For Northwest Territory and IN Territory (1787-1816) at NA, and for IN Territory and IN (1803-1962) in the Chicago Branch of the NA, see Section 10, Chapter 2

Details on all of these have been given in the pertinent sections of Chapter 2. Further detail on them may be obtained in:

___NA Staff, GENEALOGICAL RESEARCH IN THE NATIONAL ARCHIVES, NA, Washington, DC, 1982.

The numerous records of the NA may be examined in Washington in person or by a hired researcher. Microfilm copies of many of the major records and/or their indexes may also be seen in Regional Branches of the National Archives (NARB) which are located in or near Atlanta (1557 St. Joseph Ave., East Point, GA 30344), Boston (380 Trapelo Rd., Waltham, MA 02154), Chicago (7358 S. Pulaski Rd., Chicago, IL 60629), Denver (Bldg. 48, Federal Center, Denver, CO 80225), Fort Worth (501 West Felix St., Ft. Worth, TX 76115), Kansas City (2312 E. Bannister Rd., Kansas City, MO 64131), Los Angeles (24000 Avila Rd., Laguna Niguel, CA 92677), New York (201 Varick St., New York, NY 10014), Philadelphia (9th and Market Sts., Philadelphia, PA 19107), San Francisco (1000 Commodore Dr., San Bruno, CA 94066), and Seattle (6125 Sand Point Way, NE, Seattle, WA 98115). Take special note of the Chicago Branch in Chicago, IL. It holds many IN census records, Revolutionary War service, pension, and bounty land records, US Courts of IN, naturalizations in US Circuit and District Courts, Internal Revenue tax records 1862-66, IN Union service records 1861-65, and the IN non-population census schedules.

Many of the NA records pertaining to IN, as was noted in detail in Chapters 2 and 3, are also available at ISL, PLC, ACPL, and the FHL (FHC), and some are available at LGL and RL. In addition, practically any local library in the US can borrow NA microfilms for you from AGLL (American Genealogical Lending Library, PO Box 329, Bountiful, UT 84011). Or you may borrow from them directly. Included are NA census records and military records (Revolutionary War, War of 1812, Mexican War, Civil War).

---

9. Regional libraries (RL)

Regional libraries (RL) in IN are defined as those libraries which have sizable genealogical collections for the region, rather than just for the immediate locality. Included among them are:

___Anderson Public Library, 111 East 12th Street, Anderson, IN, 46016, Phone 1-(317)-641-2442.

___Bartholomew County Public Library, 5th and Lafayette Streets, Columbus, IN 47201, Phone 1-(812)-379-1266.

___Crawfordsville District Public Library, 222 S. Washington, Crawfordsville, IN 47933, Phone 1-(317)-362-9493.

___Evansville-Vanderburgh County Public Library, 22 SE Fifth St., Evansville, IN 47708, Phone 1-(812)-428-8218.

___Gary Public Library, 220 W. 5th Avenue, Gary, IN 46402, Phone 1-(218)-886-2484.

___New Albany-Floyd County Public Library, 180 W. Spring St., New Albany, IN 47150, Phone 1-(812)-949-3527.

___Morrison-Reeves Library, 80 N. 6th Street, Richmond, IN 47374, Phone 1-(317)-966-8291.

___South Bend Public Library, 122 W. Wayne Street, South Bend, IN 46530, Phone 1-(219)-282-4625.

___Vigo County Public Library, One Library Square, Terre Haute, IN 47807, Phone 1-(812)-232-1113.

___Valparaiso Public Library, 107 Jefferson Street, Valparaiso, IN 46383, Phone 1-(219)-462-0524.

___Wabash Carnegie Public Library, 188 W. Hill St., Wabash, IN 46992, Phone 1-(219)-563-2572.

When a visit is made to any of these libraries, your first endeavor is to search the card and/or computer catalog. You can remember what to look for with the acronymn SLANT. A detailed treatment of its use was given back in Section 1 of this chapter. This procedure should give you very good coverage of the library holdings which are indexed in the catalog. The second endeavor at any of these libraries is to ask about any special indexes, catalogs, collections, finding aids, or materials which might be pertinent to your search. You should make it your aim particularly to inquire about Bible, cemetery, church, map, manuscript, military, mortuary, and newspaper materials. In some cases, microform (microfilm, microfiche, microcard) records are not included in the regular catalog but are separately indexed. It is important that you be alert to this possibility.

10. Local repositories

Local libraries, court houses, and other repositories (LL, CH, LR) are located in every county seat, and sometimes libraries and other repositories will be found in other towns in the county. The most significant libraries are listed under the counties in Chapter 4. At the libraries, it is important for you to inquire about other record repositories in the county: cemeteries, churches, mortuaries, newspaper offices, organization offices, schools, society offices. Please look back at the last third of Section 1 for information about Court Houses, and remember that they should be visited only after going to the library.

11. Large genealogical libraries (LGL)

Spread around the US there are a number of large genealogical libraries (LGL) which have at least some IN genealogical source materials. In general, those libraries nearest IN are the ones that have the larger IN collections, but there are exceptions. Among these libraries are the following:

___In AL: Birmingham Public Library, Library at Samford University in Birmingham, AL Archives and History Department in Montgomery, in AZ: Southern AZ Genealogical Society in Tucson, in AR: AR Genealogical Society in Little Rock, AR History Commission in Little Rock, Little Rock Public Library, in CA: CA Genealogical Society in San Francisco, Los Angeles Public Library, San Diego Public Library, San Francisco Public Library, Sutro Library in San Francisco,

___In CO: Denver Public Library, in CT: CT State Library in Hartford, Godfrey Memorial Library in Middletown, in DC: Library of Congress, DAR Library, National Genealogical Society Library in Washington, in FL: FL State Library in Tallahassee, Miami-Dade Public Library, Orlando Public Library, Tampa Public Library, in

GA: Atlanta Public Library, in ID: ID Genealogical Society, in IL: Newberry Library in Chicago, in IA: IA State Department of History and Archives in Des Moines, in KY: KY Historical Society in Frankfurt, Filson Club in Louisville,

___In LA: LA State Library in Baton Rouge, in ME: ME State Library in Augusta, in MD: MD State Library in Annapolis, MD Historical Society in Baltimore, in MA: Boston Public Library, New England Historic Genealogical Society Library in Boston, in MI: Detroit Public Library, in MN: MN Public Library, in MS: MS Department of Archives and History in Jackson, in MO: Kansas City Public Library, Mid-Continent Public Library in Independence, St. Louis Public Library, In NE: NE State Historical Society in Lincoln, Omaha Public Library, in NV: Washoe County Library in Reno, in NY: NY Public Library, NY Genealogical and Biographical Society in NY City, in NC: NC State Library in Raleigh, in OH: OH Historical Society and State Library of OH both in Columbus, Western Reserve Historical Society in Cleveland, Public Library in Cincinnati, in OK: OK State Historical Society in Oklahoma City, in OR: Genealogical Forum of Portland, Portland Library Association, in PA: Historical Society of PA in Philadelphia, PA State Library in Harrisburg,

___In SC: The South Caroliniana Library in Columbia, in SD: State Historical Society in Pierre, in TN: TN State Library and Archives in Nashville, in TX: Dallas Public Library, Fort Worth Public Library, TX State Library in Austin, Houston Public Library, Clayton Library in Houston, in UT: Brigham Young University Library in Provo, in VA: VA Historical Society Library and VA State Library in Richmond, in WA: Seattle Public Library, in WV: WV Department of Archives and History in Charleston, in WI: Milwaukee Public Library, State Historical Society in Madison.

When you visit a LGL, the general procedure described earlier in this chapter should be followed: First, search the card and computer catalogs. Look under the headings summarized by SLANT: subject, location, author, name, title. Then, second, inquire about special indexes, catalogs, collections, materials, and microforms.

The above list of LGL is not inclusive. There may be other medium-sized and large libraries near you. Just because they do not appear in the above list, do not fail to check out their IN genealogical holdings.

Chapter 4

RESEARCH PROCEDURE AND COUNTY LISTINGS

■■■■■■■■■■ Now you should have a good idea of IN history, its
1. Introduction genealogical records, and the locations and avail-
■■■■■■■■■■ abilities of these records. The emphasis in the first
three chapters was on records at levels higher than
the county. Detailed information on national,
state-wide, and regional records was given, but county records were
normally treated only in general. We now will turn our focus upon the
county records, treating them in detail. We will also emphasize non-
governmental records available at the county level (such as Bible,
biography, cemetery, directories, DAR, ethnic, genealogies, histories,
manuscripts, maps, mortuary, newspaper, and periodicals). The reason
for all this attention to county records is that these records are more
likely to contain more information on your ancestors than any other type.
Such records were generally recorded by people who knew your forebears,
and they often relate to the personal details of her/his life.

In the state of IN, many of the <u>original</u> governmental records of
the counties and cities remain within the counties. Many of these original
county/city governmental records and some non-governmental records
have been <u>microfilmed</u> by the FHL, and the microfilms are available at
FHL, and by interlibrary loan through the many FHC branches throughout the US. Microfilms of many of these original records are also
available at the ISL. Some of the original county/city governmental
records and numerous non-governmental records have been <u>published</u>
either in printed volumes or as typescripts. Most of these publications are
available at ISL, ACPL, and PLC. Some are available at IHS, LGL, RL,
and LL.

This chapter, Chapter 4, will deal with county and city records in
detail. We will <u>first</u> discuss procedures for finding the county in which
your IN progenitor(s) lived. This is important because knowing that your
ancestors were simply from IN is not enough to permit genealogical
research. You need to know the county or city since many genealogically-
applicable records were kept on a local basis, and since you will often find
more than one person in IN bearing the name of your ancestor. In such
a case, the county/city location will often let you tell them apart. After
discussing ways to find the county, we will <u>second</u> suggest approaches for

doing IN genealogy, recommending the order in which the various repositories should be used.

2. Finding the county

As you will recall from Chapter 1, official IN record keeping began with the territorial period (1787), even though there had been a few records pertaining to the area which were kept by the states which initially claimed the territory, especially VA. Counties were established in the Northwest Territory beginning in 1788, and they kept records from the start. Knox County was set up in 1790 with the county seat at Vincennes. The year 1800 saw the IN Territory split from the Northwest Territory, and in 1801 Clark County came into being. As the population increased, more counties were established, and more and more of the keeping of records was shifted to them. It is, therefore, of considerable importance for you to know your IN predecessor's county in order to direct yourself efficiently to many of the pertinent records. It is also important because the local county officials probably knew your ancestor personally, and further, kept more detailed records on him, his family, his property, and his activities than did the territory or state. If you happen to know your ancestor's county, you may skip the remainder of this section. If not, your first priority must be a successful search for the county. The most efficient method for discovering the county depends on the time period during which your forebear lived in IN. We will discuss county-finding techniques for three periods of time in IN history: (a) 1789-1820, (b) 1820-1908, and (c) 1908-present.

If your forebear's time period was 1789-1820, you should look in the following major sources for your progenitor's name. Items more generally available (indexes in FHC, published and microfilm indexes in LGL) will be listed before those available chiefly in IN repositories (ISL-ISA-IHS, ACPL, PLC) or available by ordering from FHL through FHC.

___(1a) INTERNATIONAL GENEALOGICAL INDEX (IGI), IN SECTION; FAMILY SEARCH; ANCESTRAL FILE; FAMILY GROUP RECORDS COLLECTION; all available at FHL and at FHC.

___(2a) F. Rider, AMERICAN GENEALOGICAL[-BIOGRAPHICAL] INDEX, Godfrey Memorial Library, Middletown, CT, 1942-, 2 series, 1st containing 48 volumes, 2nd containing over 190 volumes.

___(3a) M. Kaminkow, GENEALOGIES IN THE LIBRARY OF CONGRESS, Magna Carta, Baltimore, MD, 1972-7, 3 volumes,

plus SUPPLEMENTS; also A COMPLEMENT TO GENEALO-
GIES IN THE LIBRARY OF CONGRESS [GENEALOGIES
IN OTHER LIBRARIES], Magna Carta, Baltimore, MD, 1981.

___(4a) Published early IN land records by Ainsworth, Bureau of Land
Management (CDROM), Clark, Cowen, Dyer, McMullin, Lux,
Smith, US House of Representatives, and Waters. See Section 20,
Chapter 2, for full references.

___(5a) W. Heiss and others, IN SOURCE BOOK, GENEALOGICAL
MATERIAL FROM THE HOOSIER GENEALOGIST, IHS,
Indianapolis, IN, 1961/90, 7 volumes. First 3 volumes indexed in
INDEX, IN SOURCE BOOKS, IHS, Indianapolis, IN, 1983.

___(6a) IN pioneer and territorial lists by Dorrel, Franklin, Fraustein,
Jackson, Lindsay, McKay, Means, Riker, and Wolfe. See Sections
6 and 17, Chapter 2, for full references.

___(7a) C. M. Franklin, INDEX TO IN WILLS THROUGH 1880,
Heritage House, Indianapolis, IN, 1987, 9 volumes.

___(8a) Early marriage indexes by Automated Archives (CDROM), ISL,
Murray, Researchers of Indianapolis, and Ridlen. See Section 22,
Chapter 2, or full references.

___(9a) Revolutionary War and War of 1812 veterans' records by Egan,
Franklin, Funk, Hatcher, O'Byrne, Sons of the American
Revolution, Sutton, and Waters. See Sections 22-23, Chapter 2,
for full references.

___(10a) The Newberry Library, THE GENEALOGICAL INDEX OF
THE NEWBERRY LIBRARY, G. K. Hall, Boston, MA, 1960, 4
volumes.

___(11a) J. B. Parker and L. de Platt, MICROFICHE INDIANA BIO-
GRAPHICAL INDEX, Genealogical Indexing Associates, West
Bountiful, UT, 1983, 16 microfiche. Available at ISL and
FHL(FHC).

Notice that item (1a) is accessible at your nearest FHC, and items (2a-
11a) are mostly publications available in many LGL. If these indexes fail
to locate your predecessor's county, two further steps should be taken: (a)
explore other indexes in ISL-ISA-IHS [see pertinent sections of Chapter
3], and (b) if your ancestor was early, since there were only 13 counties
constituted before 1815 and the population was not large, a search of
major indexes of these counties is not a forbidding route to take.

For the time period 1820-1908, the census record indexes should
constitute your first search, then other materials can be invoked, if
needed. These follow:

___(1b) CENSUS INDEXES, 1820-1910, as detailed in Section 6, Chapter 2.

___(2b) ITEMS 1a, 2a, 3a, 4a, 5a, 7a, 10a, 11a from the list above.

___(3b) Automated Archives, MARRIAGE RECORDS, INCLUDING IN THROUGH LATE 1800s, CDROM-002 and CDROM-228, AGLL, Bountiful, UT, 1993 and 1995.

___(4b) J. E. Darlington, IN TAX LISTS, 1835-48, The Author, Indianapolis, IN, 1990, 2 volumes.

___(5b) W. H. H. Terrell, REPORT OF THE ADJUTANT GENERAL OF THE STATE OF IN, The Office of the Adjutant General, Indianapolis, IN, 1865-69, 8 volumes. Index at ISA. Also on microfilm at FHL.

For the time period from 1907- forward, family members usually know the county. However, if they do not, the state-wide birth and death records provide the best source. Should you not find your ancestor in them, then some of the other sources listed below can be employed.

___(1c) INDEXES TO BIRTH RECORDS (1907-) AND DEATH RECORDS (1899-), Division of Vital Records, State Board of Health, PO Box 1964, Indianapolis, IN, 42606. See Sections 4 and 12, Chapter 2.

___(2c) CENSUS INDEX, 1920, as detailed in Section 6, Chapter 2.

___(3c) ITEMS 1a, 3a, and 5a from the list above.

___(4c) Social Security Administration, SOCIAL SECURITY DEATH INDEX, 1937-88, on four computer compact discs, at FHL and FHC.

The work of locating your IN ancestor can generally be done from where you live or nearby. This is because the key items are either indexes or indexed records which means that they can be scanned rapidly. Also, many are in published form (books or microfilms), which indicates that they are in numerous LGL outside of IN, as well as being available through FHC. Therefore, you should not have to travel too far to find many of the indexes you need. Some of the important indexes in IN repositories can be searched for you upon written request (enclose SASE). Or, if you prefer, all the above resources can be examined for you by a hired researcher in Indianapolis, IN (ISL-ISA-IHS, Division of Vital Records). This ought not to cost too much because the searches can all be made in very short time, and your hired researcher can stop when the county has been identified.

3. Research approaches

Having identified the county of your forebear's residence, you are in position to ferret out the details. This means that you need to identify what non-governmental, federal, state, and county records are available, then to locate them, and finally to examine them in detail. The most useful non-governmental records have been discussed in Chapter 2 (atlas, Bible, biography, cemetery, church, city directory, county/city history, court, DAR, ethnic, gazetteer, genealogical compilation, genealogical index, genealogical periodical, land, manuscript, map, mortuary, newspaper, regional publication). The federal governmental records which are most important for consideration have also been treated in Chapter 2 (census, court, military, naturalization). State governmental records which are of the greatest utility for genealogical research are examined in Chapter 2 (birth, court, death, divorce, land, marriage, military, tax). And the types of records which were generated by IN's counties are listed in Chapter 3 (Section 1), and they were discussed in general in Chapter 2. To remind you of the various types of county governmental records, the list from Chapter 3 is repeated here:

___Auditor: county commissioner minutes, personal tax, poll tax, property tax, township assessors' budget records

___County Clerk: adoptions, bonds, circuit court records, court of common pleas records, divorces, estray records, guardianships, licenses, marriages, naturalizations, probate records, superior court records, voter registrations, wills

___County Commissioners: commissioners' minutes, military veterans' burials, survey maps

___County Health Department: births, deaths

___County Public Welfare Department: old-age, dependent children, and welfare records

___Recorder: cemetery records, deeds, land grants, military discharges, mortgages, plat books, quit claims, titles, voter registrations

___Registration Officer: voter registrations

___Sheriff: arrest and jail records

___Surveyor: maps, plats

___Treasurer: personal, poll, and property tax records

County and city governmental record originals are found in the counties, usually at the CH or in a special repository. Many microfilm copies of county and city governmental records are located at FHL (available through FHC), and at ISL. Most published (printed and typescript) county and city governmental records are at ISL-IHS, ACPL, PLC, and FHL(FHC). Some will be found at LGL, RL, and LL. Both the major microfilmed records and the major types of published records (both governmental and non-governmental) for the 92 IN counties will be listed in detail in later sections of this chapter. These listings have been obtained from the catalogs at FHL, ISL, ACPL, and PLC, and then compared to similar listings in works by Carty, Gooldy, Miller, Newhard, and Robinson.

The general approach for doing an utterly thorough job of researching an IN ancestor is to follow this pattern:

___1st, check all family sources (oral, records, mementos, Bible), making a continuing effort to contact more and more of the many descendants of the ancestor

___2nd, locate your forebear's county (Section 2, this Chapter)

___3rd, use the nearest LGL (catalogs, indexes, publications, microfilms)

___4th, use the nearest FHC or the FHL (IGI, Ancestral File, Family Group Records Archives, FHL Catalog surname and locality indexes, integrated census indexes, social security index), if at FHC, order the pertinent microfilms

___5th, borrow any major federal records you have not seen from AGLL (census, military)

___6th, either go to Indianapolis, IN (ISL-IHS-ISA), or hire a researcher in Indianapolis to look at microfilms and publications you have not seen

___7th, either visit the county, or hire a researcher in the county to look in the LL (catalogs, indexes, manuscripts, local records), and to visit offices of cemeteries, churches, mortuaries, newspapers, and organizations to obtain records you have not seen

___8th, then you or your researcher should go to the CH, and the offices of the county and city record keepers, and/or the county and city record repositories, to examine records you have not seen

___9th, use the NARB and NA (for further federal census, court, military, and naturalization materials)

___10th, address inquiries to pertinent Church Archives, if church records have still not been found

The precise way in which you use this scheme will be determined chiefly by how far you are from Salt Lake City, UT (FHL) and Indianapolis, IN (ISL-IHL-ISA), and the relevant IN county. The major idea that you need to recognize is that eventually you will have to go to IN, or you will need to hire a researcher there, perhaps two, one for Indianapolis, and one for the county.

In using the above steps to set forth your own research plan, you ought to think about three items. The <u>first</u> is expense. You need to balance the cost of a hired researcher over against the cost of personal visits (to Indianapolis and to the county): travel, meals, lodging. You need also to compare the costs of borrowing microfilms from your nearest FHC (a few dollars per roll) to a trip to Salt Lake City, where the films can be read off-the-shelf at no charge. Of course, your desire to visit your ancestor's area, and your desire to look at the records yourself may be an important consideration.

The <u>second</u> item is a reminder about interlibrary loans. With the exception of the microfilms of FHL (available through FHC) and those of AGLL (available personally or through your local library), very few libraries and practically no archives will lend out genealogical materials. The <u>third</u> item is also a reminder. Correspondence with librarians, governmental officials, and archivists is ordinarily of very limited use. The reason is that these helpful and hard-working federal, state, local, and private employees do not have time to do any detailed work for you because of the demanding duties of their offices. In some cases, these people will have time to look up <u>one</u> specific item for you (a land grant, a catalog entry, a deed record, a will, a military record) <u>if</u> an overall index is available. Please do not ask them for detailed data, and please do not write them a long letter. If you do write, enclose a long SASE, a check for $5 with the payee line left blank, and a <u>brief</u> request (no more than one-third page) for <u>one</u> specific item in an index or catalog. Ask them to use the check if there is a charge for their services or for copying, and if they do not have time to look themselves, that they hand the check and your letter to a researcher who can do the work.

---

4. Format of county listings

In the following sections of this chapter, you will find listings of many of the major records of the IN counties. The records are mostly county based, many of them being governmental records, and many non-governmental or private records. In addition, libraries and genealogical societies in the counties will be shown because they are valuable sources of ancestral information.

Please take a look at the next section (Section 5) which will serve as an example of the format of the county listings. This section deals with Adams County. <u>First</u>, the name of the county is given, then the dates on which the county was formed and organized (if they differ), along with the parent county or counties. This is followed by the name of the county seat and the zip code of the CH. After this, you will find notes regarding losses of county records, if such has occurred.

Then you will find a listing of published, microfilmed, and CDROM records which are available outside the county. That is, these are records which can be accessed at ISL-IHS, and/or FHL(FHC), and/or ACPL. Please note that not every record will be found at all three places, but that most will. A notable number of them will also be found at PLC, and some of them most likely in RL and LL. With regard to the census listings, remember what the abbreviations refer to: T = territorial census, R = regular census records, I = index to regular census records, M = manufactures census records, F = farm census records, P = 1840 census of military pensioners, and D = mortality census records.

And finally, there will be listed the library or libraries in the county which will be essential for your genealogical quest. Following the library listing, the genealogical society or societies and pertinent historical societies in the area will be named. Since these societies sometimes undergo address changes when they elect new officers, you will be advised to contact the library for the most recent address. If any of these libraries or societies have sizeable historical and/or manuscript holdings, this will be noted by the word historical/manuscript in parentheses.

Now, a few remarks about the listings of county records need to be made. The listings are not complete, but are meant to give you a good general idea of the materials which are available. The emphasis in the listings has been in the pre-1900 period, since this is the time domain of major concern to most researchers. Further, when a set of inclusive dates is given, such as (1817-1903), it does not necessarily mean that every year is included; there may be a few gaps.

Do not forget that the listings of records under the names of the counties in this chapter represent only a fraction of what is available in the counties. A visit to the IN county (or a hired searcher) and a search of its records is an absolute must if you want to do a thorough investigation. Even though the microfilmed and published records are often those of greatest genealogical utility, the records which have not been put into microfilm or published form are very valuable, particularly the court records, and among them, especially the probate and case packets or files. These records are usually only in the county.

5. ADAMS COUNTY

Adams County, established/organized 1835/1836 from Allen and Randolph Counties. County seat Decatur (46733).

Printed/microfilmed/CDROM records (most in ISL-IHS, many in FHL/FHC, many in ACPL, some in PLC): Amish (1894-1936), biography (1881, 1887, 1918, 1930s-40s, 1979), birth (1882-1920), Catholic (1847-1988), cemetery, census (1840 RIP, 1850 RIMFD, 1860 RIMFD, 1870 RIMFD, 1880 RIMFD, 1900 RI, 1910 R, 1920 RI), DAR volumes, death (1882-1920), deed (1837-1902), German Reformed (1856-1931), history (1887, 1896, 1904, 1915, 1936, 1979, 1989), marriage (1836-1920), Mennonite (1838-1938), Methodist, periodical (1983-), probate (1838-1968), Reformed (1856-1931), tax (1839/42/43), tract (1824-54), will (1837-1968), WPA volumes.

Library: Decatur Public Library, 128 S. Third St., Decatur, IN 46733 (historical/manuscript). Society: Adams County Historical Society, PO Box 262, Decatur, IN 46733. Publishes ADAMS COUNTY TRUMPETER.

6. ALLEN COUNTY

Allen County established/organized 1824 from Randolph County and unorganized territory. County scat Fort Wayne (46802).

Printed/microfilmed/CDROM records (most in ISL-IHS, many in FHL/FHC, many in ACPL, some in PLC): atlas (1898, 1965), Baptist (1837-1931), biography (1800-1900, 1880, 1900, 1930s-40s), birth (1882-1920), Catholic (1819-1970), cemetery, census (1830 RI, 1840 RIP, 1850 RIMFD, 1860 RIMFD, 1870 RIMFD, 1880 RIMFD, 1900 RI, 1910 R, 1920 RI), circuit court (1824-35), city directory (1858-), commissioner (1824-50), DAR volumes, death (1886-1920), deed (1823-73), early land entries, Evangelical United Brethren, genealogical compilations, German Reformed, history (1868, 1872, 1880, 1889, 1900, 1905), inventory (1939), Jewish, Lutheran (1862-1970), marriage (1824-1920), Methodist (1840-80), mortuary (1874-1964), newspaper abstracts (1840-50, 1875-76), obituaries (1841-1900), periodical (1937-, 1976-), Presbyterian (1831-1959), probate (1824-95), Revolutionary veteran burials, veteran burials, will (1831-1900), WPA volumes.

Library: FHL in Ft. Wayne, Allen County Public Library, 900 Webster St., Ft. Wayne, IN 46802, Tel 1-(219)-424-7241. Society: Allen County-Fort Wayne Historical Society, 302 East Berry St., Ft. Wayne, IN 46802. Publishes BULLETIN and THE OLD FORT NEWS. Allen

County Genealogical Society of IN, PO Box 12003, Ft. Wayne, IN, 46862. Publishes ALLEN COUNTY LINES.

---

7. BARTHOLOMEW COUNTY

Bartholomew County established/organized 1821 from Jackson County and unorganized territory. County seat Columbus (47202).

Printed/microfilmed/CDROM records (most in ISL-IHS, many in FHL/FHC, many in ACPL, some in PLC): atlas (1879, 1969), Baptist (1828-1933), Bible, biography (1830-70, 1888, 1904, 1930s-40s), birth (1883-1920), Catholic (1845-1924), cemetery, census (1830 RI, 1840 RIP, 1850 RIMFD, 1860 RIMFD, 1870 RIMFD, 1880 RIMFD, 1900 RI, 1910 R, 1920 RI), Church of Christ, Church of Jesus Christ of Latter Day Saints, circuit court (1822-36), Civil War soldiers, civil court (1821-40), Civil War veterans, commissioner (1821-55), county directory (1874), court (1822-52), court of common pleas (1852-72), DAR volumes, death (1882-1920), deed (1822-1922), directory (1821), genealogical compilations, German Methodist (1883-1947), history (1874, 1879, 1885, 1888), Jewish, landowner, Lutheran (1834-1987), manuscript, marriage (1821-1951), Methodist (1856-1950), Moravian (1807-1942), mortuary (1891-1975), naturalization (1852-1916), negro (1852-55), newspaper abstracts (1872-84), obituaries (1872-93), partitions (1853-72), Presbyterian (1890-1911), probate (1821-1918), Quaker (1821-1960), Revolutionary veteran burials, road (1821-51), school (1887-1912), tract, veterans burials, veterans records, will (1822-1921), WPA volumes.

Library: Bartholomew County Public Library, 536 Fifth St., Columbus, IN 47201, Tel 1-(812)-379-1266. Society: Bartholomew County Historical Society, 524 Third St., Columbus, IN 47201. Publishes QUARTERLY CONNECTION. Bartholomew County Genealogical Society, PO Box 2455, Columbus, IN, 47202. Publishes BARTHOLOMEW COUNTY ANCESTORS.

---

8. BENTON COUNTY

Benton County established/organized 1840 from Jasper County. County seat Fowler (47944).

Printed/microfilmed/CDROM records (most in ISL-IHS, many in FHL/FHC, many in ACPL, some in PLC): biography (1883, 1899, 1987), birth (1882-1920), Catholic (1860-1988), cemetery, census (1840 RIP, 1850 RIMFD, 1860 RIMFD, 1870 RIMFD, 1880 RIMFD, 1900 RI, 1910 R, 1920 RI), death (1882-1920), deed (1835-1901), history (1883, 1925, 1930,

1942, 1984, 1987), marriage (1840-1955), partition (1860-89), Presbyterian (1870-1942), probate (1840-1920), tract (1840-75), will (1857-1924), WPA volumes.

Library: Benton County Public Library, 102 N. Van Buren Ave., Fowler, IN 47944. Society: Benton County Historical Society, 711 East Third St., Fowler, IN 47944.

---

9. BLACKFORD COUNTY

Blackford County established/organized 1838/1839 from Jay County. County seat Hartford City (47348). Printed/microfilmed/CDROM records (most in ISL-IHS, many in FHL/FHC, many in ACPL, some in PLC): biography (1887, 1914, 1930s-40s), Catholic (1842-1988), cemetery, census (1840 RIP, 1850 RIMFD, 1860 RIMFD, 1870 RIMFD, 1880 RIMFD, 1900 RI, 1910 R, 1920 RI), commissioner, court (1839-1911), death (1882-1930), deed (1836-1909), directory (1895), estray (1839-57), genealogical compilations, history (1887, 1914, 1961, 1986), inventory (1936), marriage (1839-1920), Methodist (1873-1928), mortuary, newspaper abstracts, obituaries, poor (1886-1959), Presbyterian (1843-1919), probate (1839-1921), survey (1845-66), tract (1831-53), veterans burials, will (1842-1918), WPA volumes.

Library: Hartford City Public Library, 314 N. High St., Hartford City, IN 47348. Beeson Library, 321 N. High St., Hartford City, IN 47348. Society: Blackford County Historical Society, 321 North High Street, Hartford City, IN 47348 (historical/manuscript). Montpelier Historical Society, 109 E. Huntington St., Montpelier, IN 47359 (historical/manuscript).

---

10. BOONE COUNTY

Boone County established/organized 1830 from Hendricks and Marion Counties. County seat Lebanon (46052). Some records destroyed in a fire in 1856. Printed/microfilmed/CDROM records (most in ISL-IHS, many in FHL/FHC, many in ACPL, some in PLC): atlas (1878), Baptist (1840-73), biography (1878, 1887, 1895, 1917, 1930s-40s), birth (1882-1920), Catholic (1870-1952), cemetery, census (1830 RI, 1840 RIP, 1850 RIMFD, 1860 RIMFD, 1870 RIMFD, 1880 RIMFD, 1900 RI, 1910 R, 1920 RI), DAR volumes, death (1882-1920), deed (1830-1929), history (1878, 1887, 1895, 1917, 1974), inventory (1937), Lutheran (1838-68), marriage (1831-1951), Methodist (1863-1937), mortuary (1893-1923), probate (1830-1925), tract (1822-54), veteran burials, will (1830-1925), WPA volumes.

Libraries: Lebanon Public Library, 104 E. Washington, IN 46052 (historical/manuscript). Thornton Public Library, 124 N. Market St., Thornton, IN 46071 (historical/manuscript). Society: Boone County Historical Society, PO Box 141, Lebanon, IN 46052. Publishes BOONE COUNTY HISTORICAL SOCIETY NEWSLETTER. Sullivan Museum, PO Box 182, Zionsville, IN 46077 (historical/manuscript).

11. BROWN COUNTY

Brown County established/organized 1836 from Bartholomew, Jackson, and Monroe Counties. County seat Nashville (47448). Fire in 1873 destroyed many records.

Printed/microfilmed/CDROM records (most in ISL-IHS, many in FHL/FHC, many in ACPL, some in PLC): biography (1884, 1991), cemetery, census (1840 RIP, 1850 RIMFD, 1860 RIMFD, 1870 RIMFD, 1880 RIMFD, 1900 RI, 1910 R, 1920 RI), circuit court (1836-1945), DAR volumes, death (1882-99), deed (1849-1901), genealogical compilations, history (1884, 1965, 1991), land, marriage (1836-1953), mortuary(1891-1975), naturalization (1853-89), periodical (1987-), Presbyterian (1859-1917), probate (1836-1957), will (1836-75).

Library: Brown County Public Library, 246 E. Main St., Nashville, IN 47448. Society: Brown County Historical Society, PO Box 668, Nashville, IN 47448 (historical/manuscript). Publishes BROWN COUNTY HISTORICAL SOCIETY NEWSLETTER. Brown County Genealogical Society, PO Box 1202, Nashville, IN, 47448. Publishes BROWN COUNTY GENEALOGICAL SOCIETY NEWSLETTER.

12. CARROLL COUNTY

Carroll County established/organized 1828 from Delaware and Wabash Counties and unorganized territory. County seat Delphi (46923).

Printed/microfilmed/CDROM records (most in ISL-IHS, many in FHL/FHC, many in ACPL, some in PLC): atlas (1874), Baptist (1829-43), biography (1872, 1882, 1915), birth (1882-1920), Catholic (1857-1937), cemetery, census (1830 RI, 1840 RIP, 1850 RIMFD, 1860 RIMFD, 1870 RIMFD, 1880 RIMFD, 1900 RI, 1910 R, 1920 RI), commissioner (1828-41), DAR volumes, death (1851-70, 1882-1920), deed (1829-1900), Episcopal, history (1872, 1882, 1915), marriage (1828-1920), Methodist (1857-1925), Presbyterian (1829-1971), probate (1829-99), Revolutionary veterans, tract (1824-51), voter (1850), will (1829-97), WPA volumes.

Library: Delphi Public Library, 222 E. Main St., Delphi, IN 46923 (historical/manuscript). Society: Carroll County Historical Society, PO Box 277, Delphi, IN 46923. Publishes NEWSLETTER.

13. CASS COUNTY

Cass County established/organized 1829 from Carroll County. County seat Logansport (46947). Flood in 1913 destroyed birth and death records.

Printed/microfilmed/CDROM records (most in ISL-IHS, many in FHL/FHC, many in ACPL, some in PLC): atlas (1878), Baptist (1836-70), biography (1886, 1898, 1913, 1930s-40s, 1987), birth (1882-1941), Catholic (1840-1985), cemetery, census (1830 RI, 1840 RIP, 1850 RIMFD, 1860 RIMFD, 1870 RIMFD, 1880 RIMFD, 1900 RI, 1910 R, 1920 RI), DAR volumes, death (1882-1974), deed (1830-97), directory (1892/3), genealogical compilations, history (1886, 1898, 1913, 1987), marriage (1829-1942), mortuary, newspaper abstracts (1829-78), obituaries, periodical (1985-), Presbyterian (1831-1920), probate (1829-1900), Revolutionary veterans, tax (1845), will (1831-1955), WPA volumes.

Library: Cass County Public Library, 616 E. Broadway, Logansport, IN 46947. Society: Cass County Historical Society, 1004 East Market St., Logansport, IN 46947. Cass County Genealogical Society, PO Box 373, Logansport, IN, 46947.

14. CLARK COUNTY

Clark County established/organized 1801 from Knox County. County seat Jeffersonville (47130). Some will records missing, cause not known.

Printed/microfilmed/CDROM records (most in ISL-IHS, many in FHL/FHC, many in ACPL, some in PLC): alien (1845-52), Baptist (1798-1873), biography (1880, 1889, 1909, 1930s-40s), birth (1882-1920), Catholic (1852-1985), cemetery, census (1820 RI, 1830 RI, 1840 RIP, 1850 RIMFD, 1860 RIMFD, 1870 RIMFD, 1880 RIMFD, 1900 RI, 1910 R, 1920 RI), Christian Church (1860-1960), circuit court (1801-31), Civil War veterans, commissioner (1815-52), court of common pleas (1801-31), court of quarter sessions (1801-13), DAR volumes, death (1882-1920), deed (1801-1901), estray (1801-18), Freemasons, genealogical compilations, history (1880, 1889, 1909), land (1785-1849), landowners (1872), marriage (1807-1921), Masons (1858-1958), Methodist (1801-1916), militia (1811), naturalization (1852-1928), negro (1805-10), partition (1853-69), pioneers (1885), Presbyterian (1817-1985), probate (1801-1919), Reformed (1860-1956), school (1883-84), veterans burials, voter (1802, 1809), will (1801-1918), WPA volumes.

Library: Jeffersonville Public Library, 211 Court Ave., Jeffersonville, IN 47131. Society: Clark County Historical Society, PO Box 606, Jeffersonville, IN 47130. Southern IN Genealogical Society, PO Box 665, New Albany, IN, 47151. Publishes SOUTHERN IN GENEALOGICAL SOCIETY QUARTERLY and SOUTHERN IN GENEALOGICAL SOCIETY NEWSLETTER.

15. CLAY COUNTY

Clay County established/organized 1825 from Owen, Putnam, Vigo, and Sullivan Counties. County seat Brazil (47834). Fire in 1851 destroyed most records.

Printed/microfilmed/CDROM records (most in ISL-IHS, many in FHL/FHC, many in ACPL, some in PLC): biography (1884, 1909, 1984, 1930s-40s), birth (1881-1920), Catholic (1867-1976), cemetery, census (1830 RI, 1840 RIP, 1850 RIMFD, 1860 RIMFD, 1870 RIMFD, 1880 RIMFD, 1900 RI, 1910 R, 1920 RI), DAR volumes, death (1882-1920), deed (1825-1902), genealogical compilations, GAR (1880-1908), German Reformed (1871-1960), history (1884, 1909), inventory (1939), marriage (1851-1921), Methodist (1835-1954), naturalization (1860-1906), periodical (1980-), Presbyterian (1866-1937), probate (1848-1919), Revolutionary veterans, tract (1810-55), United Brethren, will (1848-1919), WPA volumes.

Library: Brazil Public Library, 204 N. Walnut St., Brazil, IN 47834. Society: Clay County Historical Society, 100 East National Road, Brazil, IN 47834. Clay County Genealogical Society, PO Box 56, Center Point, IN, 47840. Publishes THE RESEARCHER.

16. CLINTON COUNTY

Clinton County established/organized 1830 from Tippecanoe County. County seat Frankfort (46041).

Printed/microfilmed/CDROM records (most in ISL-IHS, many in FHL/FHC, many in ACPL, some in PLC): atlas (1878, 1903, 1904), Baptist, biography (1886, 1895, 1913, 1930s-40s, 1989), birth (1882-1920), Catholic (1888-1988), cemetery, census (1830 RI, 1840 RIP, 1850 RIMFD, 1860 RIMFD, 1870 RIMFD, 1880 RIMFD, 1900 RI, 1910 R, 1920 RI), Christian Church (1868-90), Church of Christ (1852-1900), DAR volumes, death (1882-1920), deed (1829-1901), estray (1830-50), guardian (1865-84), history (1886, 1895, 1913, 1989), land patents, marriage (1830-1920), Methodist (1859-60), poor farm (1878-1915), probate (1831-1900), tract (1826-44), will (1830-1904), WPA volumes.

Library: Frankfort Public Library, 208 W. Clinton St., Frankfort, IN 46041 (historical/manuscript). Society: Clinton County Historical Society, 301 E. Clinton St., Frankfort, IN 46041. Publishes CLINTON COUNTY HISTORICAL SOCIETY AND MUSEUM NEWS. Clinton County Genealogical Society, 208 W. Clinton St., Frankfort, IN 46041.

17. CRAWFORD COUNTY

Crawford County established-/organized 1818 from Harrison, Orange, and Perry Counties. County seat English (47118).

Printed/microfilmed/CDROM records (most in ISL-IHS, many in FHL/FHC, many in ACPL, some in PLC): biography (1880, 1889), Catholic (1876-1929), cemetery, census (1820 RI, 1830 RI, 1840 RIP, 1850 RIMFD, 1860 RIMFD, 1870 RIMFD, 1880 RIMFD, 1900 RI, 1910 R, 1920 RI), Christian Church (1888-1955), deed (1818-86), genealogical compilations, guardian, history (1880, 1889, 1926), indenture (1832-70), marriage (1818-1955), naturalization (1822-96), partition (1853-75), Presbyterian (1870-1955), probate (1818-1946), tract (1804-53), will (1818-1946), WPA volumes.

Library: Crawford County Public Library, 111 W. Fifth St., English, IN 47118. Society: Crawford County Historical Society, PO Box 133, Leavenworth, IN 47137. Publishes CRAWFORD COUNTIAN. Crawford County Genealogical Society, PO Box 655, English, IN, 47118.

18. DAVIESS COUNTY

Daviess County established/organized 1817 from Knox County. County seat Washington (47501). Many records burned in fire of 1879.

Printed/microfilmed/CDROM records (most in ISL-IHS, many in FHL/FHC, many in ACPL, some in PLC): atlas (1888), Baptist (1854-86), biography (1886, 1897, 1930s-40s, 1988), birth (1882-1920), Catholic (1830-1985), cemetery, census (1830 RI, 1840 RIP, 1850 RIMFD, 1860 RIMFD, 1870 RIMFD, 1880 RIMFD, 1900 RI, 1910 R, 1920 RI), Christian Church, commissioner (1820-32), DAR volumes, death (1882-1920), deed (1817-1901), genealogical compilations, history (1886, 1988), marriage (1817-1953), Methodist (1831-76), naturalization (1856-1923), newspaper abstracts, partition (1854-71), Presbyterian (1814-1964), probate (1817-1918), tract, will (1853-1923), WPA volumes.

Library: Washington-Carnegie Public Library, 300 West Main St., Washington, IN 47501. Society: Daviess County Historical Society, PO Box 2341, Washington, IN 47501. Daviess County Genealogical Society, 703 Front St., Washington, IN, 47501. Publishes FORKS.

---

19. DEARBORN COUNTY

Dearborn County established/organized 1803 from Clark County. County seat Lawrenceburg (47025). Many records lost in fire of 1826.

Printed/microfilmed/CDROM records (most in ISL-IHS, many in FHL/FHC, many in ACPL, some in PLC): apprentice (1856-1921), atlas (1875, 1899), Baptist (1807-59), biography (1885, 1915), birth (1882-1907), Catholic (1840-1988), cemetery, census (1820 RI, 1830 RI, 1840 RIP, 1850 RIMFD, 1860 RIMFD, 1870 RIMFD, 1880 RIMFD, 1900 RI, 1910 R, 1920 RI), Church of Christ (1819-44), circuit court (1824-29), commissioner (1826-51), coroner (1887-1937), DAR volumes, death (1882-1906), deed (1821-1982), directory (1859/60, 1871/2), Evangelical (1840-1984), Evangelical and Reformed (1874-1972), genealogical compilations, guardian (1865-1972), history (1885, 1915), Lutheran (1847-1987), marriage (1826-1934), Methodist (1838-1940), naturalization (1838-90), newspaper abstracts, obituaries (1820-50), partition (1881-99), Presbyterian (1854-1939), probate (1826-1952), survey (1799-1805), Universalist (1868-1927), voter (1809, 1812), will (1824-1900).

Library: FHL in Cincinnati, Lawrenceburg Public Library, 123 W. High St., Lawrenceburg, IN 47025 (historical/manuscript). Society: Dearborn County Historical Society, Courthouse, Lawrenceburg, IN 47025.

---

20. DECATUR COUNTY

Decatur County established/organized 1822 from Delaware County and unorganized territory. County seat Greensburg (47240). Some records missing, cause not known.

Printed/microfilmed/CDROM records (most in ISL-IHS, many in FHL/FHC, many in ACPL, some in PLC): atlas (1882), Baptist (1828-1973), Bible, biography (1900, 1915, 1984) Catholic (1840-1984), cemetery, census (1830 RI, 1840 RIP, 1850 RIMFD, 1860 RIMFD, 1870 RIMFD, 1880 RIMFD, 1900 RI, 1910 R, 1920 RI), Christian Church (1849-1960), Church of Jesus Christ of Latter Day Saints, coroner (1873-1934), court (1822-48), DAR volumes, death (1882-99), deed (1822-1901), early landowners, genealogical compilations, history (1915, 1900, 1984),

Lutheran (1859-1945), marriage (1822-1950), Methodist (1857-1953), military, naturalization (1824-1923), newspaper abstracts, Presbyterian (1825-1972), probate (1826-1918), tract, veterans enrollment (1894), veterans burial, will (1822-1906).

Library: Greensburg Public Library, 114 N. Michigan St., Greensburg, IN 47240 (historical/manuscript). Society: Decatur County Historical Society, 222 N. Franklin St., Greensburg, IN 47240. Tri-County Genealogical Society, PO Box 118, Batesville, IN, 47006.

21. DEKALB COUNTY

DeKalb County established/organized 1835/1837 from Allen and Lagrange Counties. County seat Auburn (46706). Fire in 1913, probate records prior to 1850 lost.

Printed/microfilmed/CDROM records (most in ISL-IHS, many in FHL/FHC, many in ACPL, some in PLC): atlas (1880), Bible, biography (1859, 1885, 1914, 1992), birth (1882-1944), Catholic (1868-1958), cemetery, census (1840 RIP, 1850 RIMFD, 1860 RIMFD, 1870 RIMFD, 1880 RIMFD, 1900 RI, 1910 R, 1920 RI), civil court (1839-1933), DAR volumes, death (1882-1920), deed (1837-1901), genealogical compilations, guardian (1851-1954), history (1859, 1885, 1992, 1993), marriage (1837-1957), Methodist (1840-80), mortgage (1845-52), naturalization (1839-1921), pioneers, obituaries, probate (1850-1936), tract (1835-53), will (1852-1910), WPA volumes.

Library: Eckhart Public Library, 603 S. Jackson St., Auburn, IN 46706. Society: Garrett Historical Society, 201 E. Quincy St., Garrett, IN 46738.

22. DELAWARE COUNTY

Delaware County established/organized 1827 from Randolph County. County seat Muncie (47305).

Printed/microfilmed/CDROM records (most in ISL-IHS, many in FHL/FHC, many in ACPL, some in PLC): atlas (1887), biography (1894, 1908, 1930s-40s), birth (1882-1920), Catholic (1875-1945), cemetery, census (1830 RI, 1840 RIP, 1850 RIMFD, 1860 RIMFD, 1870 RIMFD, 1880 RIMFD, 1900 RI, 1910 R, 1920 RI), church records (1895-1933), Church of Jesus Christ of Latter Day Saints, city directory (1899), DAR volumes, death (1882-1920), deed (1829-1902), genealogical compilations, history (1894, 1908, 1924, 1975), inventory (1940), land, marriage (1827-1920), Methodist (1873-93), naturalization, Presbyterian, probate (1830-1931), Quaker (1876-1902),

Revolutionary veterans burials, survey (1874), tax (1843), tract, veterans burials, will (1827-1902), WPA volumes.

Library: Muncie Public Library, 301 E. Jackson St., Muncie, IN 47305. Society: Delaware County Historical Alliance, 120 E. Washington St., Muncie, IN 47308. Publishes DELAWARE COUNTY GENEALOGIST and DELAWARE COUNTY HERITAGE. Minnetrista Cultural Foundation, 1200 N. Minnetrista Parkway. Muncie, IN 47308 (historical/manuscript).

23. DUBOIS COUNTY

Dubois County established/organized 1818 from Pike County. County seat Jasper (47546). Many records lost in fire of 1839.

Printed/microfilmed/CDROM records (most in ISL-IHS, many in FHL/FHC, many in ACPL, some in PLC): biography (1885, 1938, 1942), birth (1882-1906), Catholic (1837-1985), cemetery, census (1820 RI, 1830 RI, 1840 RIP, 1850 RIMFD, 1860 RIMFD, 1870 RIMFD, 1880 RIMFD, 1900 RI, 1910 R, 1920 RI), circuit court (1840-56), coroner (1895-1911), DAR volumes, death (1882-1901), deed (1839-1901), Evangelical (1888-1946), genealogical compilations, German Evangelical (1800-1967), German immigrants, guardian (1860-1985), history (1885, 1910, 1942, 1964, 1970), indenture (1841-1909), Lutheran (1850-1985), marriage (1839-1924), Methodist (1843-1907), naturalization (1852-1928), newspaper abstracts, Presbyterian (1817-1981), probate (1860-90), stock marks (1839-84), United Church of Christ (1827-1984), will (1840-1924).

Library: Jasper Public Library, 1116 Main St., Jasper, IN 47546. Society: Dubois County Historical Society, 737 W. Eighth St., Jasper, IN 47546.

24. ELKHART COUNTY

Elkhart County established/organized 1830 from Cass and Allen Counties. County seat Goshen (46526).

Printed/microfilmed/CDROM records (most in ISL-IHS, many in FHL/FHC, many in ACPL, some in PLC): Amish, atlas (1874), biography (1885, 1893, 1905, 1939, 1930s-40s), birth (1882-1924), Brethren, Catholic (1861-1933), cemetery, census (1830 RI, 1840 RIP, 1850 RIMFD, 1860 RIMFD, 1870 RIMFD, 1880 RIMFD, 1900 RI, 1910 R, 1920 RI), circuit court (1830-1926), city directory (1885/6), Civil War soldiers, court (1853-90), DAR volumes, death (1882-1920), deed (1830-1915), Episcopalian, genealogical compilations, history (1881, 1893, 1905, 1916, 1936), marriage

(1830-1951), Methodist (1893-1963), newspaper abstracts (1831-54), partition (1853-69), probate (1830-1991), tract (1830-54), United Church of Christ (1858-1985), will (1833-1925).

Library: Elkhart County Public Library, 300 S. Second St., Elkhart, IN 46516. Nappanee Public Library, 157 N. Main St., Nappanee, IN 46550 (historical/manuscript). Society: Elkhart County Historical Society, 304 W. Vistula St., Bristol, IN 46507 (historical/manuscript). Publishes ELKHART COUNTY HISTORICAL SOCIETY NEWSLETTER. Elkhart County Genealogical Society, 1812 Jeanwood Dr., Elkhart, IN 46514. Publishes MICHIANA SEARCHER. Archives of the Mennonite Church and Mennonite Historical Library, 1700 S. Main St., Goshen, IN 46526 (historical/manuscript).

---

25. FAYETTE COUNTY

Fayette County established/organized 1819 from Franklin and Wayne Counties. County seat Connersville (47331).

Printed/microfilmed/CDROM records (most in ISL-IHS, many in FHL/FHC, many in ACPL, some in PLC): atlas (1875), biography (1885, 1899, 1917, 1939, 1930s-40s), birth (1893-99), Catholic (1853-1954), cemetery, census (1820 RI, 1830 RI, 1840 RIP, 1850 RIMFD, 1860 RIMFD, 1870 RIMFD, 1880 RIMFD, 1900 RI, 1910 R, 1920 RI), civil court (1819-91), commissioner (1819-42), court (1818-49), DAR volumes, death (1829-49, 1883-1907), deed (1814-1901), early landowner, Episcopal, genealogical compilations, history (1885, 1899, 1917), marriage (1819-1951), Methodist (1845-67, 1883-1900), partition (1853-1935), Presbyterian, probate (1819-1918), tax (1829, 1842), tract, voter (1877), will (1819-1939).

Library: Fayette County Public Library, 828 Grand Ave., Connersville, IN 47331. Historian: Fayette County Historian, 610 Marion St., Connersville, IN 47331.

---

26. FLOYD COUNTY

Floyd County established/organized 1819 from Clark and Harrison Counties. County seat New Albany (47150). Marriage records 1846-52 and a few others are missing.

Printed/microfilmed/CDROM records (most in ISL-IHS, many in FHL/FHC, many in ACPL, some in PLC): Baptist (1831-34), Bible, biography (1880, 1889, 1939, 1930s-40s), birth (1882-1920), Catholic (1835-1952), cemetery, census (1820 RI, 1830 RI, 1840 RIP, 1850 RIMFD, 1860 RIMFD, 1870 RIMFD, 1880 RIMFD, 1900 RI, 1910 R,

1920 RI), Civil War veterans, commissioner (1818-28), coroner (1880-1936), DAR volumes, death (1882-1920), deed (1818-1901), genealogical compilations, German Methodist (1863-1920), history (1880, 1889) indenture (1847-1915), land entry, marriage (1819-1922), Methodist (1828-1941), naturalization (1854-1927), negro (1853-65), New Albany city directories (Louisville for 1836-52), newspaper abstracts, obituaries, partition (1855-68), Presbyterian (1837-1917), probate (1819-1918), United Church of Christ (1837-95), veterans enrollment (1894), will (1818-37, 1853-1921), WPA volumes.

Library: FHL in New Albany, FHL in Louisville, New Albany Public Library, 180 W. Spring St., New Albany, IN 47150. Society: Southern IN Genealogical Society, PO Box 665, New Albany, IN 47150. Publishes SOUTHERN IN GENEALOGICAL SOCIETY QUARTERLY and SOUTHERN IN GENEALOGICAL SOCIETY NEWSLETTER.

27. FOUNTAIN COUNTY

Fountain County established/organized 1826 from Montgomery and Parke Counties. County seat Covington (47932).

Printed/microfilmed/CDROM records (most in ISL-IHS, many in FHL/FHC, many in ACPL, some in PLC): Baptist (1871-1901), Bible, biography (1881, 1893, 1940, 1968, 1983), birth (1887-1920), Catholic (1863-1986), cemetery, census (1830 RI, 1840 RIP, 1850 RIMFD, 1860 RIMFD, 1870 RIMFD, 1880 RIMFD, 1900 RI, 1910 R, 1920 RI), Christian Church (1840-1920), court, DAR volumes, death (1882-1920), deed (1827-87), directory (1871/2), genealogical compilations, history (1881, 1893, 1983), indenture (1847-84), Lutheran, marriage (1826-1941), mortuary, naturalization (1854-1908), partition (1856-1923), Presbyterian (1832-1925), probate (1832-1918), Quaker, Revolutionary soldiers, will (1827-1923).

Library: Covington Public Library, 620 Fifth St., Covington, IN 47932. Society: Fountain County Historical Society, PO Box 148, Kingman, IN 47952. Publishes FOUNTAIN COUNTY HISTORY.

28. FRANKLIN COUNTY

Franklin County established/organized 1811 from Clark, Dearborn, and Jefferson Counties. County seat Brookville (47012).

Printed/microfilmed/CDROM records (most in ISL-IHS, many in FHL/FHC, many in ACPL, some in PLC): apprentice (1831-1902), atlas (1882), Baptist (1817-59), biography

(1899, 1915), birth (1882-1920), Catholic (1837-1988), cemetery, census (1820 RI, 1830 RI, 1840 RIP, 1850 RIMFD, 1860 RIMFD, 1870 RIMFD, 1880 RIMFD, 1900 RI, 1910 R, 1920 RI), circuit court (1811-45), commissioner (1817-19, 1847-52), court (1815-65), court of common pleas (1811-36), DAR volumes, death (1882-1920), deed (1811-1902), estray (1811-14), genealogical compilations, history (1899, 1915), Lutheran (1836-1981), marriage (1811-1953), Methodist (1823-1989), mortuary, naturalization (1820-1976), negro (1852-56), newspaper abstracts (1827-1905), obituaries, Presbyterian (1824-1950), probate (1811-1920), stock marks (1811-39), tax (1811-49), tract (1811-97), treasurer (1836-53), United Brethren (1843-1933), United Church of Christ (1838-1988), veterans burials, will (1813-1936), WPA volumes.

Library: Brookville Public Library, 929 Main St., Brookville, IN 47006. Society: Franklin County Historical Society, Box 342, Route 4, Brookville, IN 47006. Tri-County Genealogical Society, 23184 Pocket Rd., West, Batesville, IN 47012.

29. FULTON COUNTY

Fulton County established/organized 1835 from Cass and St. Joseph Counties. County seat Rochester (46975).

Printed/microfilmed/CDROM records (most in ISL-IHS, many in FHL/FHC, many in ACPL, some in PLC): atlas (1883, 1907), Baptist (1898-1909), biography (1883, 1896, 1939, 1974, 1930s-40s, 1909-11), birth (1882-1920), Catholic (1868-1941), cemetery, census (1840 RIP, 1850 RIMFD, 1860 RIMFD, 1870 RIMFD, 1880 RIMFD, 1900 RI, 1910 R, 1920 RI), circuit court (1836-50), civil court (1853-1921), commissioner (1836-45), court (1836-72), death (1882-1920), deed (1836-1901), genealogical compilations, guardian (1837-1985), history (1896, 1909-11, 1923), inventory (1942), justice of peace (1877-1921), marriage (1836-1983), Methodist (1898-1909), newspaper abstracts, obituaries (1891-1900), partitions (1852-1920), poor farm (1871-1965), Presbyterian (1874-1925), probate (1836-1921), school (1896), tract (1834-1980), veterans discharges, will (1836-1974), WPA volumes.

Library: Fulton County Public Library, 320 W. Seventh St., Rochester, IN 46975. Society: Fulton County Historical Society, Box 89, Route 3, Rochester, IN 46975. Publishes FULTON COUNTY FOLKFINDER and FULTON COUNTY IMAGES.

30. GIBSON COUNTY

Gibson County established/organized 1813 from Knox County. County seat Princeton (47670).

Printed/microfilmed/CDROM records (most in ISL-IHS, many in FHL/FHC, many in ACPL, some in PLC): atlas (1881), Baptist (1813-45, 1874-75, 1881-1966), biography (1884, 1914, 1940, 1930s-40s), birth (1882-1920), Catholic (1844-1985), cemetery, census (1820 RI, 1830 RI, 1840 RIP, 1850 RIMFD, 1860 RIMFD, 1870 RIMFD, 1880 RIMFD, 1900 RI, 1910 R, 1920 RI), Christian Church (1823-1955), circuit court (1813-39), commissioner (1835-54), court of common pleas (1813-39), DAR volumes, death (1880-1920), deed (1813-1901), directory (1870), genealogical compilations, guardian (1863-1966), history (1884, 1897, 1914), marriage (1813-1924), Methodist (1845-1947), negro lists, newspaper abstracts (1872-1915), obituaries (1846-68), partition (1853-1918), Presbyterian (1876-1947), probate (1813-1919), Revolutionary veteran burials, tax (1819, 1826), United Church of Christ (1856-1983), will (1813-1926), WPA volumes.

Library: Princeton Public Library, 124 South Hart St., Princeton, IN 47670 (historical/manuscript). Founders Memorial Library, Oakland City College, 143 Lucretia St., Oakland City, IN 47660 (General Baptist historical/manuscript). Society: Gibson County Historical Society, PO Box 516, Princeton, IN 47670. Publishes GIBSON COUNTY LINES.

31. GRANT COUNTY

Grant County established/organized 1831 from Madison, Delaware, and Cass Counties. County seat Marion (46953).

Printed/microfilmed/CDROM records (most in ISL-IHS, many in FHL/FHC, many in ACPL, some in PLC): atlas (1877), biography (1886, 1901, 1909, 1914, 1976, 1930s-40s), Catholic (1876-1988), cemetery, census (1840 RIP, 1850 RIMFD, 1860 RIMFD, 1870 RIMFD, 1880 RIMFD, 1900 RI, 1910 R, 1920 RI), DAR volumes, deed (1831-99), genealogical compilations, history (1886, 1901, 1914), marriage (1831-1938), Methodist, newspaper abstracts (1867-86), obituaries (1867-1925), Presbyterian (1838-1945), probate (1831-98), Quaker (1825-1966), soldiers home (1866-1937), tract (1825-57), will (1839-89).

Library: Marion Public Library, 600 S. Washington St., Marion, IN 46952. Society: Grant County Historical Society, 24 Herbal Drive, Marion, IN 46952. Grant County Genealogy Club, Grant County Courthouse, Marion, IN 46952. Publishes GRANT COUNTY BEACON.

32. GREENE COUNTY

Greene County established/organized 1821 from Daviess and Sullivan Counties. County seat Bloomfield (47424). Printed/microfilmed/CDROM records (most in ISL-IHS, many in FHL/FHC, many in ACPL, some in PLC): atlas (1879), Baptist (1843-62), biography (1884, 1908, 1942, 1930s-40s, 1990), birth (1885-1920), Catholic (1872-1985), cemetery, census (1830 RI, 1840 RIP, 1850 RIMFD, 1860 RIMFD, 1870 RIMFD, 1880 RIMFD, 1900 RI, 1910 R, 1920 RI), Christian Church (1859-1953), Church of Christ, DAR volumes, death (1893-1920), deed (1822-1902), early settlers, genealogical compilations, history (1875, 1884, 1908, 1959, 1990), inventory (1939), marriage (1821-1921), Methodist (1831-1950), naturalization (1856-1906), obituaries, partition (1853-61), Presbyterian (1825-1935), probate (1823-1919), will (1825-1904), WPA volumes.

Library: Bloomfield Public Library, 125 South Franklin St., Bloomfield, IN 47424. Society: Greene County Historical Society, PO Box 516, Bloomfield, IN 47424. Publishes GREENE HISTORICAL SOCIETY NEWSLETTER.

33. HAMILTON COUNTY

Hamilton County established/organized 1823 from Delaware and Marion Counties. County seat Noblesville (46060). Printed/microfilmed/CDROM records (most in ISL-IHS, many in FHL/FHC, many in ACPL, some in PLC): apprentice (1847-87), Baptist (1838-1923), biography (1880, 1942, 1930s-40s), birth (1882-1920), Brethren, Catholic (1876-1987), cemetery, census (1830 RI, 1840 RIP, 1850 RIMFD, 1860 RIMFD, 1870 RIMFD, 1880 RIMFD, 1900 RI, 1910 R, 1920 RI), death (1882-1920), deed (1825-1901), directory (1874), genealogical compilations, history (1880, 1901), indenture (1847-87), land (1789-1849), Lutheran, marriage (1833-1922), Methodist (1859-1921), naturalization (1855-1905), obituary (1874-81), Presbyterian (1824-66), probate (1823-1937), Quaker (1820-1951), will (1823-1920), WPA volumes.

Library: FHL in Noblesville, Noblesville Public Library, One Library Plaza, Noblesville, IN 46060 (historical/manuscript). Society: Marion-Adams Historical and Genealogical Society, 308 Main St., Sheridan, IN 46069. Hamilton County Historical Society, PO Box 397, Noblesville, IN 46060. Publishes HAMILTON COUNTY HISTORICAL SOCIETY NEWSLETTER.

34. HANCOCK COUNTY

Hancock County established/organized 1827 from Madison County. County seat Greenfield (46140).

Printed/microfilmed/CDROM records (most in ISL-IHS, many in FHL/FHC, many in ACPL, some in PLC): atlas (1887), Baptist (1838-1945), biography (1882, 1895, 1916, 1942, 1976, 1930s-40s), birth (1882-1920), Catholic (1877-1942), cemetery, census (1830 RI, 1840 RIP, 1850 RIMFD, 1860 RIMFD, 1870 RIMFD, 1880 RIMFD, 1900 RI, 1910 R, 1920 RI), Church of Jesus Christ of Latter Day Saints, court (1828-59), DAR volumes, death (1882-1920), deed (1827-1905), early landowners, genealogical compilations, guardian (1853-1951), history (1882, 1895, 1916), indenture (1843-76), marriage (1826-1921), Methodist, naturalization (1854-1906), Presbyterian (1855-1937), probate (1828-1951), Quaker (1827-1952), will (1876-1908), WPA volumes.

Library: Greenfield Public Library, 700 North Broadway, Greenfield, IN 46140. Society: Hancock County Historical Society, PO Box 375, Greenfield, IN 46140. Publishes OLD LOG CHAIN.

35. HARRISON COUNTY

Harrison County established/organized 1808 from Knox and Clark Counties. County seat Corydon (47112).

Printed/microfilmed/CDROM records (most in ISL-IHS, many in FHL/FHC, many in ACPL, some in PLC): atlas (1882), Bible, biography (1880, 1899, 1942), birth (1882-1941), Catholic (1854-1988), cemetery, census (1810 RI for only Harrison and Exeter Townships, 1820 RI, 1830 RI, 1840 RIP, 1850 RIMFD, 1860 RIMFD, 1870 RIMFD, 1880 RIMFD, 1900 RI, 1910 R, 1920 RI), circuit court (1817-20), commissioner (1817-53), court (1809-25), court of common pleas (1809-19), DAR volumes, death (1882-1920), deed (1809-1901), estray (1808-17), genealogical compilations, German Evangelical Reform (1866-97), history (1880, 1899), indenture (1854-83), land (1807-1900), Lutheran (1852-1952), marriage (1809-1920), Methodist (1839-1962), militia (1817), naturalization (1855-1926), negro (1853-1963), newspaper abstracts (1820-38), partition (1853-72), Presbyterian (1841-1961), probate (1809-1923), Revolutionary soldiers, school (1846-47), tax (1813, 1844), veterans burials, voter (1809), will (1809-32), WPA volumes.

Library: Corydon Public Library, 117 West Beaver St., Corydon, IN 47112. Society: Harrison County Historical Society, 117 West Beaver St., Corydon, IN 47112. Southern IN Genealogical Society, PO Box 665, New Albany, IN, 47151. Publishes SOUTHERN IN GENEALOGICAL

SOCIETY QUARTERLY and SOUTHERN IN GENEALOGICAL SOCIETY NEWSLETTER.

36. HENDRICKS COUNTY

Hendricks County established-/organized 1824 from unorganized territory and Putnam County. County seat Danville (46122).

Printed/microfilmed/CDROM records (most in ISL-IHS, many in FHL/FHC, many in ACPL, some in PLC): apprentice (1837-49), atlas (1878), biography (1885, 1895, 1914, 1976, 1930s-40s), birth (1882-1920), Catholic (1867-2966), cemetery, census (1830 RI, 1840 RIP, 1850 RIMFD, 1860 RIMFD, 1870 RIMFD, 1880 RIMFD, 1900 RI, 1910 R, 1920 RI), Christian Church (1837-1954), Church of Jesus Christ of Latter Day Saints, circuit court (1824-41), commissioner (1831-39), DAR volumes, death (1882-1920), deed (1823-1907), Episcopal, estray (1831-39), genealogical compilations, history (1885, 1895, 1914, 1976), indenture (1837-72), insanity (1848-61), marriage (1824-1925), Methodist (1861-1940), naturalization (1852-1906), partition (1854-74), Presbyterian (1854-1914), probate (1825-1918), Quaker (1800-1966), stock marks (1824-48) tax (1841-70), tract (1821-51), voter (1826-50), will (1822-1926), WPA volumes.

Library: Danville Public Library, 101 South Indiana St., Danville, IN 46122. Society: Hendricks County Historical Society, PO Box 128, Danville, IN 46122. Publishes HENDRICKS COUNTY HISTORICAL SOCIETY BULLETIN. Hendricks County Genealogical Society, 101 South Indiana St., Danville, IN 46122. County Seat Genealogical Society, 310 Urban St., Danville, IN 46122. Publishes COUNTY SEAT SCRAPS.

37. HENRY COUNTY

Henry County established/organized 1822 from unorganized territory. County seat New Castle (47362). Some records lost in 1864 fire.

Printed/microfilmed/CDROM records (most in ISL-IHS, many in FHL/FHC, many in ACPL, some in PLC): atlas (1875, 1893), Bible, biography (1884, 1930s-40s), birth (1882-1920), cemetery, census (1830 RI, 1840 RIP, 1850 RIMFD, 1860 RIMFD, 1870 RIMFD, 1880 RIMFD, 1900 RI, 1910 R, 1920 RI), Catholic (1840-1951), Church of Jesus Christ of Latter Day Saints, city directory (1894), courtt (1825-38), death (1882-1920), deed (1824-1905), directory (1884), history (1871, 1884, 1906, 1976, 1981), land entry (1821-49), marriage (1823-1920), Methodist (1821-33, 1880-1993), newspaper abstracts (1800-1993), obituary (1886-1953), partition (1853-72), pioneers, Presbyterian (1844-

1964), probate (1828-52), Quaker (1826-1968), will (1822-1901), WPA volumes.

Library: New Castle Public Library, 376 South 15th St., New Castle, IN 47362. Society: Henry County Historical Society, 606 South 14th St., New Castle, IN 47362. Publishes HENRY COUNTY HISTORI-CAL LOG.

---

38. HOWARD COUNTY

Howard County established/organized 1844 from Carroll, Cass, Miami, Grant, and Hamilton Counties. County seat Kokomo (46901). Name of county seat was Richardville from 1844 to 1846.

Printed/microfilmed/CDROM records (most in ISL-IHS, many in FHL/FHC, many in ACPL, some in PLC): atlas (1877), biography (1883, 1898, 1930s-40s), birth (1875-1920), Catholic (1869-1969), cemetery, census (1850 RIMFD, 1860 RIMFD, 1870 RIMFD, 1880 RIMFD, 1900 RI, 1910 R, 1920 RI), Church of Jesus Christ of Latter Day Saints, DAR volumes, death (1875-1920), deed (1846-1902), history (1883, 1898), inventory (1939), land (1844-47), marriage (1844-1920), Methodist (1867-1901), probate (1844-1909), Quaker (1793-1955), tract (1842-63), will (1844-1905), WPA volumes.

Library: Kokomo-Howard County Public Library, 220 North Union St., Kokomo, IN 46901. Society: Howard County Genealogical Society, 220 N. Union St., Kokomo, IN 46901. Publishes HOWARD COUNTY GENEALOGICAL SOCIETY NEWSLETTER. North Central IN Genealogical Society, 2399 Canterbury Dr., Kokomo, IN, 46901.

---

39. HUNTINGTON COUNTY

Huntington County established/organized 1832 from Grant and Allen Counties. County seat Huntington (46750).

Printed/microfilmed/CDROM records (most in ISL-IHS, many in FHL/FHC, many in ACPL, some in PLC): atlas (1879), biography (1887, 1930s-40s), birth (1875-1920), Catholic (1853-1989), cemetery, census (1840 RIP, 1850 RIMFD, 1860 RIMFD, 1870 RIMFD, 1880 RIMFD, 1900 RI, 1910 R, 1920 RI), Christian Church, commissioner (1834-45), DAR volumes, death (1882-1920), deed (1834-99), early settlers, Evangelical (1863-1950), history (1887), land entry (1830-53), marriage (1837-1920), Methodist (1868-1916), obituary, Presbyterian (1843-1920), probate (1842-50, 1858-73),

Quaker (1867-1916), Revolutionary soldiers, tract (1830-53), will (1841-1900), WPA volumes.

Library: Huntington Public Library, 200 West Market St., Huntington, IN 46750 (historical/manuscript). Society: Huntington County Historical Society, 1041 South Jefferson St., Huntington, IN 46750. Publishes HUNTINGTON COUNTY HISTORICAL SOCIETY NEWSLETTER. United Brethren Historical Center, Richlyn Library, Huntington College, Huntington, IN 46750 (historical/manuscript).

40. JACKSON COUNTY

Jackson County established/organized 1816 from Clark, Jefferson, and Washington Counties. County seat Brownstown (47220).

Printed/microfilmed/CDROM records (most in ISL-IHS, many in FHL/FHC, many in ACPL, some in PLC): apprentice (1884-89), atlas (1878, 1900), biography (1886, 1988), Bible, birth (1882-1920), Catholic (1863-1940), cemetery, census (1820 RI, 1830 RI, 1840 RIP, 1850 RIMFD, 1860 RIMFD, 1870 RIMFD, 1880 RIMFD, 1900 RI, 1910 R, 1920 RI), DAR volumes, death (1882-1920), deed (1816-1900), Evangelical and Reformed (1860-1964), Evangelical Lutheran (1856-1982), genealogical compilations, history (1886) land, Lutheran (1838-1964), marriage (1816-1922), Methodist (1857-1917), naturalization (1852-1905), negro (1853-54), obituary (1854-85), partition (1855-57, 1873-1928), probate (1817-1918), Quaker (1816-1940), swamp (1852-80), will (1817-37, 1844-1928), WPA volumes.

Library: Jackson County Public Library, Second and Walnut Sts., Seymour, IN 47274 (historical/manuscript). Society: Jackson County Historical Society, 115 N. Sugar St., Brownstown, IN 47220. Jackson County Genealogical Society, 415 Walnut St., Seymour, IN, 47274. Publishes GENEALOGY JOTTINGS.

41. JASPER COUNTY

Jasper County established/organized 1835/1838 from White and Warren Counties. County seat Rensselaer (47978). Fire in 1864 with many records lost.

Printed/microfilmed/CDROM records (most in ISL-IHS, many in FHL/FHC, many in ACPL, some in PLC): Baptist (1851-1904), biography (1883, 1899, 1916, 1985), Bible, birth (1882-1920), cemetery, census (1840 RIP, 1850 RIMFD, 1860 RIMFD, 1870 RIMFD, 1880 RIMFD, 1900 RI, 1910 R, 1920 RI), Catholic (1845-1958), Civil War soldiers, DAR volumes, death (1882-1920), deed (1838-1907), genealogical compilations, history (1883, 1916, 1985) marriage

(1850-1920), Methodist (1883-87), Presbyterian (1847-86), probate (1865-1907), tract (1864-99), veterans burials, will (1864-99), WPA volumes.

Library: Renssalear Public Library, 208 West Susan St., Rensselear, IN 47978. Society: Jasper County Historical Society, Van Rensselaer and Indiana-114, Rensselaer, IN 47978. Jasper-Newton Counties Genealogical Society, Box 307, Route 1, Wheatfield, IN, 46392. Publishes GENEALOGY TRAILS.

42. JAY COUNTY

Jay County established/organized 1835/1836 from Delaware and Randolph Counties. County seat Portland (47371).

Printed/microfilmed/CDROM records (most in ISL-IHS, many in FHL/FHC, many in ACPL, some in PLC): atlas (1881), biography (1887, 1922. 1930s-40s, 1982), Bible, birth (1882-1920), Catholic (1862-1988), cemetery, census (1840 RIP, 1850 RIMFD, 1860 RIMFD, 1870 RIMFD, 1880 RIMFD, 1900 RI, 1910 R, 1920 RI), Civil War soldiers, commissioner (1836-50), DAR volumes, death (1882-1920), deed (1837-1921), genealogical compilations, German Reformed, history (1864, 1887, 1922, 1975, 1982), inventory (1940), land purchases, marriage (1837-1925), Methodist (1873-1953), newspaper abstracts, obituaries, partition (1850-72), probate (1838-1920), Quaker (1841-1955), tract (1832-54), will (1846-1920), WPA volumes.

Library: Jay County Public Library, 131 East Walnut St., Portland, IN 47371. Society: Jay County Historical Society, PO Box 1282, Portland, IN 47371 (historical/manuscript). Jay County Genealogical Society, PO Box 1086, Portland, IN, 47371.

43. JEFFERSON COUNTY

Jefferson County established/organized 1811 from Dearborn and Clark Counties. County seat Madison (47250).

Printed/microfilmed/CDROM records (most in ISL-IHS, many in FHL/FHC, many in ACPL, some in PLC): apprentice (1847-82), alien, Baptist (1818-1962), biography (1880, 1889, 1957), Bible, birth (1882-1907), Catholic (1837-1988), cemetery, census (1820 RI, 1830 RI, 1840 RIP, 1850 RIMFD, 1860 RIMFD, 1870 RIMFD, 1880 RIMFD, 1900 RI, 1910 R, 1920 RI), Christian Church (1837-1944), circuit court (1811-19), commissioner (1817-54), court of common pleas (1812-18), DAR volumes, death in city (1838-50), deed (1811-91), divorce (1849-67), Episcopal (1835-1917), genealogical compilations, history (1880, 1889), indenture, license (1816-37), marriage

(1811-1923), Methodist (1822-1932), militia (1861), mortuary (1840-1936), naturalization (1840-1904), negro (1853-60), newspaper abstracts (1817-87), obituary (1849-1936), orphan (1882-1918), pioneer women, Presbyterian (1812-1957), probate (1811-1940), regional directory (1871-72), tax (1827), treasurer (1812), United Church of Christ (1837-1935), voter (1817-28), will (1811-1924).

Library: Jefferson County Public Library, 420 West Main St., Madison, IN 47250. Society: Jefferson County Historical Society, 615 West First St., Madison, IN 47250 (historical/manuscript).

44. JENNINGS COUNTY

Jennings County established/organized 1817 from Jefferson and Jackson Counties. County seat Vernon (47282).

Printed/microfilmed/CDROM records (most in ISL-IHS, many in FHL/FHC, many in ACPL, some in PLC): atlas (1884), Baptist (1822-1962), Bible, biography (1880, 1889), birth (1882-1907), Catholic (1841-1988), cemetery, census (1820 RI, 1830 RI, 1840 RIP, 1850 RIMFD, 1860 RIMFD, 1870 RIMFD, 1880 RIMFD, 1900 RI, 1910 R, 1920 RI), circuit court (1817-22, 1842-1935), commissioner (1824-46), court (1818-50), DAR volumes, death (1882-1913), deed (1817-88), (1808-17), early landowners, genealogical compilations, history (1880, 1889, 1956, 1987) indenture, landowners, map, marriage (1818-1923), mortuary, naturalization (1850-1900), negro (1853-56), obituary (1885-90), Presbyterian (1817-1909), probate (1818-1920), will (1818-1935), WPA volumes.

Library: Jennings County Public Library, 143 East Walnut St., North Vernon, IN 47265. Society: Jennings County Genealogical Society, Box 227, Route 1, Scipio, IN 47273.

45. JOHNSON COUNTY

Johnson County established/organized 1823 from unorganized territory. County seat Franklin (46131).

Printed/microfilmed/CDROM records (most in ISL-IHS, many in FHL/FHC, many in ACPL, some in PLC): atlas (1866, 1881, 1900, 1984), Baptist (1835-1930), biography (1820-1900, 1888, 1913, 1930s-40s, 1942), Bible, birth (1882-1942), Catholic (1835-1968), cemetery, census (1830 RI, 1840 RIP, 1850 RIMFD, 1860 RIMFD, 1870 RIMFD, 1880 RIMFD, 1900 RI, 1910 R, 1920 RI), Christian Church (1834-1984), commissioner (1826-38), court (1823-53), DAR volumes, death (1882-1920), deed (1825-1900), directory (1874, 1895), early landowner, genealogical compilations, history (1881, 1888, 1900, 1913), land grants, marriage (1830-1920), Methodist (1850-79), mortuary, naturalization (1823-53), obituaries (1846-60), Presbyterian (1823-1953), probate (1823-1900), will (1827-1907), WPA volumes.

Library: Johnson County Public Library, 401 South State St., Franklin, IN 46131 (historical/manuscript). Masonic Library and Museum of IN, 690 State Street, Franklin, IN 46131 (historical/manuscript). Society: Johnson County Historical Society, 135 North Main St., Franklin, IN 46131 (historical/manuscript). Publishes NOSTALGIA NEWS. Franklin College Baptist Collection, 501 E. Monroe St., Franklin, IN 46131 (historical/manuscript).

46. KNOX COUNTY

Knox County established/organized 1790 as an original county. County seat Vincennes (47591). Formed in 1790 in the Northwest Territory. Was made part of IN Territory in 1800. Some records lost in fire of 1814.

Printed/microfilmed/CDROM records (most in ISL-IHS, many in FHL/FHC, many in ACPL, some in PLC): atlas (1871, 1880, 1903), Baptist (1809-1970), biography (1886, 1902, 1911, 1930s-40s), Bible, birth (1882-1920), brands, Catholic (1749-1985), cemetery, census (1820 RI, 1830 RI, 1840 RIP, 1850 RIMFD, 1860 RIMFD, 1870 RIMFD, 1880 RIMFD, 1900 RI, 1910 R, 1920 RI), circuit court (1801-31), Clark's Grant grantees, commissioner (1814-55), court of common pleas (1790-1830), DAR volumes, death (1882-1920), deed (1783-1929), directory (1891-92), early settlers, Episcopal, genealogical compilations, history (1858, 1886, 1902, 1911, 1962), indenture, land (1783-1815), land office records, marriage (1807-1920), Methodist (1886-1909), mortuary (1816-94), naturalization (1852-1951), negro (1805-07), newspaper abstracts (1817-87), obituaries (1890-1910), petition (1806), poor (1821-32), Presbyterian, probate (1790-1836), veterans, enrollment (1886), Vincennes (1732-1840), voter (1809), will (1806-52), WPA volumes.

Library: Knox County Public Library, 502 North Seventh St., Vincennes, IN 47591 (historical/manuscript). Vigo Chapter DAR Library, 3 W. Scott St., Vincennes, IN 47591 (historical/manuscript). Repository: Knox County Records Library, 810 Broadway, Vincennes, IN 47591 (historical/manuscript). Lewis Historical Collections Library, LRC-22, Vincennes University, Vincennes, IN 47591 (historical/manuscript). Society: Northwest Territory Genealogical Society, Lewis Historical Library, Vincennes University, Vincennes, IN 47591.

47. KOSCIUSKO COUNTY

Kosciusko County established/-organized 1835/36 from Cass and Elkhart Counties. County seat Warsaw (46580).

Printed/microfilmed/CDROM records (most in ISL-IHS, many in FHL/FHC, many in ACPL, some in PLC): atlas (1879, 1914), biography (1887, 1902, 1911, 1930s-40s), Bible, birth (1882-1920), Brethren, Catholic (1852-1987), cemetery, census (1840 RIP, 1850 RIMFD, 1860 RIMFD, 1870 RIMFD, 1880 RIMFD, 1900 RI, 1910 R, 1920 RI), circuit court (1836-43, 1857-65), court (1836-43, 1857-65), DAR volumes, death (1882-1920), deed (1834-1900), genealogical compilations, guardian (1837-1913), history (1887, 1911, 1919, 1944, 1986), Lutheran (1844-60), marriage (1836-1921), Methodist (1893-1963), mortuary (1887-1926), naturalization (1855-1923), newspaper abstracts, obituaries, Presbyterian (1864-1928), probate (1836-1980), tax (1844, 1886, 1895), tract (1830-52), Union veterans (1865, 1890, 1894), veterans' burials, voter (1845, 1853), will (1837-1926), WPA volumes.

Library: Warsaw Public Library, 315 East Center St., Warsaw, IN 46580. Morgan Library, Grace College, 200 Seminary Drive, Winona Lake, IN 46590 (historical/manuscript). Society: Kosciusko County Historical Society, Genealogy Section, PO Box 1071, Warsaw, IN 46581 (historical/manuscript). Publishes OUR MISSING LINKS and KOSCIUSKO COUNTY NEWSLETTER.

48. LAGRANGE COUNTY

Lagrange County established/organized 1832 from Elkhart and Allen Counties. County seat Lagrange (46761).

Printed/microfilmed/CDROM records (most in ISL-IHS, many in FHL/FHC, many in ACPL, some in PLC): atlas (1874, 1893), Baptist (1837-68), biography (1882), birth (1882-1920), cemetery, census (1840 RIP, 1850 RIMFD, 1860 RIMFD, 1870 RIMFD, 1880 RIMFD, 1900 RI, 1910 R, 1920 RI), circuit court (1832-39), civil court (1832-72), commissioner (1832-49), DAR volumes, death (1882-1924), deed (1832-1902), history (1882, 1928, 1936), marriage (1832-1950), Presbyterian (1833-88), probate (1832-1923), school, tract (1831-48), veterans' burials, will (1842-1900), WPA volumes.

Library: Lagrange Public Library, 203 W. Spring St., Lagrange, IN 46761. Society: Lagrange County Historical Society, RR 1, Lagrange IN 46761. Publishes LAGRANGE COUNTY HISTORICAL SOCIETY NEWSLETTER. TriState Genealogical Society, 416 North Lakeview, Lagrange, IN 46171.

49. LAKE COUNTY

Lake County established/organized 1836/37 from Newton and Porter Counties. County seat Crown Point (46307).

Printed/microfilmed/CDROM records (most in ISL-IHS, many in FHL/FHC, many in ACPL, some in PLC): Baptist (1839-91), Bible, biography (1882, 1894, 1904, 1915, 1930s-40s), birth (1882-1941), Catholic (1846-1993), cemetery, census (1840 RIP, 1850 RIMFD, 1860 RIMFD, 1870 RIMFD, 1880 RIMFD, 1900 RI, 1910 R, 1920 RI), city directory (1891/2-), commissioner (1837-58), DAR volumes, death (1882-1920), genealogical compilations, Hammond city directory (1889, 1891-92), history (1873, 1882, 1904, 1915, 1938, 1959), marriage (1837-1920), Methodist (1888-1935), mortuary (1868-1924), naturalization (1854-1932), newspaper abstracts (1857-69), Presbyterian (1844-1934), school (1890, 1896), veterans, burials, WPA volumes.

Library: Lake County Public Library, 1919 West 81st St., Merrillville, IN 46410. Gary Public Library, 220 West 5th St., Gary, IN 46402 (historical/manuscript). Hammond Public Library and Historical Society, 464 State St., Hammond, IN 46320 (historical/manuscript). Crown Point Public Library, 214 S. Court St., Crown Point, IN 46307 (historical/manuscript). East Chicago Public Library, 2401 E. Columbus Dr., East Chicago, IN 46312 (historical/manuscript). Calumet Archives, Indiana University Northwest, 3400 Broadway, Gary, IN 46408 (historical/manuscript). Lowell Public Library, 250 S. Fremont St., Lowell, IN 46356 (historical/manuscript).

50. LA PORTE COUNTY

La Porte County established/organized 1832 from St. Joseph County. County seat La Porte (46350).

Printed/microfilmed/CDROM records (most in ISL-IHS, many in FHL/FHC, many in ACPL, some in PLC): atlas (1874), Baptist (1840-91), Bible, biography (1880, 1894, 1930s-40s), birth (1882-1920), Catholic (1837-1993), cemetery, census (1840 RIP, 1850 RIMFD, 1860 RIMFD, 1870 RIMFD, 1880 RIMFD, 1900 RI, 1910 R, 1920 RI), court (1832-1922), court of common pleas (1853-76), DAR volumes, death (1882-1920), deed (1832-1901), genealogical compilations, guardian (1834-1979), history (1876, 1880, 1966), inventory (1939), Lutheran (1871-1921), marriage (1832-1920), Methodist (1835-1933), partition (1853-1926), Presbyterian (1850-99), probate (1832-1978), school (1840s), United Church of Christ (1856-1958), Union veteran (1865-98), veterans' burials, will (1844-1921), WPA volumes.

Library: Michigan City Public Library, 100 East Fourth St., Michigan City, IN 45360. Society: La Porte County Historical Society, La Porte County Complex, La Porte, IN 46350 (historical/manuscript). La Porte County Genealogical Society, 904 Indiana Ave., La Porte, IN 46350.

---

51. LAWRENCE COUNTY

Lawrence County established/organized 1818 from Orange County. County seat Bedford (47421).

Printed/microfilmed/CDROM records (most in ISL-IHS, many in FHL/FHC, many in ACPL, some in PLC): atlas (1879), (1881-1956), Bible, biography (1914. 1930s-40s), birth (1882-1900), Catholic (1865-1983), cemetery, census (1820 RI, 1830 RI, 1840 RIP, 1850 RIMFD, 1860 RIMFD, 1870 RIMFD, 1880 RIMFD, 1900 RI, 1910 R, 1920 RI), DAR volumes, death (1882-99), deed (1819-1904), early settlers, marriage (1818-1981), naturalization (1852-1906), partition (1853-67), Presbyterian (1833-1923), probate (1818-1918), Revolutionary veterans' burials, school, tax (1822), will (1819-1918), WPA volumes.

Library: Bedford Public Library, 1323 K Street, Bedford, IN 47421. Society: Lawrence County Historical and Genealogical Society, 15 County Courthouse, Bedford, IN 47421 (historical/manuscript).

---

52. MADISON COUNTY

Madison County established/organized 1823 from unorganized territory. County seat Anderson (46015). Fire in 1880 resulted in loss of many records. Deeds from 1823 were saved.

Printed/microfilmed/CDROM records (most in ISL-IHS, many in FHL/FHC, many in ACPL, some in PLC): atlas (1901), biography (1880, 1895, 1897, 1914, 1930s-40s, 1978), birth (1882-1920), Catholic (1866-1988), cemetery, census (1830 RI, 1840 RIP, 1850 RIMFD, 1860 RIMFD, 1870 RIMFD, 1880 RIMFD, 1900 RI, 1910 R, 1920 RI), Church of Christ (1849-67), DAR volumes, death (1882-1020), deed (1823-1901), divorce (1849-80), history (1874, 1880, 1897, 1914), marriage (1840-1920), Methodist (1844-1955), mortuary (1891-1911), newspaper abstracts (1840-80), Presbyterian (1892-1924), Quaker (1823-1964), tax (1842), tract, Universalist (1859-1927), veterans' burials, will (1879-1901).

Library: Anderson Public Library, 111 East Twelfth St., Anderson, IN 46016. Society: Madison County Historical Society, PO Box 523, Anderson, IN 46015. Publishes MADISON COUNTY HISTORICAL GAZETTE, SEARCHLIGHT, and CAMP STILWELL. Archives of the

Church of God, 1100 E. Fifth St., Anderson, IN 46012 (historical/manuscript).

---

53. MARION COUNTY

Marion County established/organized 1822 from unorganized territory. County seat Indianapolis (46204).

Printed/microfilmed/CDROM records (most in ISL-IHS, many in FHL/FHC, many in ACPL, some in PLC): atlas (1889), Baptist (1826-1908), bastardy (1877-1921), Bible, biography (1870, 1876, 1884, 1893, 1930s-40s), birth (1882-1920), cemetery, census (1830 RI, 1840 RIP, 1850 RIMFD, 1860 RIMFD, 1870 RIMFD, 1880 RIMFD, 1900 RI, 1910 R, 1920 RI), Christian Church (1833-1939), Church of Jesus Christ of Latter Day Saints (1889-1941), circuit court (1822-1916), city directory (1855-), city history (1904), commissioner (1822-99), coroner (1884-87), court of common pleas (1849-73), DAR volumes, death (1882-1920), deed (1822-75), divorce (1848-88), Episcopal (1837-1955), genealogical compilations, Germans (1840-1918), German Evangelical (1855-1932), guardian (1847-1931), history (1853, 1884, 1893), index to city histories, inventory (1938), Lutheran (1836-1919), marriage (1822-1944), Methodist (1821-1973), naturalization (1832-1929), news-paper abstracts, old settlers, Presbyterian (1832-1952), probate (1822-1934), Quaker (1822-1967), tax (1829, 1835), will (1822-1939), WPA volumes.

Library: FHL in Indianapolis, Indianapolis-Marion County Public Library, PO Box 211, Indianapolis, IN 46206, IN Historical Society Library, 315 West Ohio St., Indianapolis, IN 46202 (historical/manuscript), IN State Library (and IN State Archives), 140 North Senate Ave., Indianapolis, IN 46204 (historical/manuscript), University Library and Archives, IN University-Purdue University at Indianapolis, 755 W. Michigan St., Indianapolis, IN 46202 (historical/manuscript, especially German). Christian Theological Seminary Library Archives, PO Box 88267, 1000 West 42nd St., Indianapolis, IN 46208 (Christian Church historical/manuscript). Wesleyan Church Archives and Library, PO Box 50434, 8050 Castleway Drive, Indianapolis, IN 46250. Society: IN Historical Society 315 West Ohio St., Indianapolis, IN 46202. Publishes THE HOOSIER GENEALOGIST. Marion County Historical Society, 735 Woodruff Place, East Drive, Indianapolis, IN 46201. Publishes THE CIRCULATOR.

---

54. MARSHALL COUNTY

Marshall County established/organized 1835 from St. Joseph and Elkhart Counties. County seat Plymouth (46563).

Printed/microfilmed/CDROM records (most in ISL-IHS, many in FHL/FHC, many in ACPL, some in PLC): Bible, biography (1890, 1930s-40s, 1986), Brethren (1891-1915), Catholic (1862-1989), cemetery, census (1840 RIP, 1850 RIMFD, 1860 RIMFD, 1870 RIMFD, 1880 RIMFD, 1900 RI, 1910 R, 1920 RI), circuit court (1837-1986), commissioner (1836-44), DAR volumes, deed (1835-1929), genealogical compilations, history (1890, 1908, 1923, 1963, 1973, 1986), inventory (1941), Lutheran, marriage (1836-1962), Methodist (1893-1963), naturalization (1837-1986), newspaper abstracts (1874-1900), obituary (1874-1900), partition (1853-1919), Presbyterian (1861-1948), probate (1836-1986), tax (1843), tract (1832-75), will (1836-1986), WPA volumes.

Library: Plymouth Public Library, 201 North Center St., Plymouth, IN 46563. Society: Marshall County Genealogical and Historical Society, 123 North Michigan St., Plymouth, IN 46563 (historical/manuscript). Publishes MARSHALL COUNTY HISTORICAL SOCIETY QUARTERLY.

55. MARTIN COUNTY

Martin County established/organized 1820 from Daviess and Dubois Counties. County seat Shoals (47581).

Printed/microfilmed/CDROM records (most in ISL-IHS, many in FHL/FHC, many in ACPL, some in PLC): Bible, biography (1897, 1979), birth (1880-1941), Catholic (1830-36, 1846-1985), cemetery, census (1820RI, 1830 RI, 1840 RIP, 1850 RIMFD, 1860 RIMFD, 1870 RIMFD, 1880 RIMFD, 1900 RI, 1910 R, 1920 RI), Civil War veterans, court (1832-67), DAR volumes, death (1880-1989), deed (1820-1947), estray (1848-89), history (1953, 1966), land, marriage (1820-1925), negro (1850), newspaper abstracts, poor (1883-1920), probate (1820-1930), tax (1855, 1865), tract, veterans' burial, will (1840-1930), WPA volumes.

Library: Shoals Public Library, Fourth and High Sts., Shoals, IN 47581. Society: Martin County Histvorical Society PO Box 84, Shoals, IN 47581. Martin County Genealogical Society, PO Box 45, Shoals, IN 47581. Publishes THE HOOSIER GENEALOGIST.

56. MIAMI COUNTY

Miami County established/organized 1832/1834 from Cass County. County seat Peru (46970). Fire in 1843 destroyed almost all records. Deeds were about all that survived.

Printed/microfilmed/CDROM records (most in ISL-IHS, many in FHL/FHC, many in ACPL, some in PLC): atlas (1877), Baptist (1848-77), biography (1887, 1897, 1898, 1914, 1930s-40s, 1979), birth (1870-1920), Catholic (1865-1951), cemetery, census (1840 RIP, 1850 RIMFD, 1860 RIMFD, 1870 RIMFD, 1880 RIMFD, 1900 RI, 1910 R, 1920 RI), Church of Jesus Christ of Latter Day Saints (1896-1929), commissioner (1834-53), death (1844-1974), deed (1836-99), early settlers, genealogical compilations, history (1887, 1896, 1897, 1898, 1914), inventory (1937), land (1830-52), land owners (1877), marriage (1843-1944), Methodist (1889-1919), newspaper abstracts, obituaries (1904-26), Presbyterian (1863-1924), Quaker (1852-1941), tract, United Brethren, voter (1850-1920), will (1843-1900), WPA volumes.

Library: Peru Public Library, 102 East Main St., Peru, IN 46970. Society: Miami County Historical Society, Courthouse Room 102, Peru, IN 46790. Publishes HISTORICAL BULLETIN OF MIAMI COUNTY. Miami County Genealogical Society, PO Box 542, Peru, IN 46970. Publishes GENEALOGIST MIAMI COUNTY INDIANA TRAKKER. Miami County Museum Archives, 51 N. Broadway, Peru, IN 46970 (historical/manuscript).

57. MONROE COUNTY

Monroe County established/organized 1818 from Orange County. County seat Bloomington (46204).

Printed/microfilmed/CDROM records (most in ISL-IHS, many in FHL/FHC, many in ACPL, some in PLC): atlas (1856), Baptist (1817-1910), Bible, biography (1884, 1914, 1930s-40s, 1987), birth (1882-1920), brands (1818-39), Catholic, cemetery, census (1820RI, 1830 RI, 1840 RIP, 1850 RIMFD, 1860 RIMFD, 1870 RIMFD, 1880 RIMFD, 1900 RI, 1910 R, 1920 RI), Christian Church (1827-64), commissioner (1818-32), constable (1876-1937), coroner (1896-1951), court of common pleas (1868-71), DAR volumes, death (1882-1975), deed (1818-1905), estray (1847-97), genealogical compilations, guardian ((1847-53), history (1884, 1914, 1987), inquest (1895-1927), inventory (1940), land entry (1856-64), Lutheran (1836-97), marriage (1818-1921), Methodist (1882-1965), naturalization (1854-1930), obituaries, Presbyterian (1819-1919), probate (1818-1937), school (1898-1901), tax (1842-1922), will (1818-1924), WPA volumes.

Library: FHL in Bloomington, Monroe County Public Library, 303 East Kirkwood Ave., Bloomington, IN 47408. University Libraries, IN University, Tenth St. and Jordan Ave., Bloomington, IN 47405. Society: Monroe County Historical Society, 202 East Sixth St., Bloomington, IN 47408. Monroe County Genealogical Society, 206 East Sixth St., Bloomington, IN 47408. Publishes THE MONROE COUNTY HISTORIAN.

58. MONTGOMERY COUNTY

Montgomery County established/organized 1823 from Parke and Counties. County seat Crawfordsville (47933).

Printed/microfilmed/CDROM records (most in ISL-IHS, many in FHL/FHC, many in ACPL, some in PLC): atlas (1878, 1898, 1917), Baptist (1832-1945), Bible, biography (1881, 1893, 1930s-40s, 1989), birth (1882-1920), Catholic (1824-1988), cemetery, census (1830 RI, 1840 RIP, 1850 RIMFD, 1860 RIMFD, 1870 RIMFD, 1880 RIMFD, 1900 RI, 1910 R, 1920 RI), Christian Church (1853-1920), Church of Christ (1867-1900), commissioner (1823-53), DAR volumes, death (1882-1920), deed (1822-1907), early settlers (1825), Episcopal, GAR records, genealogical compilations, German Baptist Brethren (1828-1942), history (1881, 1958), land entry, map (1864), marriage (1823-1920), Methodist (1848-1949), naturalization (1850-1930), Presbyterian (1824-1931), probate (1823-77), Quaker (1831-74), will (1823-1901), WPA volumes.

Library: Crawfordsville District Public Library, 222 South Washington St., Crawfordsville, IN 47933 (historical/manuscript). Society: Montgomery County Historical Society, 212 South Water St., Crawfordsville, IN 47933. Who's Your Ancestor Genealogical Society, 222 South Washington St., Crawfordsville, IN 47933.

59. MORGAN COUNTY

Morgan County established/organized 1822 from unorganized territory. County seat Martinsville (46151). Fire in 1876 resulted in loss of some records, chiefly marriage and probate records during 1850-76.

Printed/microfilmed/CDROM records (most in ISL-IHS, many in FHL/FHC, many in ACPL, some in PLC): Baptist (1854-1924), biography (1884), birth (1882-1920), blacks, Catholic (1868-1949), cemetery, census (1830 RI, 1840 RIP, 1850 RIMFD, 1860 RIMFD, 1870 RIMFD, 1880 RIMFD, 1900 RI, 1910 R, 1920 RI), Christian Church (1835-1961), DAR volumes, death (1882-1920), deed (1822-1901), ear marks (1822-78), genealogical compilations, history (1884, 1915), inventory (1941), justice of the peace (1874-1921), marriage (1822-1954), Methodist (1870-1948), newspaper abstracts, obituary, partition (1884-1915), pioneers, probate (1822-1919), Quaker (1822-1975), school (1871-89), tax (1840), tract, veterans' burials, will (1846-1904), WPA volumes.

Library: Morgan County Public Library, 110 South Jefferson St., Martinsville, IN 46151 (historical/manuscript). Mooresville Public Library,

166

32 West Main St., Mooresville, IN 46158 (historical/manuscript). Society: Morgan County Historical and Genealogical Society, 133 Carter St., Mooresville, IN 46158.

---

60. NEWTON COUNTY

Newton County established/organized 1859/60 from Jasper County. County seat Kentland (47951). Must not be confused with Old Newton County which was created in 1835 from Jasper County, was never organized, and was abolished in 1838 before it had functioned.

Printed/microfilmed/CDROM records (most in ISL-IHS, many in FHL/FHC, many in ACPL, some in PLC): Baptist (1840-1910), biography (1883, 1916, 1899), birth (1882-1937), Catholic (1848-1984), cemetery, census (1860 RIMFD, 1870 RIMFD, 1880 RIMFD, 1900 RI, 1910 R, 1920 RI), death (1882-1937), deed (1859-1903), history (1883, 1911, 1916, 1955, 1991), marriage (1860-1920), probate (1861-1900), will (1860-1902), WPA volumes.

Library: Kentland-Jefferson Township Public Library, 201 East Graham St., Kentland, IN 47951. Society: Newton County Historical Society, PO Box 103, Kentland, IN 47951.

---

61. NOBLE COUNTY

Noble County established/organized 1835/36 from Elkhart, Lagrange, and Allen Counties. County seat Albion (46701). Fires in 1843 and 1859, many records destroyed, but all deeds saved.

Printed/microfilmed/CDROM records (most in ISL-IHS, many in FHL/FHC, many in ACPL, some in PLC): atlas (1874, 1914), Bible, biography (1882, 1902, 1930s-40s, 1963, 1986), birth (1882-1901), Catholic (1858-1959), cemetery, census (1840 RIP, 1850 RIMFD, 1860 RIMFD, 1870 RIMFD, 1880 RIMFD, 1900 RI, 1910 R, 1920 RI), DAR volumes, death (1882-99), deed (1836-1925), genealogical compilations, guardian (1859-1928), history (1882, 1902, 1986), justice of the peace, land entry (1816-35), marriage (1859-1922), mortuary, newspapers (1835-1935), obituaries, plats (1828-75), probate (1859-1926), tax (1846-47), veterans' burials (1893-1923), will (1854-1902).

Library: Noble County Public Library, 109 North York St., Albion, IN 46701. Society: Noble County Historical Society, PO Box 152, Albion, IN 46701. Publishes PIONEER ECHOES. Noble County Genealogical Society, 109 North St., Albion, IN 46701. Publishes THE NOBLE NEWS.

62. OHIO COUNTY

Ohio County established/organized 1844 from Dearborn County. County seat Rising Sun (47040).

Printed/microfilmed/CDROM records (most in ISL-IHS, many in FHL/FHC, many in ACPL, some in PLC): atlas (1883), biography (1885), birth (1882-1904), cemetery, census (1850 RIMFD, 1860 RIMFD, 1870 RIMFD, 1880 RIMFD, 1900 RI, 1910 R, 1920 RI), death (1858-1969), deed (1844-1981), estates (1860-1907), Evangelical (1856-1901), genealogical compilations, history (1885), Lutheran (1855-1976), marriage (1818-1921), naturalization (1848-1927), Presbyterian (1836-68), probate (1844-1981), veterans' burials, will (1844-1901).

Library: Ohio County Public Library, 100 North High St., Rising Sun, IN 47040. Society: Ohio County Historical Society, 218 South Walnut St., Rising Sun, IN 47040. Publishes NEWSLETTER.

63. ORANGE COUNTY

Orange County established/organized 1816 from Knox, Gibson, and Washington Counties. County seat Paoli (47454).

Printed/ microfilmed /CDROM records (most in ISL-IHS, many in FHL/FHC, many in ACPL, some in PLC): apprentice (1848-84), Baptist (1818-52), Bible, biography (1884), birth (1882-1940), black genealogy, cemetery, census (1820RI, 1830 RI, 1840 RIP, 1850 RIMFD, 1860 RIMFD, 1870 RIMFD, 1880 RIMFD, 1900 RI, 1910 R, 1920 RI), Church of Christ, circuit court (1853-1918), commissioner (1817-28), coroner (1897-1916), DAR volumes, death (1882-1920), deed (1816-1902), funeral notices, genealogical compilations, history (1885), marriage (1816-1922), Methodist (1854-1926), naturalization (1840-1905), partition (1853-1918), Presbyterian (1894-1938), probate (1816-1943), Quaker (1816-1949), saline land (1836-45), tract (1808-68), United Brethren (1874-79), will (1816-1943), WPA volumes.

Library: Paoli Public Library, 10 NE Court Square, Paoli, IN 47454. Society: Orange County Genealogical Society, PO Box 344, Paoli, IN 47454. Publishes ORANGE PEELINGS.

64. OWEN COUNTY

Owen County established/organized 1819 from Daviess and Sullivan Counties. County seat Spencer (47460).

Printed/microfilmed/CDROM records (most in ISL-IHS, many in FHL/FHC, many in ACPL, some in PLC): Baptist (1822-85), biography (1884, 1890,

1930s-40s, 1994), birth (1882-1920), cemetery, census (1820RI, 1830 RI, 1840 RIP, 1850 RIMFD, 1860 RIMFD, 1870 RIMFD, 1880 RIMFD, 1900 RI, 1910 R, 1920 RI), Church of Christ, DAR volumes, death (1882-1920), deed (1819-1902), genealogical compilations, history (1884, 1890, 1994), marriage (1819-1952), Methodist (1846-52, 1878-1923), naturalization (1854-1937), partition (1854-63), Presbyterian (1848-77, 1891-1921), probate (1819-1923), tax (1819-29, 1843), will (1819-1982), WPA volumes.

Library: Spencer Public Library, 110 East Marke St., Spencer, IN 47460 (historical/manuscript). Society: Owen County Historical Society, PO Box 222, Spencer IN 47460. Owen County Historical and Genealogical Society, 110 East Market St., Spencer, IN 47460.

65. PARKE COUNTY

Parke County established/organized 1821 from Vigo County and unorganized territory. County seat Rockville (47872). Fire in 1833 resulted in loss of many records.

Printed/microfilmed/CDROM records (most in ISL-IHS, many in FHL/FHC, many in ACPL, some in PLC): atlas (1874), Baptist (1829-67), Bible, biography (1893, 1913, 1916, 1930s-40s), birth (1882-1920), cemetery, census (1830 RI, 1840 RIP, 1850 RIMFD, 1860 RIMFD, 1870 RIMFD, 1880 RIMFD, 1900 RI, 1910 R, 1920 RI), Christian Church (1878-1976), DAR volumes, death (1882-1920), deed (1820-36), genealogical compilations, guardian (1832-58), history (1880, 1913, 1916), land entry (1820-35), marriage (1829-1921), Methodist (1840-1924), naturalization (1854-1930), Presbyterian (1851-1916), probate (1833-1900), Quaker (1821-1957), tax (1851), United Brethren, United Society of Believers (1821-1911), will (1833-1906), WPA volumes.

Library: Rockville Public Library, 106 North Market St., Rockville, IN 47872 (historical/manuscript). Society: Parke County Historical Society, 505 East Oak Dr., Rockville, IN 47872.

66. PERRY COUNTY

Perry County established/organized 1814 from Gibson and Warrick Counties. County seat Cannelton (47520). Some vital records lost in flood of 1937.

Printed/microfilmed/CDROMrecords (most in ISL-IHS, many in FHL/FHC, many in ACPL, some in PLC): apprentice (1853-79), atlas (1861), biography (1885, 1930s-40s, 1977), birth (1882-1920), Catholic (1837-1988), cemetery, census (1820RI, 1830 RI, 1840 RIP, 1850 RIMFD, 1860 RIMFD, 1870 RIMFD, 1880 RIMFD,

1900 RI, 1910 R, 1920 RI), commissioner (1847-51), death (1882-1920), deed (1815-86), genealogical compilations, history (1885, 1916, 1977), marriage (1814-1922), naturalization (1890-1951), probate (1816-1919), school (1899-1900), tax (1835), will (1816-79), WPA volumes.

Library: Cannelton Public Library, West Sixth St., Cannelton, IN 47520. Society: Perry County Historical Society, 538 Eleventh St., Cannelton, IN 47520. Southern IN Genealogical Society, PO Box 665, New Albany, IN 47520. Publishes THE SOUTHERN IN GENEALOGICAL SOCIETY QUARTERLY and THE SOUTHERN IN GENEALOGICAL SOCIETY NEWSLETTER.

67. PIKE COUNTY

Pike County established/organized 1817 from Gibson and Perry Counties. County seat Petersburg (47567).

Printed/microfilmed/CDROM records (most in ISL-IHS, many in FHL/FHC, many in ACPL, some in PLC): atlas (1881), Baptist (1867-1926), biography (1885, 1942, 1978, 1987), birth (1882-1920), Catholic (1886-1945), cemetery, census (1820RI, 1830 RI, 1840 RIP, 1850 RIMFD, 1860 RIMFD, 1870 RIMFD, 1880 RIMFD, 1900 RI, 1910 R, 1920 RI), commissioner (1817-39), death (1896-1920), deed (1817-1905), GAR records, genealogical compilations, guardian (1817-1967), history (1885, 1942, 1976, 1978, 1987), indentures (1853-73), landowners (1877), Lutheran (1892-1985), marriage (1817-1922), Methodist (1832-63), naturalization (1857-1925), obituaries, orphans, partition (1853-1956), pioneer families, probate (1831-90), school (1837-52), stock marks, voter (1887-1920), will (1817-1920), WPA volumes.

Library: Pike County Public Library, 1104 Main St., Petersburg, IN 47567. Society: Pike County Historical Society, 1104 Main St., Petersburg, IN 47567. Publishes OUR NEWSLETTER.

68. PORTER COUNTY

Porter County established/organized 1835/1836 from St. Joseph County. County seat Valparaiso (46383).

Printed/microfilmed/CDROM records (most in ISL-IHS, many in FHL/FHC, many in ACPL, some in PLC): atlas (1876), Baptist (1831-77, 1882-1900), biography (1882, 1894, 1912, 1930s-40s), birth (1884-1919), Catholic (1858-1993), cemetery, census (1840 RIP, 1850 RIMFD, 1860 RIMFD, 1870 RIMFD, 1880 RIMFD, 1900 RI, 1910 R, 1920 RI), circuit court (1862-1914), city history, commissioner (1836-45), court of common pleas (1853-72), DAR volumes, death (1884-1930), deed (1836-1901), genealogical compilations, guardian (1870-1938), history (1882, 1894, 1912, 1956, 1959), marriage (1836-1921), Methodist (1856-1925), mortuary (1892-1905), naturalization (1849-1955), obituaries (1847-1950), partition (1854-1914), Presbyterian (1844-1916), probate (1838-1925), will (1839-1933).

Library: Porter County Public Library, 103 Jefferson St., Valparaiso, IN 46383. Society: Northwest IN Genealogical Society, 154 Granite St., Valparaiso, IN 46383. Publishes TWIGS. Historical Society of Porter County, 153 S. Franklin St., Valparaiso, IN 46383 (historical/manuscript).

69. POSEY COUNTY

Posey County established/organized 1814 from Warrick County. County seat Mount Vernon (47620).

Printed/microfilmed/CDROM records (most in ISL-IHS, many in FHL/FHC, many in ACPL, some in PLC): atlas (1900), Baptist (1806-1955), Bible, biography (1882, 1886, 1930s-40s, 1993), birth (1882-1920), Catholic (1844-1985), cemetery, census (1820RI, 1830 RI, 1840 RIP, 1850 RIMFD, 1860 RIMFD, 1870 RIMFD, 1880 RIMFD, 1900 RI, 1910 R, 1920 RI), Church of Christ (1841-1941), circuit court (1815-29), commissioner (1817-55), county directory (1870, 1882, 1899), death (1882-1920), deed (1815-1902), early settlers, Episcopal (1838-1934), genealogical compilations, Germans in the New Harmony Society (1814-26), history (1882, 1886, 1913, 1983), inventory (1940), land grants (1812-1921), marriage (1814-1920), Methodist (1845-1920), mortuary (1891-1906), newspaper abstracts (1825-1978), obituaries (1861-1975), partition (1853-1907), probate (1815-1918), tax (1842, 1850s), will (1815-1923), WPA volumes.

Library: Alexandrian Public Library, 115 West Fifth St., Mount Vernon, IN 47620. Historic New Harmony Archives, PO Box 578, 506 Main St., New Harmony, IN 47631 (historical/manuscript). Society: Posey County Historical Society, PO Box 171, Mount Vernon, IN 47620. New Harmony Workingmen's Institute, PO Box 369, New Harmony, IN 47631 (historical/manuscript).

70. PULASKI COUNTY

Pulaski County established/organized 1835/1839 from Cass and St. Joseph Counties. County seat Winamac (46996).

Printed/microfilmed/CDROM records (most in ISL-IHS, many in FHL/FHC, many in ACPL, some in PLC): biography (1883, 1899, 1983), Catholic (1846-1964), cemetery, census (1840 RIP, 1850 RIMFD, 1860 RIMFD, 1870 RIMFD, 1880 RIMFD, 1900 RI, 1910 R, 1920 RI), circuit court (1869-1923), court (1853-93), DAR volumes, death (1882-1920), deed (1840-1901), GAR records, genealogical compilations, guardian (1861-74), history (1883, 1983), marriage (1839-1920), Methodist, newspaper abstracts (1860-95), Presbyterian (1890-1947), probate (1839-1923), swamp land (1852-89), tract (1838-76), veterans' discharge, will (1843-1925), WPA volumes.

Library: Pulaski County Public Library, 121 South Riverside Dr., Winamac, IN 46996. Society: Pulaski County Historical Society, 400 South Market St., Winamac, IN 46996. Pulaski County Genealogical Society, PO Box 265, Winamac, IN 46996. Publishes PULASKI COUNTY GENEALOGICAL NEWESLETTER.

71. PUTNAM COUNTY

Putnam County established/organized 1822 from Vigo and Owen Counties and unorganized territory. County seat Greencastle (46135).

Printed/microfilmed/CDROM records (most in ISL-IHS, many in FHL/FHC, many in ACPL, some in PLC): atlas (1879), Baptist (1823-1929), biography (1887, 1930s-40s), birth (1882-1920), Catholic (1860-1988), cemetery, census (1830 RI, 1840 RIP, 1850 RIMFD, 1860 RIMFD, 1870 RIMFD, 1880 RIMFD, 1900 RI, 1910 R, 1920 RI), DAR volumes, death (1880-1920), deed (1824-1903), genealogical compilations, guardian (1885-1919), history (1887, 1966, 1982), indenture (1854-85), landowner (1879), marriage (1822-1923), Methodist (1822-1961), naturalization (1854-1906), Presbyterian (1825-1956), probate (1825-1918), school (1837-1907), tax (1841, 1845), will (1823-1921), WPA volumes.

Library: Putnam County Public Library, 120 East Walnut St., Greencastle, IN 46135. West Library, DePauw University, Greencastle, IN 46135 (Methodist historical/manuscript). Society: Putnam County Historical Society, Roy O. West Library, Greencastle, IN 46135. Putnam County Genealogical Club, Box 28, Route 1, Bainbridge, IN 46105.

72. RANDOLPH COUNTY

Randolph County established/organized 1818 from Wayne County. County seat Winchester (47394). Do not confuse this Randolph County with OLD Randolph County which was formed in the Northwest Territory in 1795, became a county in the IN Territory in 1800, and became a county in the Illinois Territory in 1809.

Printed/microfilmed/CDROM records (most in ISL-IHS, many in FHL/FHC, many in ACPL, some in PLC): atlas (1874), Baptist (1831-1912), biography (1882, 1894, 1896, 1930s-40s), birth (1882-1907), Catholic (1866-1987), cemetery, census (1820RI, 1830 RI, 1840 RIP, 1850 RIMFD, 1860 RIMFD, 1870 RIMFD, 1880 RIMFD, 1900 RI, 1910 R, 1920 RI), Church of Jesus Christ of Latter Day Saints, court (1819-81), death (1882-1900), deed (1818-1903), genealogical compilations, guardian (1865-1918), history (1882, 1896), land entry, marriage (1819-1900), Methodist (1895-98), mortuary, newspaper abstracts, Quaker (1818-1958), probate (1819-1921), tract, veterans' burials, will (1819-1906).

Library: Winchester Public Library, 125 North East St., Winchester, IN 47394. Society: Randolph County Historical/Genealogical Society, Box 61, Route 3, Winchester, IN 47394. Publishes HISTORICAL/GENEALOGICAL SOCIETY OF RANDOLPH COUNTY NEWSLETTER.

73. RIPLEY COUNTY

Ripley County established/organized 1816/1818 from Dearborn and Jefferson Counties. County seat Versailles (47042).

Printed/microfilmed/CDROM records (most in ISL-IHS, many in FHL/FHC, many in ACPL, some in PLC): apprentice (1833-53), atlas (1883), Baptist (1820-1912), biography (1972, 1982, 1989), birth (1882-1906), Catholic (1836-1988), cemetery, census (1820RI, 1830 RI, 1840 RIP, 1850 RIMFD, 1860 RIMFD, 1870 RIMFD, 1880 RIMFD, 1900 RI, 1910 R, 1920 RI), Christian Church (1881-1977), coroner (1897-1928), court (1839-51), DAR volumes, death (1882-1900), deed (1818-89), early landowners, Evangelical (1842-1987), genealogical compilations and manuscripts, history (1982, 1989), indenture (1853-1905), marriage (1818-1922), Methodist (1833-1987), naturalization (1837-1928), obituaries, partition (1854-1917), Presbyterian (1849-1908), probate (1818-1918), Revolutionary veteran burials, voter (1853), will (1818-1922).

Library: Batesville Public Library, 131 North Walnut Blvd., Batesville, IN 47006. Society: Ripley County Historical Society, PO Box 525, Versailles, IN 47042. Publishes RIPLEY COUNTY HISTORICAL SOCIETY BULLETIN. Tri-County Genealogical Society, 23184 Pocket Rd. West, Batesville, IN 47006.

74. RUSH COUNTY

Rush County established/organized 1822 from unorganized territory. County seat Rushville (46173).

Printed/microfilmed/CDROM records (most in ISL-IHS, many in FHL/FHC, many in ACPL, some in PLC): atlas (1879), Baptist (1823-53), biography (1888, 1921, 1930s-40s), Catholic (1868-1956), cemetery, census (1830 RI, 1840 RIP, 1850 RIMFD, 1860 RIMFD, 1870 RIMFD, 1880 RIMFD, 1900 RI, 1910 R, 1920 RI), Christian Church (1849-1952), commissioner (1822-44), coroner (1893-1932), court (1822-57), DAR volumes, deed (1820-1901), early landowners, history (1888, 1899, 1921, 1985), marriage (1822-1911), naturalization (1857-1927), partition (1853-1937), Presbyterian (1839-1966), probate (1822-1921), Quaker (1836-1963), will (1822-38, 1843-1907), WPA volumes.

Library: Rushville Public Library, 130 West Third St., Rushville, IN 46173 (historical/manuscript). Society: Rush County Historical Society, 614 North Jackson St., Rushville, IN 46173.

75. ST. JOSEPH COUNTY

St. Joseph County established/organized 1818 from Cass County. County seat South Bend (46601).

Printed/microfilmed/CDROM records (most in ISL-IHS, many in FHL/FHC, many in ACPL, some in PLC): atlas (1875, 1895), Bible, biography (1880, 1893, 1901, 1907, 1923, 1930s-40s), birth (1882-1920), Brethren (1880-1972), Catholic (1830-1989), cemetery, census (1820RI, 1830 RI, 1840 RIP, 1850 RIMFD, 1860 RIMFD, 1870 RIMFD, 1880 RIMFD, 1900 RI, 1910 R, 1920 RI), Christian Church (1851-1914), city directory (1871-), commissioner (1830-44), court (1853-1901), DAR volumes, death (1882-1920), deed (1830-1901), Episcopal (1837-1937), foreign born (1850-80), GAR records, genealogical compilations, German Evangelical (1846-1930), guardian (1837-1920), history (1880, 1893, 1901, 1907, 1923, 1927), IOOF records, land patents, Lutheran (1863-1988), marriage (1830-1920), Methodist (1830-1988), naturalization, newspaper index (1858-1981), obituary (1841-1970), partition (1880-1938), Presbyterian (1834-1990), probate (1833-1920), Swedish Evangelical (1849-1960), tax (1884), United Church of Christ (1856-1989), voter (1821-1922), will (1830-1929), WPA volumes.

Library: FHL in South Bend, South Bend Public Library, 304 South Main St., South Bend IN 46601. Mishawaka-Penn Public Library, 209 Lincoln Way East, Mishawaka, IN 46544 (historical/manuscript). Hesburg Library, University of Notre Dame, Notre Dame, IN 46556 (historical/manuscript). Society: Northern IN Historical Society, 112 South Lafayette Blvd., South Bend, IN 46601 (historical/manuscript). Publishes ST. JOSEPH VALLEY RECORD. South Bend Area Genealogical Society, 53119 Oakmont Park Dr., West, South Bend, IN

46637. Publishes SOUTH BEND AREA GENEALOGICAL QUARTERLY.

76. SCOTT COUNTY

Scott County established/organized 1820 from Clark, Jefferson, Jennings, Washington, and Jackson Counties. County seat Scottsburg (47170).

Printed/microfilmed/CDROM records (most in ISL-IHS, many in FHL/FHC, many in ACPL, some in PLC): alien (1817-94), atlas (1889), Baptist (1823-1909), Bible, biography (1880, 1889), birth (1882-1907), cemetery, census (1820RI, 1830 RI, 1840 RIP, 1850 RIMFD, 1860 RIMFD, 1870 RIMFD, 1880 RIMFD, 1900 RI, 1910 R, 1920 RI), Civil War veterans, commissioner (1820-65), DAR volumes, deed (1820-1910), entry (1819-28), genealogical compilations, history (1880, 1889), immigrants (1817-94), marriage (1820-1921), Methodist (1863-1905), naturalization (1852-1900), obituaries, pioneers, Presbyterian (1837-1950), probate (1820-1919), tax (1839), will (1821-1923).

Library: Scott County Public Library, 108 South Main St., Scottsburg, IN 47170. Society: Scott County Historical Society, PO Box 245, Scottsburg, IN 47170. Scott County Genealogical Society, 5764 South IN State Road 203, Lexington, IN 47138. Publishes THE SCOTT COUNTY GENEALOGICAL SOCIETY NEWSLETTER.

77. SHELBY COUNTY

Shelby County established/organized 1822 from unorganized territory. County seat Shelbyville (46176).

Printed/microfilmed/CDROM records (most in ISL-IHS, many in FHL/FHC, many in ACPL, some in PLC): Baptist, Bible, biography (1887, 1909, 1930s-40s), birth (1882-1920), Catholic (1837-1961), cemetery, census (1830 RI, 1840 RIP, 1850 RIMFD, 1860 RIMFD, 1870 RIMFD, 1880 RIMFD, 1900 RI, 1910 R, 1920 RI), court (1822-76), death (1878-1981), deed (1822-1902), early landowners, estray, estate (1836-1940), genealogical compilations, guardian (1836-1940), history (1887, 1909), inventory (1940), marriage (1822-1952), Methodist (1847-1942), naturalization (1822-1908), newspaper abstracts, partition (1853-91), Presbyterian (1831-53, 1867-99), probate (1822-1940), tax (1828, 1842, 1843, 1847), veterans' enrollment (1886), will (1822-1906), WPA volumes.

Library: Shelbyville Public Library, 57 W. Broadway, Shelbyville IN 46176. Society: Shelby County Historical Society, PO Box 74, Shelbyville, IN 46176 (historical/manuscript). Shelby County Genealogical Society, PO Box 434, Shelbyville, IN 46176. Publishes FORE BEARS PAWS.

78. SPENCER COUNTY

Spencer County established/organized 1818 from Perry and Warrick Counties. County seat Rockport (47635). Fire in 1833 with some loss of records.

Printed/microfilmed/CDROM records (most in ISL-IHS, many in FHL/FHC, many in ACPL, some in PLC): atlas (1879), Baptist (1816-1977), biography (1885), birth (1882-1920), Catholic (1852-1986), cemetery, census (1820RI, 1830 RI, 1840 RIP, 1850 RIMFD, 1860 RIMFD, 1870 RIMFD, 1880 RIMFD, 1900 RI, 1910 R, 1920 RI), DAR volumes, death (1882-1920), dccd (1818-86), genealogical compilations, German Episcopal (1847-1907), guardian (1850-1950), history (1885), indentures (1836-55), Lutheran (1854-1982), marriage (1818-1921), Methodist (1835-1986), mortuary, naturalization (1852-1907), newspaper abstracts (1844-1925), obituaries (1844-1925), partition (1853-69), Presbyterian (1841-1951), probate (1818-1921), United Brethren (1881-1958), United Church of Christ (1814-1978), voter (1842), will (1818-1933), WPA volumes.

Library: Spencer County Public Library, 210 Walnut St., Rockport, IN 47635 (historical/manuscript). Society: Spencer County Historical Society, 210 Walnut St., Rockport, IN 47635. Publishes NEWSLETTER.

79. STARKE COUNTY

Starke County established/organized in 1835/1850 from St. Joseph County. County seat Knox (46534).

Printed/microfilmed/CDROM records (most in ISL-IHS, many in FHL/FHC, many in ACPL, some in PLC): biography (1894), birth (1894-1938), Catholic (1882-1993), cemetery, census (1850 RIMFD, 1860 RIMFD, 1870 RIMFD, 1880 RIMFD, 1900 RI, 1910 R, 1920 RI), Christian Church (1873-75), commissioner (1850-60), death (1894-1938), deed (1850-1900), early landowners, genealogical compilations, guardian (1873-1927), history (1894, 1902, 1950), Lutheran (1887-1948), marriage (1850-1938), Methodist (1891-1928), obituary, plat (1893), probate (1850-1936), swamp land (1853-76), will (1850-98), WPA volumes.

Library: Starke County Public Library, 54 East Washington St., Knox, IN 46534.

80. STEUBEN COUNTY

Steuben County established/organized 1835/1837 from Lagrange County. County seat Angola (46703).

Printed/microfilmed/CDROM records (most in ISL-IHS, many in FHL/FHC, many in ACPL, some in PLC): atlas (1880), biography (1885), cemetery, census (1840 RIP, 1850 RIMFD, 1860 RIMFD, 1870 RIMFD, 1880 RIMFD, 1900 RI, 1910 R, 1920 RI), court (1868-71), DAR volumes, deed (1837-1901), early settlers, genealogical compilations, history (1885), marriage (1837-1950), probate (1837-1921), tract (1835-55), veterans (1888-89), will (1845-1924).

Library: Carnegie Public Library, 322 South Wayne St., Angola, IN 46703 (historical/manuscript). Society: Steuben County Historical Society, 127 Powers St., Angola, IN 46703.

81. SULLIVAN COUNTY

Sullivan County established/organized 1817 from Knox County. County seat Sullivan (47882). Most records lost in fire in 1850.

Printed/microfilmed/CDROM records (most in ISL-IHS, many in FHL/FHC, many in ACPL, some in PLC): atlas (1899), biography (1884, 1967, 1977, 1991), birth (1882-1941), canal (1854-1950), Catholic (1853-1938), cemetery, census (1820RI, 1830 RI, 1840 RIP, 1850 RIMFD, 1860 RIMFD, 1870 RIMFD, 1880 RIMFD, 1900 RI, 1910 R, 1920 RI), DAR volumes, death (1882-1920), deed (1850-1901), early settlers, genealogical compilations, history (1884, 1909, 1967, 1977, 1991), marriage (1817-1952), Methodist (1856-1946), naturalization (1864-1905), partition (1853-1963), Presbyterian (1816-1930), probate (1850-1922), will (1844-1901), WPA volumes.

Library: Sullivan County Public Library, 100 South Crowder St., Sullivan, IN 47882 (historical/manuscript). Society: Sullivan County Historical Society and Sullivan County Genealogical Society, PO Box 326, Sullivan, IN 47882. Society Publishes SULLIVAN COUNTY HISTORICAL SOCIETY NEWSLETTER.

82. SWITZERLAND COUNTY

Switzerland County established/organized 1814 from Dearborn and Jefferson Counties. County seat Vevay (47043).

Printed/microfilmed/CDROM records (most in ISL-IHS, many in FHL/FHC, many in ACPL, some in PLC): atlas (1883), Baptist (1818-1949), biography index, birth (1882-

1907), Catholic (1873-1988), , cemetery, census (1820RI, 1830 RI, 1840 RIP, 1850 RIMFD, 1860 RIMFD, 1870 RIMFD, 1880 RIMFD, 1900 RI, 1910 R, 1920 RI), death (1882-1900), deed (1814-1900), genealogical compilations, history (1924, 1969), inventory (1940), Lutheran (1855-1917), marriage (1814-1925), Methodist (1862-1921), naturalization (1858-60), Presbyterian (1836-1925), probate (1814-1947), Revolutionary veteran burials, will (1823-1919), WPA volumes.

Library: Switzerland County Public Library, PO Box 133, Vevay, IN 47043. Society: Switzerland County Historical Society, PO Box 201, Vevay, IN 47043 (historical/manuscript).

83. TIPPECANOE COUNTY

Tippecanoe County established/organized 1826 from Parke County and unorganized territory. County seat Lafayette (47901).

Printed/microfilmed/CDROM records (most in ISL-IHS, many in FHL/FHC, many in ACPL, some in PLC): apprentice (1844-99), alien (1826-1907), atlas (1878), Bible, biography (1888, 1899, 1909, 1930s-40s, 1990), birth (1882-1941), Catholic (1857-1988), cemetery, census (1830 RI, 1840 RIP, 1850 RIMFD, 1860 RIMFD, 1870 RIMFD, 1880 RIMFD, 1900 RI, 1910 R, 1920 RI), Christian Church (1873-1921), circuit court (1827-67), commissioner (1818-32), county asylum (1872-1945), court of common pleas (1848-65), DAR volumes, death (1882-1920), deed (1826-1970), Episcopal (1837-1928), estray (1827-47), genealogical compilations, guardian (1830-1905), history (1888, 1909, 1976, 1982, 1990), indenture (1833-99), inventory (1941), Lutheran (1852-1951), marriage (1826-1941), Methodist (1825-1963), naturalization (1833-1955), plat, Presbyterian (1828-1940), probate (1827-1969), Quaker (1827-1985), survey (1836-1916), tax (1843-76), United Brethren (1858-1969), will (1818-1969), WPA volumes.

Library: FHL in West Lafayette, Tippecanoe County Public Library, 627 South Street, Lafayette, IN 47901 (historical/manuscript). West Lafayette Public Library, 208 West Columbia St., West Lafayette, IN 47906. Society: Tippecanoe County Historical Association, 909 South St., Lafayette, IN 47901 (historical/manuscript). Publishes WEATENOTES. Tippecanoe County Area Genealogical Society, 909 South St., Lafayette, IN 47901. Publishes TIPCOA NEWSLETTER.

84. TIPTON COUNTY

Tipton County established/organized 1844 from Hamilton, Cass, and Miami Counties. County seat Tipton (46072).

Printed/microfilmed/CDROM records (most in ISL-IHS, many in FHL/FHC, many in ACPL, some in PLC): biography (1884, 1898, 1914, 1930s-40s), cemetery, census (1850 RIMFD, 1860 RIMFD, 1870 RIMFD, 1880 RIMFD, 1900 RI, 1910 R, 1920 RI), Christian Church (1857-1985), DAR volumes, death (1882-1907), deed (1844-1902), history (1883, 1914), inventory (1941), Lutheran (1859-93), marriage (1844-1905), mortuary (1895-1981), naturalization (1854-1930), Presbyterian (1873-1941), probate (1844-1904), Quaker (1836-1979), will (1844-1930).

Library: Tipton County Public Library, 127 East Madison St., Tipton, IN 46072 (historical/manuscript). Society: Tipton County Historical Society, Box 61, RR#1, Tipton, IN 46072.

85. UNION COUNTY

Union County established/organized 1821 from Fayette, Franklin, and Wayne Counties. County seat Liberty (47353).

Printed/microfilmed/CDROMrecords (most in ISL-IHS, many in FHL/FHC, many in ACPL, some in PLC): atlas (1884), biography (1884, 1899, 1930s-40s, 1989), Catholic (1872-1922),cemetery, census (1830 RI, 1840 RIP, 1850 RIMFD, 1860 RIMFD, 1870 RIMFD, 1880 RIMFD, 1900 RI, 1910 R, 1920 RI), court (1821-45), DAR volumes, deed (1821-1901), genealogical compilations, history (1884, 1899, 1989), land entry, marriage (1821-1951), Methodist (1845-67, 1896-1920), naturalization (1860-1939), Presbyterian (1830-51), probate (1821-1918), Quaker (1817-1945), will (1821-1932).

Library: Union County Public Library, 2 East Seminary St., Liberty, IN 47353. Society: Union County Historical Society, Railroad St., Liberty, IN 47353.

86. VANDERBURGH COUNTY

Vanderburgh County established/organized 1818 from Gibson, Posey, and Warrick Counties. County seat Evansville (47708).

Printed/microfilmed/CDROM records (most in ISL-IHS, many in FHL/FHC, many in ACPL, some in PLC): atlas (1880), Baptist (1847-1956), Bible, biography (1873, 1889, 1897, 1906, 1910, 1930s-40s, 1988), birth (1882-1920), Catholic (1837-1985)), cemetery, census (1820RI, 1830 RI, 1840 RIP, 1850 RIMFD, 1860 RIMFD, 1870 RIMFD, 1880 RIMFD, 1900 RI, 1910 R, 1920 RI), church records book, city directory (1858-), commissioner (1818-44), coroner (1870-87), DAR volumes, death (1882-1920), deed (1818-1902), divorce (1818-1942), Episcopal (1842-1946), genealogical compilations, German Evangelical (1864-1933), history (1873, 1889, 1897, 1910, 1988), inventory (1939), Lutheran (1818-1986), marriage (1818-1921), Methodist (1845-1972), mortuary (1889-99), naturalization (1837-1980), newspaper (1821-25), plat (1906), Presbyterian (1821-1975), probate (1820-1986), tract (1805-53), will (1820-1986), WPA volumes.

Library: FHL in Evansville, Evansville-Vanderburgh County Public Library, 22 S.E. Fifth St., Evansville, IN 47708 (historical/manuscript). Willard Library, Regional and Family History Center, 21 First Ave., Evansville, IN 47710 (local and regional historical/manuscript). Society: Tri-State Genealogical Society, 21 First Ave., Evansville, IN 47712. Publishes TRI-STATE PACKET. Vanderburgh County Historical Society, 201 N.W. Fourth St., Evansville, IN 47712. Evansville Museum of Arts and Science, 411 S.E. Riverside Dr., Evansville, IN 47713 (historical/manuscript).

87. VERMILLION COUNTY

Vermillion County established/organized 1824 from Parke County. County seat Newport (47966).

Printed/microfilmed/CDROM records (most in ISL-IHS, many in FHL/FHC, many in ACPL, some in PLC): atlas (1909), Baptist, biography (1888, 1913, 1963, 1969), birth (1882-1920), Catholic (1878-1987), cemetery, census (1830 RI, 1840 RIP, 1850 RIMFD, 1860 RIMFD, 1870 RIMFD, 1880 RIMFD, 1900 RI, 1910 R, 1920 RI), commissioner (1824-44), death (1882-1920), genealogical compilations, history (1888, 1913, 1963, 1969), index of persons and firms, marriage (1824-1920), Methodist (1877-1904), newspaper abstracts (1892-1924), Quaker (1873-1982), WPA volumes.

Library: Newport Public Library, Newport, IN 47966. Clinton Public Library, 313 S. Fourth St., Clinton, IN 47842 (historical/-manuscript).

88. VIGO COUNTY

Vigo County established/organized 1818 from Sullivan County. County seat Terre Haute (47807).

Printed/microfilmed/CDROM records (most in ISL-IHS, many in FHL/FHC, many in ACPL, some in PLC): atlas (1874), Baptist, Bible, biography (1880, 1891, 1908, 1930s-40s), birth (1882-1920), Catholic (1837-1988), cemetery, census (1820 RI, 1830 RI, 1840 RIP, 1850 RIMFD, 1860 RIMFD, 1870 RIMFD, 1880 RIMFD, 1900 RI, 1910 R, 1920 RI), city census (1829,

1835), commissioner (1829-44), court (1818-20), DAR volumes, death (1882-1920), deed (1818-86), genealogical compilations, guardian (1819-1927), history (1880, 1891, 1900, 1908), indenture (1826-86), marriage (1818-1951), Methodist (1837-1958), naturalization (1856-1906), newspaper abstracts, probate (1818-1927), Quaker (1818-74), school (1867-95), tax (1828), tract (1816-20), veterans' burial, will (1818-1919), WPA volumes.

Library: FHL in Terre Haute, Vigo County Public Library, One Library Square, Terre Haute, IN 47807 (historical/manuscript). Society: Vigo County Historical Society, 1411 S. Sixth St., Terre Haute, IN 47807 (historical/manuscript). Wabash Valley Genealogical Society, 2906 East Morris Ave., Terre Haute, IN 47805. Publishes SYCAMORE LEAVES.

89. WABASH COUNTY

Wabash County established/organized 1832/1835 from Cass and Grant Counties. County seat Wabash (46992). Some records lost in fire of 1870.

Printed/microfilmed/CDROM records (most in ISL-IHS, many in FHL/FHC, many in ACPL, some in PLC): biography (1884, 1901, 1930s-40s, 1976), birth (1871-86), brands (1846-78), Catholic (1846-1988), cemetery, census (1840 RIP, 1850 RIMFD, 1860 RIMFD, 1870 RIMFD, 1880 RIMFD, 1900 RI, 1910 R, 1920 RI), Christian Church, commissioner (1835-68), deed (1835-97), genealogical compilations, history (1884, 1976), Lutheran, marriage (1835-99), Methodist (1882-84), naturalization (1854-1929), newspaper abstracts (1849-63, 1876-96), obituaries (1848-99), probate (1842-94), tax (1835-40, 1847), tract (1826-50), will (1842-94).

Library: Wabash-Carnegie Public Library, 188 West Hill St., Wabash, IN 46992 (historical/manuscript). North Manchester Public Library, 204 West Main St., North Manchester, IN 46992 (historical/manuscript). Manchester College Archives, Manchester College, North Manchester, IN 46962 (Church of the Brethren, German Baptist historical/manuscript). Society: Wabash County Historical Society, 89 West Hill St., Wabash, IN 46992 (Museum has historical/manuscript). Publishes WABASH COUNTY HISTORICAL NEWSLETTER.

90. WARREN COUNTY

Warren County established/organized 1827 from Fountain County. County seat Williamsport (47993).

Printed/microfilmed/CDROM records (most in ISL-IHS, many in FHL/FHC, many in ACPL, some in PLC): atlas (1877), biography (1883,

1899, 1981-2, 1982), birth (1882-1920), census (1830 RI, 1840 RIP, 1850 RIMFD, 1860 RIMFD, 1870 RIMFD, 1880 RIMFD, 1900 RI, 1910 R, 1920 RI), DAR volumes, death (1882-1920), deed (1827-1901), genealogical compilations, history (1883, 1966, 1981-2, 1982), indenture (1837-1903), marriage (1827-1953), Methodist (1831-1966), plat (1865), probate (1829-50), stock marks (1827-1928), tract (1825-1952), will (1830-1928), WPA volumes.

Library: Williamsport Public Library, 9 Fall St., Williamsport, IN 47993. Society: Warren County Historical Society, PO Box 176, Williamsport, IN 47993. Publishes WARREN COUNTY REFLECTIONS.

91. WARRICK COUNTY

Warrick County established/organized 1813 from Knox County. County seat Boonville (47601).

Printed/microfilmed/CDROM records (most in ISL-IHS, many in FHL/FHC, many in ACPL, some in PLC): apprentice (1831-1907), atlas (1880), Bible, biography (1885, 1907, 1909, 1930s-40s), birth (1882-1920), brands (1818-39), Catholic (1865-1985), cemetery, census (1820RI, 1830 RI, 1840 RIP, 1850 RIMFD, 1860 RIMFD, 1870 RIMFD, 1880 RIMFD, 1900 RI, 1910 R, 1920 RI), circuit court (1813-38), commissioner (1813-53), court of nisi (1813), DAR volumes, death (1882-1920), deed (1813-1901), genealogical compilations, German Evangelical, history (1885, 1909, 1981), inventory (1940), index to Clark's records, marriage (1813-1921), Methodist (1845-1956), mortuary (1885-1919), naturalization (1852-1906), newspaper abstracts (1878-97), obituaries (1878-97), partition (1881-1941), pioneers, plat (1907), probate (1813-1920), Revolutionary War pensions, stock marks (1819-87), tract, United Church of Christ (1813-1934), will (1818-1924), WPA volumes.

Library: Boonville Public Library, 611 West Main St., Boonville, IN 47601. Society: Warrick County Museum, 117 South First St., Boonville, IN 47601.

92. WASHINGTON COUNTY

Washington County established/organized 1810 from Clark, Harrison, and Jefferson Counties. County seat Salem (47167).

Printed/microfilmed/CDROM records (most in ISL-IHS, many in FHL/FHC, many in ACPL, some in PLC): apprentice (1828-91), atlas (1878), Baptist (1810-1960), Bible, biography (1880, 1889, 1916, 1976), birth (1882-1924), Catholic (1896-

1963), cemetery, census (1820 RI, 1830 RI, 1840 RIP, 1850 RIMFD, 1860 RIMFD, 1870 RIMFD, 1880 RIMFD, 1900 RI, 1910 R, 1920 RI), Christian Church (1842-1902), Church of Christ (1868-1959), circuit court (1814-18), commissioner (1817-1923), court (1831-69), court of common pleas (1814-1919), DAR volumes, death (1882-1925), deed (1814-1911), genealogical compilations, guardian (1820-77), history (1880, 1884, 1889, 1916, 1976), indenture (1828-91), marriage (1815-1920), Methodist (1863-79, 1888-1950), mortuary (1873-80), naturalization (1892-1929), negro (1853-61), newspaper abstracts, obituaries (1849-1965), pioneers, poll (1844-73), Presbyterian (1816-1966), probate (1814-1927), Quaker (1814-1941), school (1866-95), tax (1843-46), tract (1810-59), will (1814-1929), WPA volumes.

Library: Salem Public Library, 212 North Main St., Salem, IN 47167. Society: Washington County Historical Society, 307 East Market St., Salem, IN 47167 (historical/manuscript). Publishes NEWSLETTER. Southern IN Genealogical Society, PO Box 665, New Albany, IN 47150. Publishes SOUTHERN IN GENEALOGICAL SOCIETY QUAR-TERLY and SOUTHERN IN GENEALOGICAL SOCIETY NEWS-LETTER.

93. WAYNE COUNTY

Wayne County established/organized 1811 from Clark and Dearborn Counties. County seat Richmond (47375). Must not be confused with OLD-OLD Wayne County, formed in Northwest Territory in 1796, fell outside of Indiana Territory when it was set up in 1800. Neither must it be confused with OLD Wayne County which was organized in IN Territory in 1803 and went to MI Territory in 1805.

Printed/microfilmed/CDROM records (most in ISL-IHS, many in FHL/FHC, many in ACPL, some in PLC): apprentice (1828-98), atlas (1874, 1893), Bible, biography (1872, 1884, 1899, 1912, 1930s-40s, 1976), birth (1882-1920), Catholic (1845-1969), cemetery, census (1820 RI, 1830 RI, 1840 RIP, 1850 RIMFD, 1860 RIMFD, 1870 RIMFD, 1880 RIMFD, 1900 RI, 1910 R, 1920 RI), Christian Church (1859-1925), Church of Christ (1897-1948), circuit court (1814-27), Civil War soldiers, com-missioner (1811-35), DAR volumes, death (1882-1920), deed (1811-1910), directory (1857, 1859, 1860/1, 1863, 1870/1-), Episcopal (1837-1945), genealogical compilations, history (1872, 1884, 1899, 1912, 1976), inden-ture (1828-98), land entry (1805-38), landowner (1893), Lutheran (1832-1984), marriage (1811-1951), Methodist (1844-1955), mortuary (1851-76, 1886-1958), naturalization (1830-40, 1851-1929), newspaper abstracts (1822-1988), partition (1857-1905), pioneers (1875, 1945), Presbyterian

(1828-53, 1870-1943), probate (1818-1921), Quaker (1809-1966), school (1874-1924), stock marks (1815-22), trustees (1880-1950), United Brethren, will (1812-1920), WPA volumes.

Library: Morrison-Reeves Public Library, 80 North Sixth St., Richmond, IN 47374. Lilly Library, Earlham College, National Road West, Richmond, IN 47374 (Quaker historical/manuscript). Cambridge City Public Library, 33 West Main St., Cambridge City, IN 47327 (historical/manuscript). Society: Wayne County Historical Association, 1150 North A St., Richmond, IN 47374 (historical/manuscript). Wayne County Genealogical Society, 1150 North A St., Richmond, IN 47374. Publishes NEWSLETTER.

94. WELLS COUNTY

Wells County established/organized 1835-/37 from Allen, Delaware, and Randolph Counties. County seat Bluffton (46714).

Printed/microfilmed/CDROMrecords (most in ISL-IHS, many in FHL/FHC, many in ACPL, some in PLC): atlas (1881), Baptist (1842-77), biography (1887, 1903, 1918), birth (1883-1920), Catholic (1876-1919), cemetery, census (1840 RIP, 1850 RIMFD, 1860 RIMFD, 1870 RIMFD, 1880 RIMFD, 1900 RI, 1910 R, 1920 RI), death (1883-1920), deed (1838-99), genealogical compilations, history (1881, 1887, 1903, 1918), inventory (1941), land entry (to 1835), marriage (1837-1974), mortuary (1865-1975), probate (1838-1900), will (1838-1901), WPA volumes.

Library: Bluffton Public Library, 223 West Washington, Bluffton, IN 46714. Society: Wells County Historical Society, 420 West Market St., Bluffton, IN 46714 (historical/manuscript).

95. WHITE COUNTY

White County established/organized 1834 from Carroll County. County seat Monticello (47960).

Printed/microfilmed/CDROMrecords (most in ISL-IHS, many in FHL/FHC, many in ACPL, some in PLC): atlas (1896), Baptist (1898-1972), biography (1883, 1899, 1915), birth (1882-1920), Catholic (1874-1988), cemetery, census (1840 RIP, 1850 RIMFD, 1860 RIMFD, 1870 RIMFD, 1880 RIMFD, 1900 RI, 1910 R, 1920 RI), death (1882-1920), genealogical compilations, history (1883, 1899, 1915), marriage (1834-1920), Methodist (1857-1903), plat (1896), probate (1835-1900), tract (1829-54), voter (1883-1931), will (1835-95), WPA volumes.

Library: Monticello Public Library, 101 South Bluff St., Monticello, IN 47960. Monon Public Library, 427 North Market St.,

Monon, IN 47959. Society: White County Historical Society, 101 South Bluff St., Monticello, IN 47960 (historical/manuscript). White County Genealogical Society, PO Box 884, Monticello, IN 47960.

---

96. WHITLEY COUNTY

Whitley County established/organized 1835/38 from Elkhart and Allen Counties. County seat Columbia City (46725).

Printed/microfilmed/CDROM records (most in ISL-IHS, many in FHL/FHC, many in ACPL, some in PLC): biography (1882), Catholic (1860-1988), cemetery, census (1840 RIP, 1850 RIMFD, 1860 RIMFD, 1870 RIMFD, 1880 RIMFD, 1900 RI, 1910 R, 1920 RI), court of common pleas (1853-92), DAR volumes, death (1882-1920), deed (1838-1923), genealogical compilations, guardian (1876-1931), history (1882), indenture (1857-87), land entry (1813-84), landowners (1862), Lutheran, marriage (1838-1925), obituaries (1858-1930), Presbyterian (1853-1928), probate (1839-1925), tax (1838), will (1839-1928).

Library: Peabody Library, 203 East Main St., Columbia City, IN 46725. South Whitley-Cleveland Township Public Library, 201 East Front St., South Whitley, IN 46787. Society: Whitley County Historical Society, 108 West Jefferson St., Columbia City, IN 46725 (historical/manuscript). Publishes THE BULLETIN OF THE WHITLEY COUNTY HISTORICAL SOCIETY.

Books by George K. Schweitzer

CIVIL WAR GENEALOGY. A 93-paged book of 316 sources for tracing your Civil War ancestor. Chapters include I: The Civil War, II: The Archives, III: National Publications, IV: State Publications, V: Local Sources, VI: Military Unit Histories, VII: Civil War Events.

GEORGIA GENEALOGICAL RESEARCH. A 238-paged book containing 1303 sources for tracing your GA ancestor along with detailed instructions. Chapters include I: GA Background, II: Types of Records, III: Record Locations, IV: Research Procedure and County Listings (detailed listing of records available for each of the 159 GA counties).

HANDBOOK OF GENEALOGICAL SOURCES. A 252-paged book describing all major and many minor sources of genealogical information with precise and detailed instructions for obtaining data from them.

INDIANA GENEALOGICAL RESEARCH. A 189-paged book containing 1044 sources for tracing your IN ancestor along with detailed instructions. Chapters include I: IN Background, II: Types of Records, III: Record Locations, IV: Research Procedure and County Listings (detailed listing of records available for each of the 92 IN counties).

KENTUCKY GENEALOGICAL RESEARCH. A 167-paged book containing 1191 sources for tracing your KY ancestor along with detailed instructions. Chapters include I: KY Background, II: Types of Records, III: Record Locations, IV: Research Procedure and County Listings (detailed listing of records available for each of the 120 KY counties).

MARYLAND GENEALOGICAL RESEARCH. A 208-paged book containing 1176 sources for tracing your MD ancestor along with detailed instructions. Chapters include I: MD Background, II: Types of Records, III: Record Locations, IV: Research Procedure and County Listings (detailed listing of records available for each of the 23MD counties and for Baltimore City).

MASSACHUSETTS GENEALOGICAL RESEARCH. A 279-paged book containing 1709 sources for tracing your MA ancestor along with detailed instructions. Chapters include I: MA Background, II: Types of Records, III: Record Locations, IV: Research Procedure and County-Town-City Listings (detailed listing of records available for each of the 14 MA counties and the 351 cities-towns).

NEW YORK GENEALOGICAL RESEARCH. A 252-paged book containing 1426 sources for tracing your NY ancestor along with detailed instructions. Chapters include I: NY Background, II: Types of Records, III: Record Locations, IV: Research Procedure and NY City Record Listings (detailed listing of records available for the 5 counties of NY City), V: Record Listings for Other Counties (detailed listing of records available for each of the other 57 NY counties).

NORTH CAROLINA GENEALOGICAL RESEARCH. A 169-paged book containing 1233 sources for tracing your NC ancestor along with detailed instructions. Chapters include I: NC Background, II: Types of Records, III: Record Locations, IV: Research Procedure and County Listings (detailed listing of records available for each of the 100 NC counties).

OHIO GENEALOGICAL RESEARCH. A 212-paged book containing 1241 sources for tracing your OH ancestor along with detailed instructions. Chapters include I: OH Background, II: Types of Records, III: Record Locations, IV: Research Procedure and County Listings (detailed listing of records available for each of the 100 OH counties).

PENNSYLVANIA GENEALOGICAL RESEARCH. A 201-paged book containing 1309 sources for tracing your PA ancestor along with detailed instructions. Chapters include I: PA Background, II: Types of Records, III: Record Locations, IV: Research Procedure and County Listings (detailed listing of records available for each of the 67 PA counties).

REVOLUTIONARY WAR GENEALOGY. A 110-paged book containing 407 sources for tracing your Revolutionary War ancestor. Chapters include I: Revolutionary War History, II: The Archives, III: National Publications, IV: State Publications, V: Local Sources, VI: Military Unit Histories, VII: Sites and Museums.

SOUTH CAROLINA GENEALOGICAL RESEARCH. A 170-paged book containing 1107 sources for tracing your SC ancestor along with detailed instructions. Chapters include I: SC Background, II: Types of Records, III: Record Locations, IV: Research Procedure and County Listings (detailed listing of records available for each of the 47 SC counties and districts).

TENNESSEE GENEALOGICAL RESEARCH. A 132-paged book containing 1073 sources for tracing your TN ancestor along with detailed instructions. Chapters include I: TN Background, II: Types of Records, III: Record Locations, IV: Research Procedure and County Listings (detailed listing of records available for each of the 96 TN counties).

VIRGINIA GENEALOGICAL RESEARCH. A 216-paged book containing 1273 sources for tracing your VA ancestor along with detailed instructions. Chapters include I: VA Background, II: Types of Records, III: Record Locations, IV: Research Procedure and County Listings (detailed listing of records available for each of the 100 VA counties and 41 major cities).

WAR OF 1812 GENEALOGY. A 75-paged book of 289 sources for tracing your War of 1812 ancestor. Chapters include I: History of the War, II: Service Records, III: Bounty Land and Pension Records, IV: National and State Publications, V: Local Sources, VI: Military Unit Histories, VII: Sites and Events.

All of the above books may be ordered from Dr. George K. Schweitzer at the address given on the title page. Or send a long SASE for a FREE descriptive leaflet on any or all of the books.